The Seven Stages *of* Motherhood

Ann Pleshette Murphy joined *Good Morning America* as parenting expert in November 1998. Since then, more than 200 "American Family" segments have aired before five million viewers. In 2002, two of her segments received a media award from the National Council on Family Relations, and a segment on teen drivers received an award from MADD in 2003. She was for ten years the Editor-in-Chief of *Parents* magazine and currently has a bi-monthly column, 'Mom Know-How', in *Family Circle*. Ann is a cum laude graduate of Harvard University, where she majored in psychology, and currently resides in New York City with her husband and two children.

http://www.annpleshettemurphy.com

Ann Pleshette Murphy

The Seven Stages *of* Motherhood

Making the Most of Your Life as a Mum

PAN BOOKS

First published 2004 by Aaron A. Knopf
a division of Random House, Inc., New York

This edition published 2004 by Boxtree
an imprint of Pan Macmillan, a division of Macmillan Publishers Limited
20 New Wharf Road, London N1 9RR
Basingstoke and Oxford
Associated companies throughout the world
www.panmacmillan.com

ISBN-13: 978-1-4472-4929-0

A CIP catalogue record for this book is available from
the British Library.

Printed and bound by CPI Group (UK) Ltd, Croydon, CR0 4YY

To Steve, the love of my life,
and to Madeleine and Nick,
who are my life

CONTENTS

Introduction   ix

Stage 1
Altered States: *Pregnancy, Birth, and the Fourth Trimester*   3

Stage 2
Finding Your Footing, Finding Yourself:
Months Four Through Twelve   67

Stage 3
Letting Go: *The Toddler Years, One and Two*   88

Stage 4
Trying to Do It All: *The Preschool Years, Three to Six*   110

Stage 5
Reading the Compass to God-Knows-Where: *Years Six to Ten*   144

Stage 6
Living in the Gray Zone: *The Preteen Years, Ten to Thirteen*   181

Stage 7
It Gets Easier . . . and Then They Leave:
The Teen Years, Thirteen to Eighteen   215

Conclusion   244
Notes   249
Bibliography   257
Acknowledgments   263
Index   265

INTRODUCTION

Motherhood: It's the defining event in a woman's life, a seismic trans-formation, a path we travel forever. But most of the literature on motherhood neglects the mother. We're coached on the how-tos, not the why-mes. We're encouraged to stand in our children's shoes, while our own shoes gather dust. As we learn to read our kids' signals, anticipate their needs, and accommodate their demands, we rarely take the time to reflect on where we are or where we want to be. The result is that even the most confident mom often feels unsure of her footing. And those of us who aren't so sanguine worry that we're headed in the wrong direction entirely, dragging our children along this path toward God-knows-where.

When Maddie and Nick were babies, I devoured every child-development tome I could lay my hands on. The fact that I was edit-ing the leading parenthood magazine in the country gave me access to the best and the brightest among baby experts. Drs. Spock and Brazel-ton were on my speed dial. But rarely did a day go by that I wasn't painfully aware of my rookie rating. Second-guessing became second nature. I was great at giving other people advice about bedtime rituals or picky eaters, but I routinely spent two hours trying to get Maddie to bed—even resorting to crawling out of her room on my hands and knees to avoid making the floor creak.

With Nick, my "been there, done that" status helped a little, but the first boy in a long line of Pleshette-Murphy girls made it clear from birth that he was composed of a completely different set of chromosomes than his sister. For every stretch of road I felt prepared to walk, there were four unexpected turns that brought me face-to-face with my own insecurities.

When I left *Parents* to write this book, Maddie and Nick were thirteen and nine, respectively, and I was the parenting contributor to *Good Morning America*. Viewers who e-mailed me questions routinely addressed me as "Dr. Murphy," conferring a degree of expertise and a credential I hardly deserved, but I did have decades of cumulative knowledge. Not my own, but that of the hundreds of moms, child-development experts, and researchers I had met and interviewed over the years. If there was one thing I learned, it was the simple yet ironic fact that motherhood is the great equalizer; become a mother and join a sorority that bridges millennia and miles. But as much as we all have in common, each of us is unique, and as quickly as our children change, we do, too. The mother your baby knew is not the same person ten months, let alone ten years, later. Child number three experiences a different mom than the one his older siblings knew. And, of course, the entire family evolves and develops along with each child. As Erik Erikson observed in *Childhood and Society,* "This weak and changing little being moves the whole family along. Babies control and bring up their families as much as they are controlled by them; in fact, we may say that the family brings up a baby by being brought up by him."[1]

We watch our children grow and change at a furious rate, panting to keep up or, if we're lucky, to stay one step ahead, and in so doing we develop muscles, new ways of thinking, and a whole new self-concept. One eminent psychologist characterized our evolution as a kind of contained vertical progression, a building that grows taller but remains solidly rooted in place. Our children, on the other hand, are always pushing outward and away: "While children move themselves as individuals separate from their mothers, women evolve from one maternal identity to another," writes Rozsika Parker in her book *Torn in Two*. "Thus they move from being a mother supporting a head, to a mother pushing a buggy, to a mother holding a hand, to a mother waving a hand, to a mother waiting for a hand to hold. *But always a mother*. Theirs is a 'vertical' development compared to their children's more 'horizontal' growth away from them."[2]

No matter how we choose to characterize our maternal development, we accept that we'll never be the same, that there's no going back. Yet our children want us to remain the same, to be that predictable, unconditionally loving anchor they need to cling to. Sometimes we can pull it off. When the storm clouds gather we're there, unchanging and available, giving of ourselves in ways we never dreamed possible. But there are other times when our own needs must come first, or when our ability to be flexible and empathic is undermined by anxiety, fatigue, anger, work, other relationships, past hurts, or all of the above.

How do you attend to your own developmental needs at each stage of your child's life? And why is that so important? That's what this book is about. I want mothers to realize that every stage of a child's life presents specific challenges and there are good, bad, and better ways of handling those issues, but it's only by turning the telescope around that you can focus on what's really important. "Knowing thyself" is never more critical than when those two little stripes of pink show up in the plastic window.

One of my favorite illustrations of this comes from *Nature's Thumbprint*, a book on identical twins and the age-old nature/nurture question. The authors describe identical girls, separated at birth and raised by very different moms. Interviewed about their girls' (then two and a half) behavior, one of the mothers complained bitterly about her daughter's eating habits. "She won't touch anything I give her. No mashed potatoes, no bananas. Nothing without cinnamon. Everything has to have cinnamon on it. I'm really at my wit's end with her about this." The other mother, asked about her daughter's eating habits, replied, "She eats well. As a matter of fact, as long as I put cinnamon on her food she'll eat anything."[3]

We don't have to put cinnamon on everything to raise happy, healthy children. But we do have to spend as much time (or just enough time) on our own physical, emotional, cognitive, and social growth to make the most of the years we spend raising our kids. And those years will fly by so fast it takes your breath away. Mothers with older children will tell you that when you stand on the bridge you've built and watch your children cross over and away into adulthood, you'll experience the pain of regret along with elation. You mourn the moments that slipped through your fingers and at the same time realize that very few of the mistakes you made really mattered in the long run. One thing is certain: If you happen to glance into the water below, you'll see a reflection that is formed, dissolved, then formed again by countless memories, cast like pebbles by the children you love.

The Seven Stages *of* Motherhood

Stage 1

❧

Altered States

Pregnancy, Birth, and the Fourth Trimester

I was thirty-one when I became pregnant with our first child. From the moment my obstetrician gave us the good news, I began to fantasize about our baby, to picture myself as a mother. The hazy sonogram image I carried in my wallet, the fetal heartbeat, those first fluttery kicks changed my sense of who I was and who I was becoming. Long before my husband, Steve, and I settled on our baby's name, Molly, I had turned a dramatic corner. Just how sharp that corner really was I would discover in an agonizing way.

Molly died two days after her birth, tearing a hole in our lives. Even though I knew that I could have done nothing to prevent her death, which was due to a highly rare form of intrauterine growth retardation, I suffered profound feelings of worthlessness and guilt. During the succeeding weeks, Steve and I held on to each other, sharing our sadness and loss. Then Steve returned to work and I recuperated at home. As the news spread, a love tide of condolence notes poured in from family and friends, colleagues, acquaintances, people we saw often and others we hardly knew. I found myself reading and rereading every word—whether a multipage letter or a treacly Hallmark card. I hoarded the notes, counted them, organized and sorted them. Opening the mail became a kind of obsession, the one pastime I craved during an otherwise desolate period.

Only when I was pregnant with Maddie the following year did I understand why the letters had meant so much. Having planned for months to be a mother, redefining myself in terms of our baby and our new life as a family, I suddenly felt as though I had no purpose, no handle on where to go from there. I had lost not only a chance to hold and love our baby, I was deprived of my new identity. For the better part of a year, I had carried a vision of myself and of Molly that informed every minute of my day and affected my dreams at night. Losing her meant losing me—or at least an experience of myself I wanted desperately to embrace.

I hoarded the letters not because of what they said but because they reminded me that I was also a friend, cousin, employee, colleague, daughter, sister, aunt. The more letters I received, the more I was connected to these other roles and the easier it became to retrace my steps. I slowly reclaimed my old self, began to feel on solid ground again, but I never really stepped back completely from the place I had entered eight months before. Even if I had never conceived another child, I would have forever defined myself as a mother.

Most of us become mothers in our minds the minute that second pink line blooms in the plastic window or the call to the doctor's office confirms the news. We breathe a little differently, see a different reflection in the mirror long before our contours actually change. I doubt the Dalai Lama could clear his mind of thoughts of the future were he lucky enough to experience pregnancy, because being pregnant is all about the future. We may go about the mundane business of our lives—having supper with our spouse, catching a movie with friends, going to work, taking a walk in the park—but we're already acutely aware that nothing will ever be the same, that our own personal history, and that of our baby-to-be, is about to change in ways that are thrilling and terrifying. The psychologist Daphne de Marneffe aptly describes this sense of "history in the making" as all the more awe-inspiring in the context of our day-to-day lives: "We are both part of the cycle of life and the march of history. This is an incarnation, and even as we stroll to the drugstore to pick up some toothbrushes, or maybe even partly because of the strange contrast between them, it can inspire awe. That sense of awe is often one adoptive parents express as well, in evoking the experience of joining destinies with their child."[1]

In many ways, your fantasies about the future are as important as the little cluster of cells floating inside you. Pregnancy is a three-in-one deal: There's the physical baby you're carrying, the imagined one in your dreams, and your picture of yourself as a mother. They're all important, all part of what makes pregnancy the seminal journey of any woman's life. From the minute you find out you're pregnant, you feel as though you've wandered into a totally new neighborhood. You daydream about running behind your towheaded toddler on the beach or reading *Charlotte's Web* to your rapt first-grader or shopping with your preteen, and you begin to reshape a sense of who you are.

Most of us don't take the time to indulge in these fantasies or to give voice to them, especially if they tip precariously toward the dark side. Heavyhearted visions of loneliness, fatigue, and unwanted fat get pushed aside whenever someone asks, "Are you excited?" or "How are you feeling?" It's far easier to assume that we can accommodate a small earthquake than to contemplate the sidewalk splitting open or giant boulders tumbling from the sky.

The New Macho Mom

When I found out I was pregnant the second time, my anxiety was understandably high, but once everything seemed normal, I hurtled ahead, adjusting my frenetic routine as little as possible. One morning I was running late to the office, and in my frantic sprint into the subway car I slipped, slamming my head against the edge of the door. By the time the train arrived at the next stop, I looked as though my unborn baby was about to spring Athena-like from my swelling forehead and several of my fellow straphangers were advising me to "get the hell off and put some ice on that thing."

I wound up at my parents' apartment a few blocks away, where my father, an obstetrician-gynecologist, ministered to my sore head and bruised ego. "You have to slow down, darling," he admonished, placing an ice pack on my throbbing brow. "You're pregnant." I realized later that he had stated the obvious because I was ignoring the obvious, racing through my days with a ferocious determination to prove I could still do it all, that nothing had changed. I'm sure I was running as fast as I could out of fear—fear that if I indulged in fantasies about this baby, in images of myself as a mom, of Steve as a dad—I might suffer the same loss and disappointment we had our first time. But even after an amniocentesis reassured us that everything was fine, I kept a tight rein on my fantasies and a tight schedule at work.

Although I'm sure there are women who adopt an eighteenth-century approach to their pregnancies, fainting onto chaises or taking to their beds, most of the moms I spoke to copped a decidedly macho attitude toward their nine months. Morning sickness was slightly embarrassing but not paralyzing; fatigue was just something they'd work around; hemorrhoids, heartburn, varicose veins—not so bad. Even today's maternity wardrobes seem designed with a "what's the big deal with big" attitude. Evidently, there's a lot of pressure on today's moms to treat pregnancy as a minor inconvenience and to barrel ahead with the confidence of Seabiscuit.

In many ways this shift in perspective is positive; we've come a long way from the days when anything having to do with a woman's reproductive tract was considered X-rated and childbirth itself akin to a medical problem. In the 1700s, pregnant women were "confined" and expected to wear clothing that made burnooses look revealing. Before World War II pregnancy was rarely described as such. Women were "with child" or "in the family way" or "had a bun in the oven." And no nineteenth-century man in his right mind ever announced, "We're pregnant!"

Not only has the language of pregnancy changed in the past few decades, but the acceptance of expectant mothers in the workplace, in the media, in bikinis has made it possible to strut your stuff and maintain the status quo for as long as you want. And it's wonderful if your pregnancy goes so smoothly that you can continue to work and play with Energizer Bunny stamina. When Nick's beloved third-grade teacher became pregnant for the first time, her ebullience made Kathie Lee Gifford look lethargic. In addition to teaching full-time, she kept up a rigorous workout routine, practically jogging into the delivery room. And her happy-mom motor was clearly revved up the day I ran into her on the street. (*She* was running; I was not.) "I feel really, really good," she said, panting as she jogged in place. "Only three weeks to go!" I wished her luck and told her I would call her after the baby arrived. But as she trotted away I worried that she might be setting herself up for disappointment—not in terms of the experience of being a mom but in entertaining the fantasy that even after the baby arrived she would just jog through life at the same self-determined pace.

There are plenty of evolutionary explanations as to why we carry our babies for nine long months, but I'm convinced that those last few weeks, when our bodily changes (and quite a few functions) seem totally out of control, are an apt metaphor for motherhood. "If you think you look and feel completely different now," Mother Nature laughs, "then just wait." Long before you can't see your feet, you should be putting them up—literally and psychologically. As you'll learn, the shock of the new (baby, that is) can knock you sideways, especially if you've harbored the fantasy that becoming a mom represents a little bump in the road. Accepting that you're looking at a Mount Fuji–sized change and giving yourself the time and space to plan for your new life and, more important, for your new sense of yourself makes a lot more sense than investing in a chic maternity wardrobe you hope will double as back-to-work wear.

"I realize now that I just wasn't facing the fact that our lives would be totally different," Emily admitted a few months after her daughter was born. "It happened so quickly—we weren't really trying to conceive—I guess I didn't really admit to being pregnant. Like we didn't assemble the crib until about a week before Isabella was born. I kept putting it off; on one level, I just couldn't believe it was happening."

Few *can* believe it. How is it possible to fully imagine what and how you'll feel when the fluttering inside you is a miraculous fact of your life, when there's an actual baby in that room you're wallpapering with cute little ducks. Shelly, a twenty-six-year-old saleswoman who was expecting her first baby when I interviewed her, never really stopped to think about *why* she wanted to be a mom. In fact, as she admitted during the course of our conversation, the pregnancy had not been planned: "I'm still having a hard time believing that I'm going to be a mom. Even my coworkers were really surprised when I told them I was pregnant, because I have a low tolerance for typical kid behavior. I work in retail, and when a baby has a tantrum in the store, basically I have to leave. I'm so frustrated by what I see parents doing or not doing in those situations. So I guess I'm worried that I might be just like them."

Actually, most of us assume we won't be "just like them," that we'll manage to soothe an inconsolable infant or prevent a preschooler's supermarket meltdown or negotiate a successful peace treaty with an angry adolescent. The novelist Fay Weldon once commented that "the greatest advantage of not having children must be that you can go on believing that you are a nice person: once you have children, you realize how wars start."[2]

Weldon's cynicism notwithstanding, there's no reason to believe you won't be a nice person once you're a mom; you just won't be the *same* person. Ever. And for many of us, that sense of change, of evolution, is exactly why pregnancy is so fiercely exciting. As the psychologist Harriet Lerner aptly says, "Any woman who doesn't fear for her *own* future when she becomes a mother is sleepwalking or perhaps in a coma."[3]

Good-bye to All That

Most moms-to-be experience moments of panic, when the irreversibility of pregnancy feels very scary. Even if you desperately want to be a mom, there's always ambivalence about saying good-bye to your old self. Among the women I spoke to who had postponed motherhood, a significant proportion had experienced the paradoxical conflict between embracing their excitement about becoming moms and sacrificing the image of themselves they had worked long and hard to craft. For Leslie, an accomplished, beautiful business executive, the anticipated changes of motherhood induced what felt, at times, like mourning. "As excited as I was to be pregnant, the first trimester was really rough emotionally. I think I felt two things: this huge lack of control, and loss. I just kept thinking about how I was giving up my career and losing my body and making lots of sacrifices. I had no morning sickness or cravings; I didn't put on a lot of weight. But I definitely found the emotional adjustment to losing a chapter in my life very hard to take." In what she described as a slightly defiant act, Leslie continued to indulge in a glass of wine when she wanted one and to play down the myriad health warnings that bombarded her. She seemed to be saying, "Hey, I know this baby is going to change my life, but I don't want to give up who I am."

In "Soliloquy," from the musical *Carousel,* expectant dad Billy Bigelow goes from swaggering tough guy to insecure "bum with no money" as he imagines fathering a boy, then a girl. His poignant transformation makes the song one of the most lyrical explorations of how impending parenthood forces us to see ourselves in a whole new light. There's no question that ruminating over the kind of person you want to be for your baby can keep you up all night. "I'm already thinking about how she will see me, what kind of a person I am now and what I want to change about myself," Elise told me when she was about five months pregnant. As she fantasized about hanging out with her baby, going places and interacting, she found herself consciously deciding to change the way she presented herself. "Getting pregnant has forced me to clean up my act. To be more poised, more grown-up, I suppose. Even though I realize the baby can't hear me, I find that I'm not swearing as much as I used to. Maybe that's silly, but it's part of imagining how I want our child to see me."

Ambivalent and somewhat anxious about becoming a mom, Shelly claimed that she rarely fantasized about what her relationship with her baby would be like. "I don't have a picture of it really," she admitted. "I guess I don't think about the relationship we'll have very much." Other moms had elaborate images of playing with and holding and feeding their babies. Lisa, who was expecting her first girl (she had two boys), waxed rhapsodic about the shopping trips she and her daughter would take together. She had even figured out what they might order for lunch.

In *The Birth of a Mother,* Dr. Daniel Stern describes an interesting shift in our fantasies about our babies toward the eighth or ninth month of pregnancy: "Instead of the imagined baby becoming even more fully drawn, almost the opposite occurs. Recent studies suggest that at this time, the mother starts to undo this highly elaborated imagined baby. She allows the mental picture to fade, and in a sense starts to dismantle and even hide the imagined baby from herself." According to Stern, we may "clear the decks" so that our expectations are not disappointed when the actual baby arrives, an adjustment that is particularly valuable among mothers who give birth prematurely. "The mother [of a preemie] will not have had enough time to undo her imagined baby. She and the real baby now suffer doubly. Not only is the real baby less developed than normally expected, but the mother compares it to her often unrealistically idealized, imaginary baby who is still too vivid in her mind."[4]

By far the most difficult phase of my first pregnancy was the weeks preceding Molly's birth, when I knew that she would never be normal. The anger I experienced toward the doctors who had failed to diagnose her problem until the end of my seventh month battled daily with numbing grief. I had to let go of the soft-focus fantasies of a smiling, pink-cheeked baby, curled up in my loving arms, and to accept that my life would be much harder and so unfair. With the help of a therapist, I was able to admit how angry I was, to say through choking sobs, "Sometimes I hate Molly!" and then to deal with the sickening guilt those feelings provoked.

I was also able to share my feelings with Steve, who of course was struggling with his own load of guilt and anger and anxiety. I leaned on him with a force that might have toppled weaker mates, and although he confessed later how torturous it had been to feel impotent to affect any meaningful change, he helped me on a daily basis. I never had to wonder what kind of a father he would be.

Dream Dad

Given what we had gone through the first time, Steve's elevated concern when I conceived again made my pregnancy with Maddie a time of heightened involvement and togetherness. He was there for me in ways that ran the gamut from massaging my swollen ankles to making certain our obstetrician told us absolutely everything. When I balked about "bothering the doctor with a dumb question," he picked up the phone and called. He also took over completely the organization of Maddie's room, giving the ceiling a fresh coat of paint days before she arrived. "I don't want her staring at cracks and water stains!" he explained only somewhat facetiously.

We were in step in many ways, completely in denial in others. I can't remember ever sitting down to talk about our roles or about how Steve might adjust his schedule once his week of paternity leave came to an end; nor did our ridiculously lame Lamaze class prepare either of us for the practical demands of a new baby. I suppose I assumed that, as the eldest of four, Steve would know something about diapers and midnight feedings, and I suppose I didn't want to question whether he felt his identity was on the line, because that would mean thinking about my own. Or perhaps it was my total self-absorption (particularly toward the end of my pregnancy) that precluded my stopping to consider fully how Steve felt about becoming a dad. Like an egocentric toddler who thinks everyone sees the world just as she does, I assumed Steve approached the big day with similar fears, hopes, images of the future. But then again, I never bothered to ask.

Perhaps the biggest challenge in considering one's spouse and thinking about the kind of dad he'll be is managing to separate fantasy from reality. If your husband is a member of Workaholics Anonymous, then chances are he will not spend mornings lying next to you in bed, gazing through tear-glazed eyes at his newborn. More likely he'll be primed to spend more time out on the hunt, fulfilling his role as provider.

Several moms I spoke to knew from the start that the early months would be flown solo. They harbored no fantasies of Dad racing to the nursery for the midnight feeding or leaving his office early to take the baby to the pediatrician. Toward the end of her pregnancy, my friend Elise had come to terms with what her highly driven spouse would be like and, more important, what they might be like as a team: "Even though there is a part of me that wants Brian to be very involved in the baby's care and feeding, I know that he hasn't really thought about that stuff. He just doesn't go there. I think about it all the time. Also, I'm pretty headstrong about how I want things done, and if he is very involved, I'm sure ultimately there will be some issue that we won't see eye to eye on."

One of the more novel—not necessarily more sage—solutions to the prospect of having to share the baby care came from a self-confessed "type-A" expectant mom, married to a "total type-A" guy. Four weeks shy of her due date, MaryAnn told me that she had refused to read any books on the how-tos of baby care. "I've intentionally not learned things. I have sisters with kids, so I've been around newborns. But I have not read any of the books about having a baby because I don't want the leg up. I don't want to know more than Doug. He's a great uncle to the kids once they can throw a ball, but the newborns, well, suffice it to say, I don't think he's ever changed a diaper, so I specifically want a clean slate so we can learn together. Once I tell him three things he'll assume I know everything and then he'll look to me for how to do X or Y. I'd rather we figure it out together."

Convinced that her husband "wouldn't be around much," Shelly pictured herself alone and exhausted: "When I imagine motherhood, I think I'll be really tired at the end of the day. I worry that I'm going to be bored and lonely. I don't think John will be very helpful. I worry that he won't be there a lot of the time." As sad as Shelly sounded, and although her life might well have turned out different and better, at least her mental preparation for motherhood included fantasies that many women are too ashamed or anxious to share.

When my friend Chloe became pregnant six weeks after she and her husband were married, her first thought was to have an abortion. The timing was all wrong. They were just starting out together as a couple, and she had been accepted to graduate school. "I was really upset and angry," she recalled. But one night Chris pulled out a photo of his daughter by his first wife and said, "Look, you have to decide, but this is why I would want you to go ahead: I love Allison so much. You just can't imagine what it's like to feel this way."

As it turned out, Chloe and Chris found that their son's arrival early in their marriage grounded them. It was a tough time. Chris had taken a job he didn't like in order to be at home while Chloe attended grad school, and finances were tight. "I think had we not been parents, we might not have made it," she said.

Of course, having a baby to heal a troubled marriage or to trap a spouse is so patently misguided that it's become a hackneyed staple of afternoon soaps. Surprisingly, in a study of reasons American couples stated for having kids, "to bring spouse closer" ranked number one.[5] And many pregnant women say they experience a deepening intimacy and connection with their husbands.

Elise described a sense of having crossed over into a new stage in her relationship with her husband, Brian: "First we were a couple, living together. Then we got married and felt an even stronger connection. But this is even closer than that. I can't imagine how intense and deep it will be when we actually have a baby in our lives."

As close as she felt to Brian, Elise admitted that it drove her crazy when he told friends, "*We're* pregnant." Having gone through many months of fertility treatments and riding the arduous physical and emotional roller coaster that these treatments entailed, she laughed at the notion that the pregnancy was shared: "You know right away there is an imbalance. When you're doing fertility treatments, you're tested five days after you get your period, and you start shooting yourself up with drugs and doing whatever you have to. And what does your husband do? He ejaculates into a cup. And now that I am pregnant, as enthusiastic as Brian is, nothing's changed for him really. He didn't have nausea for four months. He wasn't unbelievably exhausted or moody. He gets up and goes to work and can't understand why I have trouble getting out of bed. Life has changed for him intellectually, but it's changed for me physically, emotionally, and intellectually. I mean there is not a single aspect of my life that has been untouched by this."

Expecting your husband to walk in matched steps with you to the delivery room and, having panted and perspired and wept alongside you, to react to your baby's arrival with the same mix of emotions is not only unrealistic, it's unfair—to both of you. Just as you cannot possibly share pregnancy and childbirth, you won't share parenthood, even if he does 50 percent of the child care. Love for the baby, your sense of yourselves as parents, commitment to career, and attention to each other are just a few of the areas in your marriage in which you may suddenly fly off in different directions. Too few of us take the time to anticipate the strain these changes may bring and work on our marriage before the baby arrives. If we're married to someone whose career occupies center stage, we sing that tune from *Guys and Dolls,* "Marry the Man Today," and assume that the baby's arrival will affect a total personality adjustment. Perhaps—but why not voice your concerns, air your grievances, state your preferences, and establish your priorities a few months before you're too tired to even talk?

Big

Going through the most dramatic physical changes you've ever experienced, watching your body transform completely, and thinking every day about this little person growing inside you is aptly described by most moms as "miraculous." In her lovely memoir, *The Blue Jay's Dance: A Birth Year,* Louise Erdrich recalls experiencing her body as a separate place: "I'm not me. I feel myself becoming less a person than a place, inhabited, a foreign land."[6]

Tami, who has a high-powered job in publishing, got pregnant in her thirties, survived two months of constant nausea ("I ate plain pasta and crackers for breakfast, lunch, and dinner"), and experienced a dramatic change in her response to her body: "The first thing that changed was my boobs. They were enormous—I mean, three times the size. And, believe me, I didn't need any more on top! I have plenty of heft. People would just stare at them, and that made me really uncomfortable. Then, when I popped, at about four months, I would look at myself as if I were looking at someone else. My body had changed so much. It was as if some alien inhabited my body—which I guess it had—but I went through a couple of months of pure denial. I would actually try to get dressed in my prepregnancy clothes. Now that I'm past the nausea and the anxiety and the testing, I feel great. I'm aware of being this host—or hostess—to a mysterious miracle. And I'm just amazed."

I remember lying in bed toward the end of my pregnancy, feeling Maddie press a tiny heel against my palm as I ran my hand over my preternaturally large abdomen, and laughing aloud at this wacky phenomenon. It was just mind-blowing to think about having a baby inside me. As my friend Elise wisely noted, "Look, it took me five years to go through puberty. And now in nine months, I have experienced many more changes in my body."

During the first trimester, when morning sickness, fatigue, sore breasts, and hormonal changes are often most acute, it's natural to feel as though you've lost control of your body. Even if you have few unpleasant symptoms, the mere prospect of kissing your figure good-bye can be really distressing. Leslie had witnessed the transformation of two close friends, both of whom put on a lot of weight, suffered through terrible morning sickness, and complained about a host of ugly ailments, so even when the first few weeks of her pregnancy were relatively symptom-free, she dreaded and resented the physical changes she imagined would ambush her at any moment. "I had always defined myself as intelligent, interesting, and attractive. I'm very tall and slender, and I had had a great dating life before I got married. So I worried I would gain a lot of weight and lose control of my body. I didn't know when I would pop, when my waistline would disappear, when I would stop feeling attractive. It was very tough emotionally in the beginning." She found the second and third trimesters much easier. "When I didn't gain weight but had this kind of Buddha belly, I actually felt okay with my body."

MaryAnn, whose job involved giving presentations, often to large groups, found it excruciating during the first trimester to stand up in front of two hundred people. "I was so uncomfortable in my skin, and you can't tell anyone. My clothes were tight and uncomfortable, but I didn't want to buy two sizes up and then have to buy maternity clothes."

Like MaryAnn, Dierdre, who got married when she was four months pregnant, struggled through a summer of hating how she looked. "We went on a cruise for our honeymoon at a point when my body didn't look really pregnant, just fat. That was hard. But then I came to terms with it. I thought of my body as a house for our baby, and the bigger I got, the safer the baby would be."

Jordan, who had had a lot of negative body-image issues when she was a teenager, adored being pregnant. "It was the only time I felt great about my body—not in the sense of feeling sexy or exceptionally beautiful—but simply because I knew I looked exactly as I should look," she explained. "For the first time in my life I could get dressed for work in minutes, instead of trying on forty different outfits and not feeling comfortable in any of them. It was such a relief to dress in maternity clothes and not have to suck in my belly or worry if I looked okay."

Loving your pregnant shape is a lot easier when it's accompanied by other positive changes. MaryAnn found that her skin looked beautiful and that she felt awkward but energized. Still, there were moments when she mourned the loss of her "sexy self" and was aware of comparing herself to nonpregnant women. "You definitely still want to feel sexy, knowing that you're about to do the most unsexy thing in the world, which is to give birth and become a mom, so when you see these beautiful women walking down the street, you think, 'Oh, man, am I never going to be a head turner once I have a kid in a stroller?'"

Definitely Not Sexy

Hunter Tylo, one of the stars of *Melrose Place*, successfully sued the producers of the show for millions of dollars because she believed that she could portray a seductive vixen even if pregnant. I would have *paid* millions of dollars to look like Hunter Tylo during my pregnancy or just to feel a little less like the Pillsbury Dough Girl. Most of us don't think "alluring" when we're bent over the toilet much of the day or completely wiped out at night. And by the time the morning sickness passes and the first-trimester fatigue abates, our boobs may be bigger, but so is the rest of us. I remember rolling into bed toward the end of my pregnancy, lying like a beached whale next to my inveterately amorous spouse, and finding the prospect of sex almost laughable. I just couldn't believe Steve could find my enormous belly or stretch marks a turn-on. I kept hearing Dr. Ruth's Viennese-rich voice reminding me that "zee brain is zee most important sexual organ." Especially true when you can't see below your breasts!

Of course, a sense of humor is key to maintaining a healthy sex life during your pregnancy. "I actually burst out laughing one night when I happened to catch a glimpse of us in our bedroom mirror," one mom said, laughing all over again. "I had had my eyes closed, and as I was getting into it, I guess I kind of forgot what I looked like, so at first I didn't know what I was looking at. We looked like a scene from one of those nature shows about the mating habits of giant bullfrogs or something!"

Other women talked about the advantages of not having to worry about contraception ("much more spontaneous"), of feeling more easily aroused as their pregnancies progressed (there's some evidence that increased blood flow to the pelvic area can be stimulating), of having to "be a little creative." "We tried some new positions," Diane recalled. "And I guess it was good that Greg became kind of fascinated by my body in a nonsexual way. He would lie next to me and stroke my belly and admire my body. It was really sweet—and that made us feel closer." Tami's husband loved her pregnant body. "He treats me like this icon of womanhood, this beautiful, sexy, life-bearing goddess."

One mom's husband told her she tasted different. "At first I was kind of grossed out," she told me, "but then it was really intriguing. I finally got up the nerve to ask my obstetrician about it, and she explained that your vagina can feel, look, and I guess taste different. When I told my husband he was right, he strutted around like he was some kind of connoisseur."

Leslie, who had had no problems reaching an orgasm before she became pregnant, saw her libido and her enjoyment of sex hit an all-time low. "At first I thought it was just because I was going through a lot of emotional turmoil. But by my second trimester, when I read in lots of books that women are often pretty horny, I realized I was the antithesis. Sex was the absolute last thing on my mind. It was hard to have an orgasm, and I had to reassure Josh that it was all about me, not him, because suddenly our sex life was nonexistent."

Imagining that the baby is in bed with you—even if said baby is the size of a lima bean and in the dark (literally) regarding what's happening—can definitely put a damper on your sex life. This was an issue for only a handful of moms, but several more told me that their husbands were preoccupied by fantasies (read wishful thinking) of hurting the baby. When the gorgeous Cindy Crawford shared this myth with me, I told her to tell her also-gorgeous husband not to flatter himself!

Of course, there are prospective dads whose libidos downshift dramatically as their wives get bigger and more awkward. But among the moms I interviewed, this was rarely the case. "I think we had a lot of sex during my pregnancy because everyone had warned us that we would be too exhausted to do it once the baby arrived!" one Chicago mom in her twenties said with a laugh.

Unsolicited Advice and Advances

Getting touched by one's husband may not be a problem; in fact, it's wonderful to have him kiss your giant belly or sing to the baby or admire your beautiful breasts and glowing skin. It's quite another thing to feel like one of those hands-on exhibits in a science museum ("Touch Mom's big hard tummy! You might even feel the fetus kick!"). Still, you'll be amazed by the number of strangers who feel compelled to pat your belly, ask you highly personal questions, or share a trove of pregnancy tales guaranteed to freak you out.

My personal favorite came from a woman at a cocktail party, who, spotting my maternity dress, torpedoed across the room, introduced herself hastily, and then launched into a revolting account of her friend's eighth-month ordeal: "She developed this problem with her salivary glands," she said, spitting a little herself, perhaps for the sake of verisimilitude. "So she drooled all the time. She had to carry a cup around all day—even at her office." Of course, I didn't have the where-withal to drool on *her* shoes or to ask why the hell she thought I needed to hear that particular story. I just stood mutely, soaking it all in, and spent the next twenty-four hours anxiously waiting for foam to begin to pour out of my mouth. Looking back, I see it a bit like a *Seinfeld* episode; back then it felt more like Stephen King.

Elise's close friends and family were a tad more tactful. "I find that people I am very close with, friends who know me and are sympathetic, tell me things that I really want to know," she said. "But people I know less well—friends of friends or, come to think of it, total strangers—burden me with horror stories."

Long after I gave birth, a wise obstetrician told me that he advises his patients to deal with unsolicited horror stories (and gratuitous advice) by nodding politely and then making lists in their head. "Just smile and think what groceries you need to buy, the contents of your closet—anything that makes it impossible to listen to their baloney."

For Elise it was easier to just say, "You know, I'm sorry that you had that experience, but I'd rather not hear any more. It upsets me." She also did not have the problem of unsolicited touching. "Maybe because I'm close to six feet tall, so I didn't look too cute or cuddly. People didn't gravitate my way, but I know someone who responded to a little old man's patting her belly by rubbing the top of his bald head!"

Everyone is different when it comes to being touched. Some moms find the intrusiveness appalling; others shrug it off. One mom told me she liked it ("It felt like blessings!"). Sandra recalled total strangers on the New York subway coming over to touch her. "Most times they would ask if they could touch my belly, but even when I said, 'But you're a total stranger,' they just had their hands on me. One guy came up to me and told me he thought pregnant women were really hot. I just said, 'Are you kidding me? No!' He got the message."

Noelle, a high school chemistry teacher, understood her students' fascination with her pregnant shape, although at first their touching made her "very uncomfortable." As a teacher, she wanted to encourage their curiosity and to answer their questions, but not at the expense of maintaining clear boundaries. "A lot of those accepted boundaries disappear when you're pregnant, especially among children."

There's no question that your sense of personal space alters completely as your pregnancy progresses. If you've always been the kind of person who walks into a crowded room and commands attention, either because of your personality or because of your physique, then you may not feel as though the world is very different, despite your own metamorphosis. But if you happen to be very petite or shy or both, then suddenly taking up more space—literally and in terms of others' attention—can make you feel big and powerful. There's no way to be a wallflower when you stick out like a giant flowering topiary. You walk into a room and heads turn; you board a bus and a little ripple of attention fans out as the women try to glare the seated males out of their feigned sleep.

I distinctly remember the first time I rode a bus a few weeks after giving birth to Maddie, and missing my pregnant shape and the attention I inevitably drew. (Not that any of those seated males had leapt to his feet when I was eight months along.) I didn't like being "back to normal," just another exhausted-looking, slightly pudgy commuter. I wanted to reexperience those knowing smiles from moms with toddlers and that sense of being singled out.

In his lovely short story "When Everyone Was Pregnant," John Updike describes a summer when his wife and several of her friends were pregnant: "How they would float across the sand like billowed sails. Shakespeare, Titania to Oberon: 'We have laughed to see the sails conceive, / And grow big-bellied with the wanton wind.' In their sun-paled maternity bathing suits, the pregnant young women. Tugging behind them the toddlers already born, like dinghies."[7] Reading that, I remember how like some beautiful ship or fully ripened fruit I felt toward the end of my pregnancy; I was a walking promise, inviting smiles and blessings from perfect strangers as I sailed through my day.

Pregnant at Work

Receiving unexpected attention in public was decidedly different from the responses I received at my job. My boss, a loving but definitely old-school type, greeted my pregnancy with enthusiasm, then quickly—and not too subtly—started to work around me. Suddenly I had far fewer assignments, I wasn't included in long-term planning sessions, and I was no longer the first of his consiglieri to be called with a question. It angered me, but I found as I spoke to other pregnant working moms that my experience was mild compared with many of theirs.

There's a healthy body of literature on the ways in which working women are often blatantly or subtly eased out of the inner circle once their pregnancies are announced or their physical change pronounced. Despite laws protecting pregnant women's jobs, guaranteeing maternity leave, and stipulating what constitutes discrimination, the latter can occur in ways that may not threaten your livelihood but will definitely shake your sense of yourself. As one of the first women in her department to have children, Sandra found that the attention she received was a mixed blessing. "Although I liked being told I looked great and I enjoyed their interest in my pregnancy, I also felt a little cut off. Television work is intense and fast-paced. People wouldn't tell me about certain meetings, because they knew I was going to be on maternity leave soon—or maybe they had kind of written me off by that point. But I wanted to be given the opportunity to attend or not."

Our feelings toward our jobs change as well. As the big day approaches, there's no way in the world you're not going to question what you're doing and how your baby's arrival on the planet will shift your priorities, affect your schedule, impact the goals you may have taken for granted until now. For Erica, a self-employed psychologist, the change in her feelings about work were fueled by a dread of "dropping off the career ladder." When I spoke to her, she was nursing Bryce, then five months old, and blissfully happy to be working part-time, but she vividly recalled her anxiety during her pregnancy: "I had reached a place in my career when I was enjoying a certain degree of renown and making my mark professionally. I was terrified of a drop after the baby. It was very frightening, and no matter how many times mothers told me I would feel differently, I couldn't imagine what it would be like."

The flash point in MaryAnn's pregnancy occurred a few weeks before her due date, when it seemed impossible to schedule a childbirth-education class convenient to both her and her busy spouse. "I had been telling myself that becoming parents would just be something new in our marriage and that our lives would continue," she recalled.

"But over the weekend, we had this big fight about the birthing class. Doug's got this huge presentation. And I've got a huge presentation, but I'm willing to find the time. So I'm yelling, 'What's more important? Your presentation or the baby?'" MaryAnn was quick to attribute the blowout to "a lot of emotions going on," including her profound fear that her love for the baby would derail her career: "Loving a baby is not the same as when you fall in love with your husband—with your husband you don't have the option to stay home with him all day. It's not like you get swept away and your life gets out of control. It's very scary to think I could be so in love with the baby that it would undermine everything I've built myself on."

Implicit in MaryAnn's eloquent and honest description of her feelings is the assumption that falling passionately in love with her baby and, perhaps, wanting to stay home guarantees an obliteration of "everything I've built myself on." As Daphne de Marneffe discusses throughout her book on the tension maternal love creates for all mothers, "One reason it is hard for any of us to think about maternal desire is that the life changes implied by those desires, the identity we will need to assume, seems radically at odds with the kind of goal-oriented activity that leads to success in social terms. To choose to redirect one's energies toward mothering means not only a change in one's use of time (not to mention one's economic standing or security), but often a drastic reformulation of one's orientation toward control, independence, and even one's prior identity."[8]

It hadn't occurred to MaryAnn, as it rarely occurs to most working mothers, that staying home full-time might radically change her sense of herself but not necessarily for the worse. Opening up to imagining a range of ways to be a mother is the most important work you can do during your pregnancy. Did I practice what I'm preaching? Suffice it to say, I worked until the day before Maddie was born, and Nick escaped being delivered on the floor of my office at *Parents* magazine only by virtue of my hysterical assistant threatening to call the building's one-eyed security guard if I didn't "leave right now!" Earlier that morning, as I was getting Maddie ready for preschool, I had felt a little pluck somewhere deep inside, but the sensation was so distant and uneventful (no Human Niagara Falls followed, as it had when my water broke with Maddie) that I assumed I had imagined it. By the time I arrived at my office, my elegant maternity dress (I had an important luncheon that day) was, shall we say, a bit damp, and although I had no labor pains, I knew this was it. Still, I lingered at my desk, trying in vain to finish my editorial column before I went uptown to my OB-GYN's office.

How's that for a model of what *not* to do? Although I don't advocate staying home for weeks before your baby's birth if you're only going to rewallpaper the nursery or watch afternoon soaps, I do believe in stopping long enough to consider what is about to happen. Talk to your spouse; write in a journal; take the risk that self-contemplation always requires. It is difficult, even painful, to let go of an image of yourself and to consider how a change in your identity will affect your work, friendships, marriage—your whole life. But when we lock ourselves into certain roles simply because we're afraid of imagining anything else, we deny ourselves a chance to consider the ways in which we yearn for and fear motherhood.

The Truth About Childbirth

As we hurtle toward childbirth, thoughts and feelings about losing our sense of ourselves, of facing an unknowable future, are easily overwhelmed by fears about labor and delivery. "Knowledge is power" may be your mantra as you attend childbirth classes, quiz your obstetrician or midwife about what to expect, and read books on everything from water births to active births to spiritual births to at-home births. When the printed word fails to satisfy the hunger to know "what it's really like," you're likely to turn to relatives, friends, even total strangers to tell you about their experiences.[9]

One of the reasons we turn to other women for support and advice may be that in some deep, atavistic way, we know we can't go it alone. In *Woman: An Intimate Geography,* Natalie Angier points out that we are the only species among whom birth is a shared experience. Think about your cat disappearing for a week, only to be discovered in some darkened corner of your closet nursing a litter of mewling kittens. Thanks to our evolutionary history, the human mother needs help. "She needs help so badly that she begins to panic shortly before the birth. She starts to anticipate pain and difficulty, and she feels lost and vulnerable, but the anxiety is not pathological, it is not the byproduct of the hormonal maelstrom of late-stage gestation, as some have said. It is rational anxiety, and as human as our opposable thumbs, our depilated breasts, and our Lamaze classes."[10]

For most pregnant moms, their number-one question is "Will I be able to stand the pain?" Whether you need anesthesia to get your teeth cleaned or you laugh off root canal, the prospect of pushing a fully formed, melon-sized head out of your vagina makes skydiving sound like a spa treatment. I remember standing in a supermarket when a *National Enquirer* headline assaulted me: COMA MOM WAKES DURING LABOR. The message was clear: Even if you've been brain-dead for nine months, the pain will snap you out of it!

The problem is, you're unlikely to get a straight answer regarding birth. And you'll certainly not get a *short* one. There is nothing mothers like to talk about more than the exhausting, exhilarating, terrifying, and sometimes comical hours surrounding their child's birth. But if you're interested in hearing about the most thrilling and satisfying moments in a woman's life, told with a vividness and clarity unaffected by time, then by all means pour yourself a cup of coffee, pull up a chair, and ask.

And since you didn't ask, but this is my book, I'll start with my own childbirth tales. The night Maddie arrived, I had decided to follow the folk wisdom about garlicky food inducing labor and had indulged in a giant bowl of spaghetti and meatballs. Suffice it to say, I haven't eaten a meatball since. Steve and I had just finished watching one of my favorite movies on TV when my water broke at midnight. That little internal pluck followed by the involuntary expulsion of warm liquid all over our new bedspread made it pretty clear what was happening, but Steve seemed genuinely flabbergasted. "What do you *mean* you're in labor!" he whinnied, as a kind of Jim Carrey eyesbulging expression exploded on his face. When I reiterated in my most soothing voice that the big moment was imminent, he rushed to brew a giant pot of coffee, so he could stay up with me. I protested that he should take advantage of the next few hours to sleep. "No, no," he insisted. "I'm going to stay awake with you and time your contractions." Two giant mugs of black coffee later, he was out cold.

I began timing my contractions, taking the slow, controlled Lamaze breaths I had dutifully practiced over the past few weeks. By the time I woke Steve, four hours later, the pain that gripped my lower torso

every five minutes led to more breath holding than controlled panting. I kept running (well, waddling) to the bathroom, as though all I
had was a bad case of the runs, but obviously that was not what my
body was trying to expel.

We headed for the hospital (via a cab whose driver spent so much
time glancing anxiously into the rearview mirror that Steve had to tell
him to keep his eyes on the road), where I vaguely recall checking in.
All I wanted was some relief from the pain, which was frightening in
its unrelenting intensity. I do remember thinking—as I threw up my
garlicky meatballs—that no one had warned me about this. (I never
went into labor with Molly, who was delivered via an emergency
C-section.) Yes, I knew it would hurt, that I might want an epidural,
but I didn't expect the contractions to make me puke, hold my breath,
beg for help. When my obstetrician finally appeared and asked if I
wanted anything for the pain, I screamed, "ARE YOU KIDDING?"
Who the hell would say no?

Of course there are thousands of moms who give birth with little or
no pain relief. And I salute them one and all. But it's unfair and wrong
to perpetuate the myth that stoicism makes the mom. After all, the
Barbary macaque monkey swings through trees while in labor, stopping a couple of times to check out what's happening down there but
eventually just reaching back and scooping up her baby with her free
hand. A little holding and yelping and then she's back in the swing of
things—literally.[11] Is she a superior simian because she seems to feel
less pain than some other species clutching a branch and howling in
another part of the jungle? As far as I know, those Barbary macaques
may be a bunch of sluts, without a maternal bone in their bodies. The
point is, you could line up the ten greatest moms on earth and discover that half of them were out cold during their kids' births.

That said, it's extremely important to know in advance what your
options may be. One of the toughest aspects of labor and birth is
feeling totally out of control. It's not only the intensity of the pain
that's hard to take, it's the unrelenting, inexorable nature of the
birth process that often seems unbearable. Even Dawn, a self-confessed
marathon-running stoic, told me that she was unprepared for the fear
generated by her lack of control during labor. "People say that you forget the pain, the trauma, but I don't understand how you ever forget
it. I felt totally out of control, which was the hardest part. Just lying

there in that bed, just trying to shake it off, with everyone saying, 'Visualize, breathe.' And I couldn't even function."

There will be plenty of opportunities for emotionally painful acts of selflessness during the years ahead. If you need pain relief, go for it. For Dawn—and definitely for me—an epidural provided the perfect cocktail of pain relief and muscle control. I remember feeling as though I were floating in a warm bath, and although I could feel the pressure of the contractions, the pain had vanished.

In what seemed like a matter of minutes, my obstetrician was telling me, "You're ten centimeters. Let's go!" and Steve and I were flying along the corridor to the delivery room. By the time Nick was born, the hospital had renovated its maternity ward, so when the moment came to push, my beautifully appointed labor room became the delivery room. The furniture adjusted to my needs—not the other way around—an apt metaphor for the changes in maternal care that have occurred over the past few decades.

There's no question that we have more say over our birth experiences than in the days when Dr. Patronize banished Dad to the cigar-choked waiting room, put Mom to sleep, and used forceps to pull the baby out. Lamaze and other relaxation techniques, improved pain-management options, and the participation of husbands, partners, parents, even children definitely make childbirth less like a dreaded illness and more like a celebration.

For Laura, who went into labor three weeks early, a crash course in Lamaze helped enormously during the final and most difficult stages of labor. "I remember thinking when we were taking the course, 'How the heck is breathing going to help?' But it definitely gave me something to focus on and alleviated some of the pain. I didn't find it that bad." Laura was so unfazed during the actual delivery that one of the nurses joked, "It's like you're at the mall!" And Laura admits that she felt as though she was in "this other world," a state of mind not induced by an anesthetic cocktail.

The physical challenge of birth was intimately linked to the emotional and spiritual aspects of the experience for Phoebe, who delivered both her babies at home. During nine hours of hard labor with her first daughter, Malaika, a large cast of friends and family coached her with her breathing, gave her massages, chanted prayers, even bathed her. "It was really empowering," she said dreamily. "We did everything ourselves, and I just accepted the pain as a powerful, mystical experience, something a woman is meant to have."

Phoebe, pregnant with her second baby, was in the park with Malaika, then three, when her labor started in earnest. "This time I knew it was going to be painful, and I tried to embrace it and learn more, because it is such a blessing to give birth. We stayed in the park, walking around. We even went to a concert and were laughing and dancing. My mom and my best friend—who's like a sister—were there, and when we got home I finished cleaning the house, putting clean sheets on the beds. At seven p.m. I got in the bath with Malaika, and then she and my mom went out for pizza. At eight, the labor was very intense and it lasted until almost ten, when she was born. My husband was there about an hour before she was born, and I definitely was waiting for him, because when he arrived, I felt relieved and relaxed. When the midwife arrived, I was fully dilated. I got into a kind of squatting position, with my husband behind me and my friend in front of me, and I just pushed against them with all my might. Five pushes, and Aiya was born."

For those of you who are reading this and thinking you would like to take out a contract on Phoebe's head, bear in mind that childbirth is not a competitive sport. She's the first to say that whatever gets you through the experience, whatever helps you wrest some control over the pain, the fatigue, the fear, is what works. And that may be screaming or chanting, cursing or crying—or all of the above. Squeezing the feeling out of Steve's hand helped me a lot, as did blaming him for the meatballs. Massage, music, or medication should be available if and when you need them—not just when the doctor dictates.

Before You Push, Be Pushy

The problem for many women is that our desire to be a "good girl,"[12] a "good patient," runs high. This is especially true in a hospital setting. At home women are often freer to act however they want, to move or say or do whatever makes them comfortable, without thoughts of offending or annoying "the staff." This is definitely not how I felt the night Steve and I arrived at the hospital. Having been raised by an obstetrician-gynecologist, I was taught that the white lab coat, like a royal Greek chiton, elevates the wearer slighter closer to Mount Olympus. My OB-GYN was certainly breathing more rarified air than I was as I panted my way through the first stages of labor. An hour after I checked in, all my plans to be assertive about fetal monitors, walking epidurals, or ice chips seemed to evaporate.

My reluctance to speak up even extended to the recovery stage, when I was wheeled into a storage room because the hospital didn't have a bed ready for me. As I lay there, staring at boxes of Kotex and paper towels (believe me, I was not hallucinating), it occurred to me that this was a hell of a lot worse than getting a lousy table at my favorite restaurant—something I would have had no problem demanding to change. Yet I just lay there as nurses scurried in and out, grabbing supplies and commiserating about the inexcusable lack of beds.

Apparently my passivity was not a function of my doctor-God confusion. I have a friend who makes Rosie O'Donnell look shy, who admitted that she was obsequious, even coy, with the hospital staff. "Maybe it was because I felt so vulnerable, so like a child myself during the whole experience," she explained. "I just didn't have those 'Do it 'cause I say so!' chops together at all. I just lay there thanking them for showing up."

Alyce, whose son was three weeks old when we met, still harbored bitterness toward the hospital staff. "I had to ask for everything. And when you're under all this pressure, not to mention pain, to then also have to be assertive—it made me really mad. For example, I wanted to walk during my labor. We had been told during our Lamaze class that it often helped to walk, but they insisted I stay on the monitor. So, sure enough, we asked the labor nurse, and she said, Well, you need to be on the monitor, but let me ask your doctor. An hour later she came back and said okay. If I hadn't taken the class, I wouldn't have known to ask. As it was, I had to wait over an hour to get an answer."

According to a recent survey of nearly sixteen hundred women, the good news is that Alyce's experience seems to be the exception, not the rule.[13] Of the women surveyed, 96 percent reported satisfaction with the care they received during childbirth. Close to that number (94 percent) said they were treated "with kindness and understanding"; 87 percent said they were "free to make their own decisions."

For moms who have an unplanned C-section—often after hours of hard labor—relief and joy may be miserably tainted by disappointment and bitterness. "The terrible thing about the C-section was that I felt all that pressure beforehand to go through a natural birth, and then, during labor, the doctors and everybody were pulling me in different directions," Alyce recalled. "And I just didn't feel like anyone was on my side." Alyce's bitterness extended to the doula she hired to help her during delivery. "She actually told me that Nathaniel's jaundice was due to the cesarean. And I just said to her, 'That's not true, it has nothing to do with it,' but I was really upset, because I began to question all the other things she had told me. And you're so much more vulnerable at that point, you don't really know anything, so it's particularly upsetting to have the people you trust undermine your confidence in them."

Alyce's experience underscores how important it is to be prepared for the possibility of a C-section and to understand why it might happen. A recent study found that women who had planned C-sections "showed a more positive reaction to their experience than unplanned C-section women." Other research supports the idea that the more in control a mom feels before and during birth, the less likely she is to suffer from postpartum depression and to report that childbirth was a positive experience. ("Mothers whose actual experience differed significantly from their expected experience showed an increase in depressive symptoms from antepartum to postpartum. The mothers with an internal locus of control were both more satisfied with their childbirth experience and showed less of an increase in depressive symptoms.")[14]

For approximately one in five moms, a cesarean will be deemed the safest and perhaps the only way to deliver their babies.[15] Discussing the reasons your doctor might suggest a cesarean well in advance of your due date can spare you disappointment, frustration, and anger.

Giving Birth

There should be a song for women to sing at this moment, or a prayer to recite. But perhaps there is none because there are no words strong enough to name that moment. Like every mother since the first mother, I was overcome and bereft, exalted and ravaged. I had crossed over from girlhood. I beheld myself as an infant in my mother's arms and caught a glimpse of my own death. I wept without knowing whether I rejoiced or mourned. My mothers and their mothers were with me as I held my baby.

From The Red Tent by Anita Diamant[16]

If motherhood is a push-pull dance of connection and separation, independence and dependence, then birth is the ultimate pas de deux. For nine months the baby is inside you; there is no separation—psychological or physical. Then, once the umbilical cord is cut, the baby is considered separate, independent of you. But as Joyce Block says in *Motherhood as Metamorphosis,* "What is physically self-evident is not always psychically real."[17] It's impossible to witness that slippery miracle making his entrance into the world and not feel highly connected and painfully alone, at once enlarged and diminished. One thing is certain: Whether you're positioned in such a way as to witness your baby's final slide into life or prone on an operating table with a curtain separating you from your cesarean incision, the sight of your fully formed newborn unfolding like a flower before your eyes will be one you never, ever forget.

For Katherine, who had a cesarean, seeing her baby "lifted up over the screen" was a kind of shock. "Of course, this was what we were waiting for—how could it possibly have been any different? But there was this very pronounced sense of her birth. I felt tremendously close to her, still connected with her, but I also had a very strong sense of her as an individual, especially when I watched the nurse walk away with her."

Phoebe, who gave birth at home, recalls marveling at her daughter's body and realizing that, in a way, she was giving birth to herself. "I thought about the fact that I was being reborn along with Malaika. And then I thought about the miraculous promise of her anatomy, that someday her perfect, tiny vagina would be able to do what I had done. It was just fantastic!"

Giving birth is transformative and transitional, a culmination and a beginning; it brings a sense of oneness and of separateness, cataclysmic upheaval and intense focus. It is an experience so charged with stress, fear, pain, joy, relief, and gratitude that it quickly becomes our war story of courage, strength, and survival.

"I had a vaginal birth," Erica recalled. "I was crying. I don't think I was thinking, I was just emotional. I looked at him, and what I thought was, 'My God, he's so big!' I just didn't imagine that this big, beautiful baby could come out of me, and I just wanted to look at him and look at him. It was the best feeling in the world." Asked if her baby fulfilled her fantasies, she was quick to reply, "He exceeded my fantasies."

Other moms felt weirdly detached. After a painful and very long labor and delivery, Dawn found her daughter's actual presence in her arms an odd out-of-body experience. "I remember that I was going through an inventory. I was like, 'Okay, she has two eyes, ten fingers. Let me see her toes.' I was staring at her, examining her, pulling her apart in that way. While Danny, from the second she was born, he was just bawling, 'She's beautiful! She's gorgeous! She's perfect!' I was just kind of checking her out and trying to take it all in, sitting back and watching her."

I remember feeling terrified of Nick when he was born. Unlike Maddie, who had peeped gently and gazed into my eyes from under her little stocking cap, Nick screamed like a wildcat when my obstetrician put him on my chest. I was actually relieved when the nurse took him away for his Apgar test. Several moms confessed that after the ordeal of childbirth, they were beyond exhausted—physically and emotionally. "I wept from fatigue and relief," Nancy told me. "But I think everyone assumed I was weeping from joy. I guess I was happy, but I can't remember wanting anything but to close my eyes and shut everything out for a while."

So what is this bonding business all about? Despite a few persuasive studies of infant attachment, there remains as much myth as medical truth to the study of mother love. The two researchers most responsible for the debate were Marshall Klaus and John Kennell, whose book *Maternal-Infant Bonding* was published in 1976. They postulated that during the period immediately postpartum, mothers were plunged into a highly sensitive state, a hormonally enriched pool of love, when they were primed to bond with their infants. Klaus and Kennell emphasized the importance of allowing at least thirty minutes of private contact between mother and baby after birth, including placing the baby on the mother's breast, so she could caress and feed him.[18]

Thanks to their research—and lots of other work on attachment that followed—you were probably given your baby to hold and breast-feed after birth. And that's obviously very good news. The bad news is that moms who don't feel an immediate pull toward their babies, who are too wiped out or overwhelmed to "bond," are often made to feel that they're freaks.

Love at First Sight—Sometimes

If you happen to fall into the "Whoa, who the heck is this?" camp or feel guilty because your first postpartum thought was, "Oh, God, please let me sleep," bear in mind that most of what we know about the neurochemistry of mother love comes from animal research. For obvious reasons, researchers can't manipulate the hormone levels in human mothers' brains, so they do most of their research on rodents. Klaus and Kennell based much of their research on goats and sheep. Apparently, if ewes don't bond immediately with their babies, and the latter wander out into the pasture and get mixed up with all the other little lambies, the ewes don't know who is who (or whose ewe is who—or ewe . . .). Needless to say, you're not a sheep, and feeling somewhat detached, even put off by your baby, is in no way maladaptive during the first few weeks postpartum.

Chances are, you will look at your baby and experience a ferocious love—feeling more like a lion than a lamb. When you hold your newborn against your bare skin, cradle her between hand and heart, stroke and pat her, you're likely to feel a pull, an intimacy, an intense longing for more. I remember how bereft I felt when the maternity-ward nurse would come to take Maddie back to the newborn nursery so I could rest after feeding her. One morning I padded down the hospital hall to have a peek and found Maddie crying in protest during a highly efficient but unnecessarily abrupt diaper change. I wanted to hurl my body through the glass, to save her from Nurse Cruella's icy wipes.

Katherine, whose baby was born by cesarean section in the United Kingdom, described an "instantaneous, absolute, wonderful connection" with her baby. In fact, she was furious when she heard her husband refer to their daughter as "it" when he telephoned family and friends with the big news. "I remember how outraged I was—I mean, crying hysterically—when David said, 'Oh, *it's* fine,' and I just felt as though he was denying her being an individual. I was really upset."

The fact that childbirth brings about more dramatic physical changes than any experience other than death speaks volumes in describing how fully saturated and drained one feels immediately postpartum.[19] As with every other moment in our emotional experience as mothers, there is not a "right" way to react. As anthropologist Sarah Blaffer Hrdy observes, other animals have very specific ways of acting immediately following the birth of their young, but "there are no 'fixed action patterns' universally exhibited by new mothers in *Homo sapiens* comparable to mammalian mothers licking babies and biting off the amniotic sac." Yummy! No, we don't tend to lick our babies or eat our placentas or engage in any particular "species-specific" way. Euphoria is neither the only nor the "typical" reaction to a baby's arrival.[20]

Whether or not you fall head over heels in love with your baby in the delivery room says absolutely nothing about your relative "goodness" as a mother. But your reaction to childbirth and to the intense emotions you experience provides important clues to your strengths and weaknesses, hot buttons and hidden talents. It pays to note how this first and most dramatic challenge of motherhood made you feel, because there will be myriad times in the years ahead when you will once again experience exhaustion, fear, euphoria, and the feeling of being out of control. Recognizing that you tend to shut down emotionally when you're anxious or that losing control makes you see red or that exhaustion goes hand in hand with panic gives you a chance to work on those weak spots as your child grows.

Settling In

The first few days after you bring your baby home tend to feel slightly surreal. There's a sense of blurred boundaries, of feeling as though you've been turned inside out. Sleep deprivation plays a part, as do hormonal changes, but there's also enormous emotional/psychological fallout from the birth experience. I definitely recall the odd feeling of being separate yet powerfully connected to Maddie. Every day, usually when no one could hear me, I would whisper, "I can't believe you're here" or "Are those really your toes?" because the miraculous sense of her otherness blew me away. When she turned her head toward me in response to a question (as all newborns do when they hear their mother's voice) and locked her eyes with mine, I held my breath reverently.

In a lovely essay adapted from her journals, the novelist Elizabeth Berg described waking up in the mornings following her daughter's birth and automatically putting her hand to her stomach, looking for her pregnant shape. "I worry about you, lost-looking in a crib that seems gigantic. I check on you a million times a day as you sleep there, your head nudged into the corner of the bumper pad. Is it familiar to you, that feeling of having your head pressed against something? Is that why you determinedly make your way there, regardless of where in the crib I lay you down? I am glad to have you out in the world with me at last, but sometimes we miss the way we used to be. Thus it is that I wake up and put my hand to my empty womb; thus it is that you inch your way up toward a memory, seeking a kind of solace in your sleep. We have not left pregnancy behind completely, either of us. We remember together."[21]

As clear and keen as mothers are about their birth experiences, most of them claim a kind of amnesia about their first weeks at home. I certainly have no memory of what I did all day when Maddie was a week or two old. I see myself shuffling around our tiny apartment, various pads shifting and rustling like the soughing of some big tired tree. I do remember that I found a pile of neatly folded burping cloths in the refrigerator one morning and that having a conversation complete with adverbs and adjectives was practically impossible. And, like many moms I spoke to, I rarely knew if it was day or night.

"I actually didn't remember certain visitors who came by to see me," my friend Nicole told me, which was no surprise, because I had been one of them. What was truly amazing, however, was how energized and alert she had seemed when I stopped by—only a few hours after she had given birth to twins. "I can't believe how great you seem," I had gushed, admiring her beautiful rosy cheeks and glowing eyes.

"I feel good," she said. And then proceeded to make a fuss over the gift I had brought. She even volunteered to walk me down the hallway to see the babies, but I insisted she rest. "I actually have a lot of energy!" she chirped. Now I know that we were conversing in her dreams.

For many moms, elation, relief, and an energy high make the initial postpartum period far better than they had anticipated. Kathleen, who gave birth to her son on a beautiful California Christmas Day, ascribed her "intense euphoria" to feeling cleansed of the hormones that had made her nauseated for nine months. "I never felt better in my life than I did that day and in the weeks that followed. I would wake up at night and be soaked with perspiration, but I felt as though all of the bad stuff that had made me sick was being flushed out of me. And during the days, I was so up and happy—it was wonderful."

Elise, also a California mom, found that "the euphoria lasted for days." Having been told that she would want to sleep and sleep, Elise was too excited to close her eyes. "I would just wake up and look at Ella and want to hold her. She slept so much that when she woke up and looked around, it was so exciting. I didn't want to miss it."

Fatigue, Fear, and Fragility

Unfortunately, for most mothers this adrenaline high doesn't last. Bone-numbing exhaustion, painful episiotomy sutures, sore nipples, hemorrhoids, unexplained weepiness, and ravenous hunger can easily overwhelm even the most blissed-out new mom. In fact, a couple of weeks after giving birth, you're likely to feel betrayed—by your body, your doctor or midwife, the articles and books you read, and by every mother who somehow neglected to mention how tough the first few weeks can be.

"No one told me how hard it would be," Stephanie confided, her anger palpable. "I felt as though I was the victim of this kind of conspiracy of silence. I guess people don't want you to be scared, but I was totally unprepared for how exhausted I was. I mean, I knew intellectually that I would be tired, but no one really prepared me. I was sick several times in the beginning, and a guy I work with said, 'Well, that's from exhaustion. Sleep deprivation *is* a form of torture.'"

In fact, if you've never seen the movie classic *Stalag 17*, rent it tonight—and try to stay awake for the critical scene during which an American POW is being tortured by the Nazi commandant. Don't worry, the scene isn't remotely disturbing. In fact, by the time the Nazis finally send the lieutenant back to his barracks, you're unlikely to experience patriotic pride or admiration for his act of heroism and strength; you're more apt to shrug and say, "Ha! That's nothing!" Because the form of torture employed is sleep deprivation. They make the poor guy stand against a wall for a couple of days. Big deal. You're deprived of sleep for weeks on end, and no one calls *you* a hero.

One mom described her state of mind as post-traumatic stress, and there's no question that childbirth is traumatic, pushing us to the edge of our physical limitations. Karen Binder-Brynes, a psychologist who specializes in post-traumatic stress disorder, says that childbirth has never been classified as a "trauma" because it's a natural and sup-posedly happy part of life, but she agrees that the pain, fear, feelings of being out of control, and thoughts of death echo many of the precipitating factors in PTSD. More important, the symptoms of the syndrome—sleeplessness, exhaustion, panic attacks, and irritability—have all been associated with the postpartum period.[22]

I recall a kind of psychological fragility, if not sheer terror, at the prospect of caring for my tiny, helpless baby. When Maddie screamed and flailed her arms, I didn't need a neurophysiologist or trauma ex-pert to tell me that my stress hormones were elevated. My every muscle tensed as I tried to calm her; then I worried that the tension in my body would exacerbate her fretfulness.

The week we brought Maddie home from the hospital, the temper-ature of her room became the lightning rod for all of my anxiety. Our adorable fifth-floor walk-up had lost its charm because of the no-toriously unreliable radiators. Metamorphosing into the proverbial mother grizzly bear, I screamed at our landlord with a ferocity that surprised (or at least awakened) anyone within a two-block radius. When he finally arrived to bleed the pipes, I stood nearby, clutching a room thermometer in my hand like a stone, threatening to bleed *him* if the heat didn't come up *right away*.

Most mothers experience similar feelings of passionate concern. The cliché of the new mom waking her sleeping baby just to make sure he's breathing is probably played out in some newborn's nursery every day. Alyce sent her husband on a wild-goose chase for a rectal ther-mometer when their newborn son felt a bit warm to the touch. "We actually had a digital ear thermometer, but I knew that those weren't the most accurate, so when it read one hundred degrees, we began to get really nervous. We had been told to call the doctor if he ran a temperature of a hundred point five, so I sent Steve up to the twenty-four-hour Duane Reade by taxi. He came back with two different rectal thermometers. And, of course, we didn't know how to use them. How far do you insert it? How much Vaseline do you put on the tip? We finally called a friend who's a pediatrician, and he went through the play-by-play, but by the time we were satisfied that Nathaniel was okay, we were totally exhausted."

Kristen found herself in a "constant state of fear." Having worried throughout her pregnancy about the baby's safety, she even asked the doctor who conducted a maternity-ward tour if obstetricians ever drop the baby when it "shoots out." When he replied, "Well, I've never dropped one," Kristen interpreted that to mean that other doctors do. For months after her son was born, Kristen was sure that someone would spill something and scald his tender skin. Or that her husband would drop him. "Let's not even get into Sudden Infant Death Syndrome and checking his breathing every hour," she said when I asked about her anxiety level. "I'm better now, but there's always some demon tapping me on the shoulder whispering in my ear that something awful will happen. I don't know if I'm crazy or suffering from post-9/11 stress or if it's hormonal."

In her book Life After Birth, Kate Figes describes how, when each of her babies was just weeks old, she saw danger everywhere: "A kitchen knife could so easily be plunged into her stomach, too great a squeeze could break her neck, or a pillow could so easily smother her. I knew that I would never kill my babies, but the images were so vivid and frequent that they were frightening and felt uncomfortably close to madness at times, for I had no control over them and couldn't prevent them from coming." As Figes points out, a psychiatrist might interpret these fantasies as "suppressed anger and a longing for release from the constant demands of a small baby," but she believes—and I tend to agree—that something very primal is at play during those early weeks.[23] Despite numbing fatigue, we are more finely tuned, more sensitive and alert to our babies' distress.

Psychiatrist Daniel Stern believes that our postpartum fears are "nature's way of assuring your baby's survival." In The Birth of a Mother, he harshly criticizes mental health professionals who label moms' worries as unconscious desires to hurt their babies: "The interpretation of a mother's vigilant responses (fears) as a manifestation of ambivalence is a misapplication of theory that I find wrong-headed and destructive rather than helpful. It serves only to wound the mother and make her doubt herself at a profound level."[24]

Just what you need—more self-doubt—especially during the first few weeks when your baby's routines are totally unpredictable and every change in his behavior is open to interpretation. When he won't sleep, you wear treads in the carpet pacing back and forth trying to soothe him. But if he happens to sleep longer than usual, you imagine the worst and rush in to see what's wrong. When the baby cries excessively, you're frantic, but a baby who never cries doesn't seem quite normal. My friend Dawn actually called 911 the night her baby threw up for the first time. "They kept saying, 'Lady, calm down and call your regular doctor,' but I was screaming that my child never vomited like this and it was an emergency."

"I was a teen parent," said Jennifer. "I remember driving home from the hospital. She was crying. And I wondered if we had to stop the car to change her diaper. I felt I knew absolutely nothing. And I was so upset by her crying."

As Alyce said during the third week of her son's life, "The biggest revelation of the first couple of days, the early weeks, was that I could imagine why someone might lose it: why there is shaken-baby syndrome, why kids get abused, or get hit. I mean, if I didn't have Steve to hand Nathaniel off to at some point . . . I could see—I don't know. It's not about being a bad mother. It's just that the situation is so overwhelming. You're sleep-deprived; you're irrational. I don't know how people do it all alone. Or do it when they're fourteen years old."

Not long after I spoke to Alyce, I called one of my closest friends, the mother of four. We had a long-standing lunch date, but when I heard her raspy, exhausted voice, I told her we could reschedule. "No, no," she said with audible desperation. "I have to get out of the house, or I'm going to shoot myself in the head." Later, over lunch, she, too, confessed how she understood why people throw their babies out of windows. "No one wants to admit that they feel this way sometimes. But on days like today when I'm sick and the kids are sick and we've been up all night—or for several nights in a row—I know that if I didn't have help, I would go nuts."

For Jackie, the mother of newborn twins, her salvation was simply giving herself permission to feel out of control, exhausted, overwhelmed, and miserable for a set period. "I'm the kind of person who has to take a situation and try to make sense out of it, to somehow put it in its place, even though it is so out of place. I said to myself, 'I know this is going to be really hard, impossible at times, for the next three months. I'm giving myself ninety days, during which I just won't know what each day is going to bring, and I have to accept that. And I really was *not* happy for the first three months. But knowing that it had nothing to do with the children, that it was about me and that it would definitely get better, saved me from going crazy sometimes."

Letting go of the expectation that life will soon get back to normal is absolutely critical during this postpartum period. There's nothing "normal" about days that merge into night, a body that balloons and sags in bizarre and sometimes painful ways, and a heart that pumps equal amounts of passion and panic. Take the pressure off yourself and plan nothing, other than ample time to sleep, eat, feed your baby, and lie in bed with your partner beside you and your little miracle between you. If you manage to take a shower or to change out of your spit-up encrusted nightgown, give yourself a well-deserved pat on the back. Then get back into bed.

Breast-feeding: This Is Not a Test . . .

Reducing your expectations about how your first few weeks postpartum should go can help minimize the stress and reduce the learning curve associated with breast-feeding. Unfortunately, most of us assume that the natural flow of milk goes hand in hand with an instinctive understanding of how to get that milk into the baby's mouth, so when breast-feeding doesn't go smoothly at first—and it often does not—a cascade of feelings follows: frustration, disappointment, guilt. Yes, nursing is one of the great milestones of motherhood, and a convenient, cost-free, healthful, and deeply satisfying experience. But to a person, the moms I interviewed admitted that their unrealistic expectations, coupled with inadequate information and support, initially made nursing seem about as natural as levitating. Whether you wind up a La Leche League spokeswoman, breast-feeding with a vengeance for years, or switch to a bottle after a few weeks, your baby will thrive. And you'll do no one any favors by treating this first challenge as a test of your mettle as a mom.

"Everyone said, 'Oh, once you get the knack of it, everything will be smooth sailing,'" recalled Alyce. "And although you hear about blocked ducts, most of the books make these problems seem like the exception, not the rule. So when I had this shooting pain down my arms every time I fed Nathaniel, I couldn't figure it out." Diagnosed with mastitis, Alyce suffered through hours of misery, compounded by the often conflicting messages she got from doctors, lactation consultants, and her well-meaning husband. "Steve was urging me to wait longer between feedings, so I could rest—which was a joke! Who can rest? According to the books, I was supposed to feed on demand—every two hours. And when I called my wonderful pediatrician, she says in this warm Zsa Zsa Gabor accent, 'Da-a-a-hling, we can only give him what we have. It's okay, give him from the bottle, or some of the expressed milk that you have,' like I've got all this stuff stocked away. And she was very nice about it, but then of course subconsciously it makes you feel very bad, because you think you don't have enough milk."

Turning to La Leche, an organization Wendy Wasserstein once dubbed "the nipple Nazis," Alyce was told to feed more, which meant she sometimes had her baby to her breast for hours. "I really felt like my breasts were gonna fall off! So finally, in the end, I couldn't take it anymore. I told Steve to crack open a bottle and we supplemented Nathaniel with some formula, and in two or three days everything started to normalize. And now, we're finally in sync and it's great."

After trying to nurse for several painful and frustrating days, Jill called in a lactation consultant. "Bryan nicknamed her 'the Breast Whisperer,' because she was so gentle and lovely. But I just found it too difficult and then Nicholas started losing weight, so I switched to formula." Physical, emotional, and logistical challenges aside, the number-one reason women stop breast-feeding is that they do not believe they have enough milk.[25] And there's no question that the whole process would be a lot easier if our breasts were transparent.

Not being able to see exactly what your baby is getting, coupled with a newborn's tendency to drift off during feedings or to lose a little weight after birth, can make bottle-feeding highly attractive.

Like most women in this country, Elise was given a hasty breast-feeding how-to in the hospital and discharged before her milk came in. "I'm pretty busty to begin with. So when my breasts were so huge, I really thought I might suffocate Ella!"

I'll never forget getting home from the hospital, settling Maddie into her new bassinet, and lying down for a brief nap, only to discover upon waking that my breasts had ballooned into two gigantic leaky torpedoes. I felt like the hapless heroine in some sick Brothers Grimm tale. I struggled to get Maddie latched on, but my nipples were twenty-five times the size of her mouth. Not that she didn't make powerful use of those tiny chapped lips; in fact, I couldn't believe how hard she sucked. By the following day, my nipples were so sore that I wept through each feeding, prompting everyone from my mother to Maddie's pediatrician to suggest I give up.

But I didn't want to give up—not just because my Martyr Mom hormones had already kicked in but because I believed that "breast was best." I imagined subjecting my innocent baby to years of ear infections, allergies, and lowered IQ scores simply because my nipples hurt. When my sister showed me the trick of placing Maddie on a pillow to raise her up and I discovered the soothing effect of warm compresses and cold cabbage leaves (they work wonders while they wilt), the pain and awkwardness of those first few days were reduced immeasurably. By Maddie's third week on the planet I had begun to enjoy nursing; by week six, I couldn't remember exactly what had been so challenging. Gazing down into her liquid brown eyes, watching her drift in and out of sleep, I felt animal-like, wholly unique and completely unoriginal all at the same moment. I felt happy, proud, competent, protective, vulnerable, strong.

I also know that had I opted for formula, Maddie would have been just fine. The quiet moments of holding her, of stroking her cheek or her downy head, of watching her boneless biscuit of a fist clasp my finger or a bit of my blouse would have been just as intensely satisfying had I been feeding her from a bottle. It's far better to give your baby formula feeling relaxed and comfortable than to nurse twisted with anxiety, resentment, or anger. Mother's milk alone isn't going to determine your child's path in life. In fact, deciding to respect your own feelings, your own needs, will probably benefit your child in ways that far outstrip the nutritional advantages of breast milk.

If you do decide to bottle-feed, you'll need to prepare yourself for the first of many guilt trips, especially if your friends or relatives are avid breast-feeders. A national survey conducted by *BabyTalk* magazine in 2001 garnered 36,000 passionate responses and underscored how divided the breast/bottle camps really are. Two out of three breast-feeders "felt sorry" for formula-fed babies, and over a third said they thought bottle-feeding moms were "selfish and lazy." One mother compared bottle-feeding to smoking. Another accused bottle-feeders of neglect, bordering on abuse.[26]

Of course, the bottle-feeders weren't so sweet either. Although 92 percent said they supported breast-feeding, their actions belied their responses: 83 percent of breast-feeders reported that they felt criticized by moms who pack bottles. According to the magazine, "Much of the criticism takes the form of looks of disapproval or derogatory remarks from other mothers while they are nursing in public."

It's a shame when this kind of competition makes the universal club of motherhood feel more like a collection of competing sororities (Ima Beta Mama versus Alpha Nu Mamas?), inherently fraught with feelings of alienation. "When Emily was born, I had so much trouble feeding her that she started to lose weight," my sister-in-law Lois recalled. A graduate of Harvard and Harvard Law School, Lois is one of the most highly accomplished and competent women I know, yet she admitted, "For the first time in my life, I really didn't know what to do and I was in a panic. I felt very alone." According to research conducted at Boston City Hospital, so-called type-A moms are more likely to breast-feed, apparently "because they're into mastering the task at hand."[27] By the same token, when something as seemingly simple as sticking your boob in your baby's mouth proves painfully challenging, moms who are used to being mistresses of their universe can find themselves anxious and frustrated.

Having had a cesarean, an experience she saw as a kind of "failure," Katherine was determined to make breast-feeding work: "I felt that if I failed to do one thing, I had to do something that was natural. So breast-feeding was very important to me. And, of course, it wasn't easy at all." The fact that her husband had grown children by his first wife ("I'm pretty sure she gave them bottles") and "was incredibly laid back about everything" seemed to fuel Katherine's frustration. She sensed that he didn't understand how important it was for her to prove that she could not only do it but do it better than Wife Number One. When her husband, trying to be supportive, suggested that she switch to formula, Katherine had "a hideous fit."

When I interviewed Alyce a few weeks after the birth of her son, she confessed to moments of feeling "really resentful and angry." But on the heels of that resentment came intense guilt. "In part, I blame all those books that say this is supposed to be feeling great, enjoyable or bonding or whatever," she complained. "I haven't reached the bonding point yet, which makes me feel like I'm weird."

Talk to any woman about the first few weeks postpartum, and unless she is in total denial, highly defensive, competitive, or a Big Fat Liar, she will admit to having felt at times incompetent, stupid, weird, angry, frustrated, or all of the above. Believe me, plenty of moms resent, dread, curse, even hate their newborns—not just for making their nipples hurt and their bodies ache with fatigue but for causing them to "fail" at what they perceive as the PSAT's of motherhood.

Experiencing "the Great Yes," No, and Maybe

Breast-feeding is not a test; functioning on two hours' sleep is an oxymoron; and getting back to normal doesn't happen until your kids go off to college—and even then your life is never quite the same as it was before you gave birth. That said, the postpartum period can and should be a time of bliss, an opportunity to marvel at and celebrate your baby's perfection, to experience what novelist Louise Erdrich describes as a "sense of oceanic oneness, the great *yes*, the wholeness" that holding and nursing your baby provides.[28]

I recall gentle times of feeding, rocking, or holding my babies as almost painfully peaceful. I would close my eyes and feel merged with my infant, calm deep in my bones, yet buzzing with a warmth that made me wonder if I was glowing in the dark. Apparently, this wasn't some sleep-deprivation-induced hallucination. Research on breast-feeding mothers, conducted in Sweden, shows that when we nurse our babies, we secrete high levels of the hormone oxytocin, which not only raises our body temperatures but also makes us feel calm and highly attached to our babies. When you caress and stroke your baby (and who can resist?), you boost your oxytocin levels even more. "The mother secretes oxytocin as she caresses her child, for her hand is feeling the soothing sensation of stroking, just as her child feels the balm of being stroked."[29]

Other neurobiological studies have led some researchers to label oxytocin the love hormone. Our own levels of oxytocin are known to peak during orgasm, and when it's injected into rodents, they act all lovey-dovey with each other, as though they just enjoyed a nice roll in the sawdust. One experiment placed infant rhesus monkeys into a cage with oxytocin-dosed virgin females; these typically disinterested monkeys played with and kissed the babies. They also became a lot friendlier to the folks in the white lab coats who were doing the research.

Another interesting study of moms, this one conducted by a psychologist in Toronto, suggested that the hormone cortisol, typically associated with the body's stress reaction, seems to play a part in a new mother's attraction to her baby's smell, increased sympathy to her infant's cries, and more involvement in his or her care.[30] There's even some anecdotal evidence that the excitement and stress felt by new adoptive mothers may trigger a similar elevation in cortisol levels. But oxytocin and cortisol aren't the only hormones coursing through your body, and neurochemistry alone doesn't explain the complicated feelings we have in the weeks following birth.

In addition to bliss, there may be times when you experience an atavistic panic or intense dread or fear. "I was so surprised at how lonely I felt—especially late at night when I was nursing," recalled Alyce. "I didn't think happy thoughts during that time—I couldn't. So my mind would focus on people who had passed away or on sad things."

Jackie, who gave birth to twin boys, worried about favoring one over the other—even when they were days old. "The biggest fear in the beginning was how to console the two of them at once, to establish trust, when you have only two arms, two hands. That was for me a huge hurdle to get over, especially when I didn't *know* them. Now I do, but back then I was constantly feeling as though I was cheating

Michael when I tended to Peter, and when I gave Peter an extra five minutes and Michael would be crying, I would think, 'I'm never going to be able to bond with both of them. I'm going to hurt Peter by spending more time with Michael in the early weeks.'"

A "difficult" baby—or one you *think* is difficult—can make bonding especially tough. Every time she wails or arches her back or strains in frustration, you question your parenting skills, your self-worth, your decision to have a baby at all. Unlike the frustration and anger we may feel when our children are toddlers or teens, the panicky despair of these early weeks can't be escaped. You don't have the time, space, or energy to step back and gain some perspective; you also have no experience. And this goes for all mothers, not just first-timers. Elizabeth, who lives in St. Louis, recalled how the arrival of her son— the second of her three children—caused a dramatic shift in how she saw herself. "Our first baby had been easy, perfect really," she explained. "But my son cried from the second he was out. He was just miserable and unhappy all the time. And so was I. I described him to everyone as 'tough,' 'demanding,' and 'extremely difficult' because he was. But gradually, I was able to see that he was just more dependent, more needy, and that wasn't necessarily a bad thing. I stopped using those negative labels and decided to just try to nurture him in a different way than I had my daughter."

Elizabeth's ability to step back and gain some perspective on her baby's behavior, in fact, to use her own ambivalence and negative feelings toward a positive end, is incredibly inspiring. In *Torn in Two: The Experience of Maternal Ambivalence,* Rozsika Parker, a British psychoanalyst, speaks eloquently about the understanding we stand to gain of ourselves and of our babies when we allow feelings of anger, frustration, even hatred to surface along with more acceptable emotions like euphoria and love: "Where motherhood is concerned, I think the conflict between love and hate actually spurs mothers on to struggle to understand and know their baby. . . . It is the troubling co-existence of love and hate that propels a mother into thinking about what goes on between herself and her child."[31]

Of course, it's a lot easier to slap a label—even an affectionate one like "feisty" or "a real bruiser"—on our "difficult" babies than to stop and think about why certain behaviors may be pushing our buttons. We often affix labels to our children before they take their first breath, and certainly by the second month of your baby's life, you're likely to have a host of nicknames at the ready. Whether you call your newborn "angel," "kitten," or "sweet pea," "spunky," "high energy," or "Motor Man," these labels will say as much about your attitude as they will about your baby's temperament. The key is to use Post-its, not a hammer and chisel, for the obvious reason that your "impossible" newborn may blossom into a dreamy toddler.

More important, *you* will develop from an insecure, conflicted, confused, overwhelmed new mom into a wise older soul, doling out advice and solace over the heads of her thriving children. Yes, I'm talking about you. As hard as it is to look at your baby and remember that a short time ago he was inside you, it's even tougher to peer into the future and imagine that you'll know exactly what to say to make him laugh or how to calm him down or how to help him help himself. Right now you hold your wailing baby and ask over and over again, "What do you *want*?" Or you cradle his tiny head in your hand and wonder, "My God, he's so fragile and helpless. How can I be expected to keep him safe?"

Why Mothers Need Mothers

One of the reasons we're so acutely aware of our newborns' helplessness is that we feel so helpless ourselves. But unlike the preceding nine months, during which you were often fussed over and pampered, treated as though *you* were a helpless baby, now you're expected to act like a grown-up, to be a mom!

Erica put it this way: "You get to be the baby when you're pregnant—you're pampered and coddled. Everyone acts protectively, if not somewhat patronizingly, toward you. When the baby is born, you have to give up that role, so you're not only mourning the loss of being together, being connected to the baby, but you're mourning the loss of not being the baby anymore."

According to psychoanalyst and author Joyce Block, "Women return via their babies to the stage where it all began."[32] Some part of our unconscious self identifies intensely with our babies; we experience a kind of fierce neediness, a feeling of vulnerability that runs counter to everyone's expectations of how we should behave. Yes, we're allowed to be exhausted, weepy, even unwashed, but to curl into a ball in bed just won't fly in most Western households.

Of course, if you happen to live in the Japanese islands of the Goto Archipelago, you're *expected* to take to your bed. There, new mothers spend at least one month wrapped almost cocoonlike with their newborns while their own mothers feed and serve them. The doting grandmothers even use a kind of singsong "motherese," underscoring their recognition of a new mother's vulnerability and helplessness.[33]

While the idea of being confined to bed for a month while your mother coos baby talk all day long would drive most moms screaming from the room, the other extreme—forty-eight hours in a hospital then, *boom,* home, with no help—is equally absurd. Unfortunately, few of the moms I interviewed anticipated how tough it would be and planned to have minimal help for a variety of reasons. "I can't afford help" or "We don't have room for someone to sleep over" or "I'd feel like a spoiled yuppie" or "I want to be alone with my husband and baby" were the most familiar tunes. To which I replied, "Borrow the money, make room on the couch, and get someone to clean and cook so you *can* spend time with the baby and with your spouse."

Steve's sister Lois remembers how much it meant when my mother-in-law provided some unsolicited TLC during her first weeks home: "When Emily was a newborn, I had a terrible time getting her to nurse. My husband and I were so freaked out. Everyone was focusing on Emily's drinking, but it was Mom who brought *me* glasses of water." I reminded her that she had done the same thing for me when I had spent the night at my in-laws'. "You and Gloria magically appeared at five a.m. to help me with Maddie. I offered to polish your haloes as I stumbled back to bed!"

A close friend, a lesbian whose partner had recently given birth to a baby girl, confided that she found herself longing for her mother's attention and involvement in their lives. "It's really weird," she said with uncharacteristic vulnerability. "I've never, ever wanted my mother around more. I've never really cared what she thought about my life or felt like I needed her. But now I want her to take care of me. Me!"

When Nick developed newborn jaundice and needed daily blood tests to monitor his bilirubin, I would drive into Manhattan from

Brooklyn to see a pediatrician near my parents' apartment, where I would stop for a visit before driving back home. I told myself that I was doing this because I loved the pediatrician so much that I just couldn't make the switch to a Brooklyn-based doctor, but I know that what I needed most of all was to be near my mother. I wanted her to take care of me for a few minutes each day—even if it meant driving an hour for her special touch. Just having her pat my hand or make me a cup of tea or watch me nurse or let me cry was like a shot of oxytocin. Sometimes just watching her rock Nick was enough to soothe my jangled nerves. I would listen to her sing to him, her pack-a-day voice running the musical gamut from C to D-flat, her hand patting a gentle syncopation on his bottom as he nestled against her shoulder, and I could almost feel her cheek against mine. When we sat together on the sofa, she would pat my arm absentmindedly in the same distinct meter, and of course that rhythm guided my own hand whenever I patted Maddie or Nick.

These days many of us don't live close to our moms. Katherine, who lives in London, found that the arrival of her children forged an emotional bridge to her mom in Edinburgh, a bittersweet shift in their relationship. "When I first moved to London and was doing my thing here, there was kind of a distancing. We saw each other on holidays and talked occasionally on the phone. But now I'm on the phone to her every other day, and we're terribly, terribly close as a result of the children."

My mother was well into her seventies when my children were born; she had three granddaughters and loved nothing more than to care for and kvell over them. (When we moved from Manhattan to Brooklyn—a whopping seven miles—she acted as though we had emigrated to Brazil.) But there are the ranks of middle-aged women to whom the grandmother mantle feels more like a lead coat, something they would prefer to leave in the closet for a few more years. "The minute we told her the big news, my mother announced that she didn't want to be called Grandma or anything like that," Lisa recalled. "At first I was really hurt, but then I realized that as an active sixty-three-year-old she felt young—and being called Grandma just made her feel really old." After much discussion ("almost as much time as we spent discussing our son's name"), her mother settled on Grammy.

"I guess she liked the idea of being associated with hip music awards!" Lisa said with a laugh.

When Grandma Second-guesses

Then there are the ranks of mothers and mothers-in-law who brandish the grandma banner with a vengeance, second-guessing your every move. "My mom was trying to be helpful," Alyce recalled. "But she had done the bottle thing—had never breast-fed—so all I would hear from her was, 'Oh, I tried with you, but my milk was bad, so you kept throwing up.' I got to the point where I had to Xerox the pages in the book that says it is not about the milk going bad, because it drove me nuts that she even thought that."

Joanne's mother kept asking her if she thought the baby was getting enough milk. "When I said yes, she would ask, 'But how do you know?' Which, of course, affected my confidence. I don't really think she meant to do that, but I almost gave up the breast-feeding because I began to seriously doubt my milk supply."

Whether Joanne's mother was motivated by competitiveness (not unusual) or concern, the result was to undermine Joanne's self-assurance. Rather than challenge her mother's motives, she questioned herself. At a time when we desperately need our mothers' support, when our emotional vulnerability is at an all-time high, it's particularly difficult to deal with ambivalence—hers and yours. Sometimes it helps to ask simply, "Why are you telling me that?" or to say, "I know you mean well, but it doesn't help me when you say/ask/share that kind of thing."

When you're a little farther down the mothering path, you can (and should) take the time to think about where your own mom was coming from, or why certain behaviors irritated her. Cynthia, the adopted daughter of a woman who could not have children, realized that her mother's surprisingly unsupportive and critical behavior was the result of intense envy, and managed a remarkable degree of compassion and tolerance. "I guess I sensed from the moment I told her I was pregnant that she was very conflicted. On the one hand, she wanted me to be happy, to succeed; on the other, it reinforced what she experienced as this major failure in her life. Of course, she would never, ever admit to me that that's how she felt, but I just knew something was up. She was very distant, very judgmental, which isn't like her at all."

Some new mothers resist asking their moms for help because they're loath to "become her," to give up a sense of themselves that is distinctly—if not aggressively—in opposition to that of Grandma. This is especially true for moms anticipating a return to work, whose own mothers stayed home full-time. Every new mother awaiting the end of her maternity leave does so with, at best, ambivalence, at worst, dread. Having in the wings (or in the living room or on the phone) a mom whose sheer presence is a reminder of choices you rejected years ago can make her "help" feel suffocating, annoying, or critical.

For Jackie, the least helpful "helper" was her mother-in-law, a first-generation immigrant whose highly traditional approach to mothering drove Jackie nuts. "What happened was that in the very beginning she came in and she wanted to try to run the show, just as she had done with *her* daughter. John does not tolerate stuff like that, which was great, because I have a lot of friends who actually run into this prob-lem and their husbands don't stand up for them. She would be over my left shoulder all the time: 'Is there enough water in the tub? You're leaving him out naked for too long. Why are you holding him that way?' That type of stuff. I tried to handle it very calmly, but it got to a point where she really started to get in my face. I thanked her very much for her advice, but I explained that I really just wanted her to be a grandmother and to leave the mothering to me. She got very offended; in fact, things got so bad that at one point I didn't hear from her at all—and she lives in our building, three floors away from us!"

If your mother is struggling with her new role or feeling jealous, rivalrous, anxious, or simply afraid of this next turn in the road, then it's going to be much harder for her to offer emotional support. Not having that support, especially during the postpartum period, can make for unexpected waves of resentment, disappointment, or just down-and-dirty anger. Even if you never expected your mother to fly in, "ooh and aah" over the baby, roll up her sleeves, and brew a pot of herbal tea, it's natural to want to be babied. And who better to do that than the person you assume knows best?

Postpartum Depression

Moms whose own mothers died before they reached adolescence have a significantly increased risk for postpartum depression, research shows.[34] One of my oldest and dearest friends lost her mother when she was ten years old. When I visited her shortly after the birth of her second child, her eyes were filled with an intense sadness. It was as though she were longing to tell me something but suddenly spoke no English; she seemed desperate to communicate her pain but sensed I wouldn't understand or could provide no relief. When we met for lunch a few months later, she described her depression as "an altered state," the equivalent of being incredibly nauseated or physically sick. "I just couldn't imagine being well. Someone would come to visit and I would think, 'How is she walking? How is she functioning?' I could barely do one thing a day. I felt this burden, this weight. It was overwhelming."

Another mom I spoke to characterized her postpartum depression as a "state of constant agitation—like there were termites eating me alive from the inside out." She just couldn't relax; despite numbing fatigue, sleep was elusive. Katherine, who had experienced intense but short-lived baby blues with her first child, Julie, was able to tell herself that her overwhelming feelings of melancholy would eventually subside. "The first time around was really very hard," she said, her face tense and worried. "But with Emma I knew it would happen, so when I found myself crying and crying all the time, I could say, 'All right, this is terrible, but it will pass.'"

And postpartum blues usually do pass. During the first few weeks after delivery, eight out of ten new mothers experience a temporary period of weepiness.[35] I remember bursting into tears over detergent commercials, feeling anxious and panicky, then enervated or bitchy. But my mood swings would not have been defined as postpartum depression, a condition that affects up to 20 percent of new mothers. PPD includes persistent feelings of hopelessness, guilt, anxiety, lack of motivation, and occasional fantasies of harming oneself or the baby.[36] Moms suffering from this kind of depression experience mood swings, lethargy, feelings of inadequacy, and anxiety. If you've had a history of depression, especially previous postpartum depression, then your risk of a repeated experience is very high (70 percent). But even if this is your first experience with serious baby blues, don't wait to get some help. Yes, the first few weeks postpartum almost always involve sleep deprivation, changes in appetite, increased anxiety, and mood swings, but if your feelings of depression and/or agitation persist, talk to your doctor or a therapist right away.

One of the most disturbing aspects of postpartum depression is the barrier it erects between you and your baby and between you and those you love. You just can't give when you're feeling empty and needy yourself. Even a mild case of the blues can make bonding feel more like bondage; it's excruciating to drag yourself out of bed and comfort a screaming infant when you're sick with fatigue or emotionally weak. Your husband may feel cut off from you, worried, or frustrated by mood swings he can't predict or control. When a close friend of Steve's called recently to tell us about his new baby, I could sense that all was not well. "How's Carrie doing?" I asked. His false cheer lasted about two minutes. "Actually, she's having a really hard time," he admitted. "She cries constantly. I don't know what's going on with her." Interestingly, Carrie had lost her mother at a young age, and although she had close relationships with her sisters, I sensed that her depression was profound and totally unexpected. She wouldn't see anyone, had stopped breast-feeding, and rarely slept. I told our friend to get her some help and to make sure that she had plenty of support from him and from close friends and family. "Even if she feels like crawling into a cave and hiding, don't let her," I advised. "The worst thing right now would be for her to be alone."

The Help Hang-up

Even as I spouted this advice, I knew how hard it would be to follow. Carrie was the kind of confident, competent career woman who has a hard time asking for help. Actually, I take that back. I think most moms have a major problem asking for help. I remember being home with my then two-month-old Maddie one rainy afternoon when the phone rang. "Karen and I just had lunch with Amy and Diane," a friend chirped. "We all thought we could come by now to see Madeleine and give you a little break."

"Sure," I squeaked, a knot forming in my stomach. I hung up the phone, quickly made my bed, and then ran around like a crazy person, trashing take-out food cartons, picking up burping cloths, tidying piles of unread newspapers. Fifteen minutes later a small horde of helpers descended. And as they gushed over Maddie's "teensy toenails" and "perfect mouth, " I scurried around serving cookies and cups of coffee. When they left, I stood over an exhausting sinkful of dirty cups and saucers and wondered why I was weeping.

The answer was simple: I had accepted "help" that I should have refused and refused help I should have accepted. I loved my friends, though I knew that they were not the baby-sitting types—particularly after a couple of lunchtime mimosas—yet I ignored my gut and agreed to their visit. Worse, I let them slide on their initial promise to give me "a little break." I became Cinderella, doing it all myself instead of asking *them* to make the coffee, serve me a cup, and clean up afterward.

Jackie knew better. She surrounded herself with friends—all fellow moms—one afternoon and just let her guard down. "I was feeling so alone, so misunderstood by John," she told me. "I had two of my girlfriends and my mother come over, and I just cried and talked and cried. And I felt so much better, I felt so supported."

Most of us associate asking for help (let alone sobbing on the couch in front of friends) with weakness or incompetence or both. I was in a bookstore recently and noticed that the self-help aisle had a new name: "Self-Improvement." Obviously, *help* has become (or perhaps has always been) a dirty word in our culture. This is especially true when it comes to parenthood. Admitting you can't go it alone, that you're overwhelmed or unsure of yourself or unhappy in your new role, just doesn't fly. It may be the norm, but it's not normal.

Make Room for Daddy

For many new moms, the logical person to turn to for help is one's spouse, but there's the rub. He's not only more of a rookie than you are, but he's exponentially and perhaps genetically less likely to admit that he doesn't know what he's doing. (Why does it take ten thousand sperm to fertilize one egg? Because none of them will stop to ask for directions.) Discovering that your spouse isn't necessarily the diaper champ you had envisioned or that he somehow manages to sleep through midnight howls that would wake the dead or that he's fleeing to the office at the crack of dawn or that he's so in love with the baby he never puts her down or that he just isn't the person you had imagined can make the loneliness of the first few weeks home even more desolate. Whatever you do, keep in mind that it takes a very long time to negotiate the shift from partners to parents. The fact is that you're never going to walk totally parallel paths; during the first few weeks postpartum your husband will struggle with a new self-image and with a desire to help you that is undermined by a relative lack of experience and a concomitant feeling of inadequacy.

The overwhelming majority of moms I spoke to found that the birth of their baby transformed even the most egalitarian marriage into a kind of *Leave It to Beaver* time warp. "It was like my husband—not my baby—was switched at birth," Julie said with a laugh. "He metamorphosed into Desi Arnaz, bumbling around the nursery, talking about taking a second mortgage to make ends meet. It was really weird."

Steve and I definitely fell into what I call the "expert/dumb apprentice trap." I remember one weekend morning when I decided to take a bath—a treat I had been denied for several weeks. I was about to step into the steaming tub when Steve shouted from the other room, "She seems to have a rash on her butt! Do we have any of that diaper cream?" I knew he would never find it, so I put my robe back on, joined him in an evaluation of the rash, a search for the cream, and a lengthy debate about exactly how much to apply. By the time the diaper was in place, my bath was cold.

This same dance played out countless times: He would defer to me or I would take over or he wouldn't jump to the rescue fast enough, so I would just do it myself. Notice how much of this traditional dynamic was a function of my impatience, presumed superiority, or tendency to second-guess. I may have resented the fact that I was doing more of the caretaking, but I was also enabling us to slip into our Dad-the-breadwinner, Mom-the-caregiver roles.

The key for most couples is to face up to your fantasies and disappointments, to discuss your expectations, fears, and anger. When the birth of their twins sent Jackie and John orbiting in different galaxies, Jackie did something many women would find too tough. "John was not supportive," she explained. "I think he wasn't used to me being out of control, calling him up crying. But I had no help. I was just one person all day long with newborn twins. And John would just get very irritated that I would call him. So I sat down and I had a very honest discussion about how I felt. I said I do not respect how you handled this whatsoever. I need to get away from you for a little while." And she did. Jackie went out to California to stay with her sister for a month. "I had to think things through, to figure what I needed from John in order to make our new life work for me," she said with a kind of shoulders-back, spine-straight assurance. "I did a lot of thinking and a lot of relaxing, and so did he, and he came out to California and met me there and we worked things out."

It's not easy to pull back or to pull out and do what Jackie did. And it may not be wise to do much of anything for the first couple of months. But if you're feeling disappointed, hurt, resentful, or angry at your spouse, don't expect him to read your mind. Tell him what you're feeling and what you need.

For Kristen, who married in her mid-thirties, getting pregnant three months after the wedding was great news. But she realizes now how little "couple practice" she and her husband, Doug, had before their baby arrived. "I wish we had had a chance to establish our marriage, to negotiate and talk about our goals. We had our first big argument recently, and it was the worst. Doug wanted to go away on a golf weekend, but he had just gone away with some other friends, and I was furious and so upset. He was silent. I think he was going to wait me out. And at first I was like, 'Over my dead body!' But then I said, 'Look, I'm not your mother and I'm not Governor Gray Davis—making the budget decision alone. We're partners.'"

According to several major research studies, having a baby is the single biggest challenge to a marriage. And even if your relationship makes it through the tough transitional times, the odds are less than one in five that you'll feel closer. In fact, one study found that half of the couples they surveyed said their relationship had seriously deteriorated or that they felt "more distanced from each other than they had been pre-pregnancy."[37]

These statistics are scary and sad if your expectations are unrealistically high. How can you *not* feel differently about each other when you have so little time to connect? How can resentments *not* build when you're exhausted and overwhelmed and unsure of your footing? The key is to make time for each other and to give your spouse ample opportunities to hang out with the baby alone. I'm not talking about handing over the baby and then watching Dad's every move. That won't work. You have to exit or to insist they go out together.

You also have to schedule regular dates. I know this sounds like all of those chirpy women's magazine articles, but many of the women who write those articles have kids, too. I can't say how many of them actually go on dates with their husbands, but we all know it's a good idea to schedule them. Here's why: If "date with Joe" isn't on the calendar, penned in with red marker, it won't happen. You'll put your relationship last—or perhaps second to last. Time for yourself will come a distant third.

Steve and I had our first postbaby date when Maddie was about three weeks old. As I recall, it lasted about forty-five minutes. We handed her over to my parents and race-walked two blocks to a small, romantic French restaurant. Sensing my nervousness or perhaps sharing it, Steve suggested we skip appetizers, then excused himself to call in "just to make sure everything's okay." Despite the fact that all was quiet on the home front, I was soon having a school-cafeteria flashback, wolfing down my duck à l'orange as though we were seriously late to class. The next thing I knew, Steve was shouting, *"L'addition!"* and we were beating a hasty retreat back to the cave.

"Back so soon?" my mother asked when we burst through the door. "What happened?"

How could I explain that our concept of "soon" was closer to "eternity" at this early stage in Maddie's life? "Well, we were a little nervous," I said apologetically. "We'll try again in a few weeks." And we did, bravely adding dessert (and about twelve minutes) to the experience.

Alyce's husband—also named Steve—made their time together last three months by taking an extended paternity leave. Despite the fact that they were both home for twelve weeks, they didn't have too many "dates," but they experienced something very few couples are able to negotiate—a chance to just hang out with each other, to figure out how this new "we-ness" should feel.

"If anybody asked me whether it's a good idea to take paternity leave and be home for three months, I would say, definitely," Alyce said, looking back. "Some people told us that it was a waste for Steve to be there the first three months. Why bother when the baby's so small? But it *is* important, because it's about spending time together and figuring out how you're going to relate to each other. And that's really what it was about. We didn't have a lot of time for tender moments, or anything like that, but we tried once a week to go out for an hour together, without the baby."

The Sex-Week Checkup (No, This Is Not a Typo)

Going out for dinner together is one thing. What you do after dinner is another. If you or your husband agree with Albert Brooks's assertion that the most boring part of sex *is* dinner, then the infamous six-week checkup will loom large on your calendar. I remember dragging myself to my OB-GYN's office, a veil of fatigue rendering me so punch-drunk that when he cheerily told me everything was fine and that I could "resume normal intercourse," I burst out laughing. What could possibly be normal about subjecting my body's sorest orifice to anything other than a warm bath? Only some long-repressed S&M fantasy could have rekindled my sex drive at that juncture.

Most moms share the feeling that six weeks is way too soon to resume anything involving a penis. In some cultures couples wait for months, even years. Moms and dads in the Abelam society in Papua New Guinea are expected to wait until their child is walking to resume sex; for the Alorese in Oceania, the big night doesn't come until the child is sitting up. And the Masai of East Africa are forbidden to have intercourse until the child has cut its teeth.[38] A recent study in the *Journal of Sex Research* found that by twelve weeks postpartum, 84 percent of couples had rekindled their sex lives. Still, the researchers point out, fatigue, adjustment to her new role, physical changes, and breast-feeding can depress a new mother's sexual desire for several months.[39]

A lot of women feel enormous guilt because they don't want to have anything to do with their husbands physically, even if sex isn't painful. As one woman described it, "After caring for the baby all day long, I get into bed and sex is the last thing on my mind. Sometimes, when he wants to make love and he starts touching my body, I feel as though I'm going to scream."

Part of what I remember going through was a feeling that Maddie had totally invaded my personal space. I was either carrying her or feeding her or holding her or cleaning up some part of her that was now on me. Sometimes our physical connection satisfied like a multi-course feast or a warm bath, and when we were apart for even a few hours, I hungered for my baby's touch the way I longed for Steve's when he had been away.

After her bath, I would lie next to Maddie and drink in her delicious fragrance, kiss and nibble her tiny feet, stroke her with my fingertips and cheeks and lips. Even in the dead of night I loved the feeling of Nick's sleep-dampened head against my neck, the curved handful of his little butt pressed against my palm. But there were just as many days, when my baby's unrelenting neediness, colic, or hunger made me feel totally cut off from the person I had been just a few weeks before. It was extremely difficult to reconcile this new experience of being bound up completely in the details of Nick's or Maddie's physical life with any previous image of myself. By the end of the day my need for sensual contact had long been saturated, while my definition of who I was had been badly shaken. When I crawled into bed, I just wanted five minutes alone in the dark with nothing but the cool sheets touching my body.

For many moms, though, the need to reconnect with their prebaby selves accelerates their desire for sex. When you're wrapped up in your baby's needs all day long, you may ache to be wrapped up in your husband's arms, to feel cared for and desirable. "I felt so connected to Brian after the baby was born," Elise recalled. "I wanted to have sex, and even though it wasn't satisfying initially, I enjoyed the closeness, the feeling that I was a woman, not just a boob!"

Feeling like you're "just a boob" or that you're very confused about your boobs can wreak havoc on your sex life. After all, our breasts play a critical part in our sexual development and in our sexual pleasure, so when they're being used in a primarily functional way for hours at a time, it can be very weird to shift gears in bed. "I spend half my life nursing the baby. I love it, but I feel as though my breasts belong to her, not to Jack," a young mom confessed. She found it close to impossible to enjoy having her husband fondle her breasts "even though it used to be a major turn-on."

Other moms love their suddenly busty selves. "I never had much on top," Felicia recalled. "So breast-feeding provided this incredible ego boost. It was such a rush—not sexual exactly, but definitely an experience that made me love my body in a way I never had."

Steve certainly never complained, even when my leaky boobs had him awash in mother's milk—a distinctly nonerotic experience. But most moms I spoke to found it a turn-off to have one's breasts spontaneously turn on, and the challenges of exhaustion, soreness, and a less-than-positive body image only exacerbated their feelings of being anything but a sex goddess.

Dawn is a high-energy, athletic thirty-two-year-old whose trim figure hardly changed during the first few months of her pregnancy. "But when I hit my second trimester, I ate a ton," she admits. "I wound up gaining forty-four pounds, and although I'm sure I'll lose the extra weight eventually—God! I certainly hope I will—it's so hard right now. I've always been really fit, really comfortable about my body, but I'm not having an easy time losing the extra weight. I feel like a blimp, which is really bugging me."

"I got pregnant very soon after we got married and fairly late in life," Helen says. "And during the times when I was dating, my appearance was a big part of how I defined myself. I was always aware of the way men checked me out. I could definitely turn on the high beams when I wanted to. Now I can't even find the time to take a shower! And when I do, I try not to look at myself in the mirror."

I remember one night shortly after Nick was born when I was breast-feeding him in our bed. I was wearing a particularly unattractive nursing bra (an attractive nursing bra may be the ultimate oxymoron) as well as a surgical mask, because I had a sore throat I worried might be contagious. Fearing that Nick felt a little warm, I decided to take his temperature. As sometimes happens when you stick a

Vaseline-coated thermometer up a baby's rear end, Nick proceeded to "pass" with projectile force his liquid meal. I sat there, my boobs hanging out of the bra, my unwashed hair splattered with baby shit, my surgical mask dangling under my chin, screaming for Steve to help me. He rushed in with a roll of paper towels, then froze in horror. "Jesus! You look like Mother from Hell! Can you rotate your head three hundred sixty degrees?"

"I'll tell *you* where to rotate if you don't help me clean this up," I growled.

Was June Cleaver a Turn-on?

Reconciling that image of myself—even after I had showered—with the woman Steve claimed to desire was often beyond my reach. And as we all know, our brains are our most important sexual organ, so if you're not thinking sexy, you're not going to be having much in the way of sexy fun. Most of the moms I spoke to said that sex and romance were a distant memory in the months following birth. "To put it mildly, I'm not feeling my most attractive," Kristen, the wife of an investment banker, said with a laugh. "And that includes feeling so stereotypical, so June Cleaver. Doug comes home from the office and I'm bursting with what the baby did today, not with what the stock market did, so I feel like we have nothing to talk about."

Like Kristen, I can recall how fatigue affected more than my sense of my physical attractiveness. An avid news junkie, I could summon neither the energy nor the enthusiasm to do more than scan the headlines of the paper—and that was only if it happened to be in view when I was nursing Maddie at the breakfast table. The result was that I felt like a moron much of the time, and worried that Steve would soon agree. I missed our conversations about work, our discussions of world events. No matter how much enthusiasm he showed for hearing about Maddie's sleep schedule, I couldn't believe that he loved the boring blob I felt I had become.

What I should have talked about were my feelings about sex, love, my body, Steve's work, anything and everything that impacted the intimate aspects of our marriage. Plenty of dads share with their wives the intense physical love of their babies and the exhaustion of caring for them during the first few weeks. They also may experience feelings of disappointment, loneliness, anxiety, and a drive to work added hours. Obviously, the upheaval in their lives can play out in the bedroom.

The shock for several mothers I spoke to was that their spouses weren't so hot to trot. Jackie said, "Men, generally, they want to get back to having sex before their wives, but in our case, it was weird. I wanted to have sex. John didn't. And so that made me feel very alone, very lonely. Even when he was lying next to me, I was just so by myself. I felt so misunderstood. I did talk to him about it. I remember asking him, 'How am I supposed to feel as a woman, that you are rejecting me physically? How do I know it's not because I gained a little weight or that my body isn't the same anymore?' He wasn't saying that, but I was feeling unattractive and undesirable."

Katy's feelings of hurt quickly turned to anger when her husband's disinterest dragged on for several months: "It was one of the hardest things I had to deal with. Our daughter was born by cesarean, so I was able to start the relationship quite soon again, and he was just not interested. I felt really rejected, even though he assured me that it had nothing to do with me—that it was his problem. But I felt like a single mother, because I had this baby stuck to me all the time. Then when I finally got back into our marital bed I found my husband still not very interested, and I thought, 'Oh, Lord, what have we done having this baby!'

Sometimes what you need more than anything is to be held, pampered, told you're amazing, seduced—not with champagne and roses but with genuine empathy and support. The husband who prepares dinner, cleans up the living room, plays with the baby while Mom enjoys a long soak in the tub, and then offers to rub her back is much more likely to get laid than the guy who uses guilt, guile, or whining to initiate sex.

"I find my husband most adorable, most attractive, when he's playing with the baby or holding her tenderly," Laura told me. "That's how I want him to be with me—sweet and loving and nurturing." When she sensed that her husband was frustrated by their stalled love life, Laura hesitated to broach the subject, but when a brief vacation without the baby afforded them a chance to really talk, she found that her feelings shifted dramatically. "It was the first time we had been alone, and we were able to really be honest about how we were feeling. We took a long walk in a park, and Jason told me that he missed our intimate bond, that he missed me in ways I had not been aware of. I realized that I do still need to take care of my husband, I do need to nurture this intimate relationship. He's so good with me, so good with the baby, I have to be good to him." Laura made a conscious effort to rekindle her sexual self, admittedly easier in a hotel room than when they returned to sleepless nights and nonstop baby care, but she found that pressuring herself paid off. "I'm actually feeling very differently now—in good ways—not in ways that make me resentful or unhappy."

Learning to Read the Baby's Signals

Feeling out of sync with your mate is intimately bound up with the struggle to understand better what your baby wants/needs during the first few weeks. It's frustrating and physically exhausting to tag-team your way through those early weeks, especially when your partner is as clueless as you are in discerning a "hungry cry" from a "fussy" or "bored" cry; at 3 a.m., all you hear is a *loud* cry. So you pace around the nursery, jiggling and singing and, in all likelihood, weeping and wailing along with your screaming baby, only to read in some book or magazine that overstimulation may be the problem.

If your baby has colic, it's imperative that you find a way to get a break, to hand her off to a patient, trustworthy relative and escape for even an hour or two. You should also check out Dr. Harvey Karp's book *The Happiest Baby on the Block: The New Way to Calm Crying and Help Your Baby Sleep Longer,* which explains how to trigger a newborn's calming reflex by applying what he calls the Five S's: swaddling; side/stomach positioning; shhhing; swinging (or gently shaking); and sucking (pacifier).[40] I have watched this approach in action with amazing results.

The good news is that even the most inconsolably colicky infants usually settle down by their third or fourth month. I realize that's a long, long time to wait when your baby's screams rival those of

Tolkien's Nazguls in their unrelenting intensity, but chanting "This, too, shall pass . . . this, too, shall pass" is far better than blaming yourself for your inability to figure out what's wrong. No one knows what causes colic exactly (it's not gas); we do know that at around eight or nine weeks, you will be able to read your baby's signals more assuredly. By then, the feeling of groping in the dark will diminish dramatically.

The fact that most newborns flash their first real smile around month two strengthens this sense of connection, often for the first time. Also, by your baby's eighth week, you may be feeling slightly more rested and less panicked. Dr. T. Berry Brazelton describes in his book *Touchpoints* how the mom of a two-month-old comes in for the baby's checkup "dressed up a bit for the big occasion."[41] At least, by now, you've probably managed to squeeze in a shower—even if the days are still consumed by your infant's myriad demands.

I'm not certain if it was exactly at that point, but somewhere around Maddie's second month on the planet I reached a stage where I was definitely more in sync with her. Perhaps my postpartum hormonal state had normalized. Not only could I respond more confidently to her needs, I could anticipate them. Maddie's cries no longer threw me into a frenzy; I could actually distinguish between hunger and boredom and frustration and do my best to help. One mom I spoke to described the initial weeks as "being on autopilot. I was overwhelmed most of the time, so I just staggered from one task to the next without really thinking about them."

For Jackie, the mother of twins, the feeling of finding her footing was so dramatic that she remembers the exact day. "I experienced a complete turnaround twelve weeks and three days after they were born. It was unbelievable! It was a Wednesday. From the beginning to the end, I had an amazing day, and I said to myself, 'Did I change overnight? Or did the babies change? Or did we change together?' Whatever it was, it was a sense of them responding to me and me feeling much more competent and comfortable with their personalities, with their needs. Recognizing what their cries meant. I remember it was such a beautiful and incredible day. It was like this lightbulb went on; it was just so bizarre."

"Having survived the first few weeks is like a badge of honor," Elise told me the day her daughter celebrated her third month on the planet. "It's the little things. I can read her signals, answer her needs. I feel like a mom and not like a lunatic!" But, as Elise was quick to point out, her life as a new mom was still a far cry from "life before birth."

Altering Our View of Our Altered State

Even after Maddie had finally slipped into a more predictable routine, I seemed to have none. Our days together were defined by an endless series of feedings, diaper changes, loads of laundry, naps. Occasionally, I would manage to shower, dress, and get Maddie out the door for a walk, but more often our days were loose and formless, coming together gradually as a series of unplanned activities. What I did from dawn to dusk could no longer be measured by the usual metrics: clock, Filofax, lists of to-dos. I had entered a different dimension, a zone where waves of emotion, not discrete blocks of time, traced the progress of my days.

As someone who was used to a fast-paced, demanding work life, I found the lack of structure and slowness of this early phase alternately rewarding and anxiety-producing. The fifteen solid balls I had juggled daily at the office were suddenly replaced by tiny, elusive bubbles. I would try to hold one in my hand, but it would evaporate just as some other bit of minutiae floated my way. When Steve asked at day's end, "What did you two do today?" I was often at a loss. "Well, I washed out Maddie's onesies in special soap. I played with her toes. I spoke to Mom for a few minutes on the phone. I think I took a shower—or maybe that was yesterday . . ."

If you are the kind of person who has a high tolerance for uncertainty and an ability to accept the feeling of being out of control at times, then early motherhood will come much easier than it did for many of the moms I interviewed. One old friend, whom I had met in first grade and who even then was destined for greatness, wound up as one of the top brass at Morgan Stanley. To say she had a demanding job would be putting it mildly. She also played semiprofessional tennis, served on several not-for-profit boards, and volunteered at a camp for emotionally disturbed children. She swore to me that she slept, but I had my doubts. For Nancy, the adjustment to being home full-time with an infant was extremely tough. She missed the solid footing and disciplined choreography of her prebaby days. "I was very disoriented being home with Jennifer all day long," she recalled. "I always thought of myself as a very organized, disciplined person by nature, but I realized that a lot of that discipline was imposed by my work and by sports. I knew I had a meeting at ten or a flight to catch at two or a game at six. Suddenly, all I had was a baby who wouldn't sleep— I mean *never*!"

Without clear goals, with little structure to our days, we can easily find the first few months with an infant suffocating and disorienting. But, of course, there are countless "goals" that are reached, even exceeded, when we care for our newborns; we just don't perceive them that way. When you respond to your baby's cries and manage to soothe him, you've accomplished a major "task"; when you tune in to your infant—by lying next to her or molding your body to hers—you're "achieving," even if those achievements are difficult to articulate or to quantify. And, of course, when you do manage to dress your baby and yourself, to go out for a walk or a drive, to call on a relative or go to a doctor's appointment, you've pulled off a three-ring circus of amazing feats. Just don't try explaining that to your colleague at the office or to childless friends. Even your spouse, if he's back at work, is likely to be so grounded in his reliable and predictable routine that, compared with the gravity-free soup you're floating in, his world can seem like a different planet.

According to psychologist Daphne de Marneffe, one of the challenges of this early phase is to learn to "accept ambiguity and fluidity . . . to stay open to new experiences and relax our need for certainty and control."[42] One of the mistakes I made while on maternity leave was trying to keep one foot in the office door, to resist surrendering to my life at home. When Nick was about ten weeks old, a month or so before my leave was up, I decided to bring him to the office for one of the magazine's regular art-edit meetings. Most of my senior staff— editors and art directors—were there, and after some oohing and aahing over Nick, we got down to business. Fifteen minutes into the meeting, he started to cry, obviously wanting to be fed. I tried to unbutton my blouse as discreetly as possible to nurse him. After all, this was *Parents* magazine; the staff was mostly women, but with twenty pairs of eyes on me (two pairs belonging to guys), I found myself distracted and awkward and tense. Worse, Nick clearly picked up on my tension, refusing to latch on and screaming like a banshee. My staffers looked as though they were in physical pain, so I excused myself and hustled Nick to the ladies' room, where we both took a deep breath and he nursed happily for twenty minutes.

One of the primary reasons I had ventured into the office at all was that I was lonely. Just that day I had watched Maddie, then three and a half, skip out the door with her baby-sitter, and I had burst into tears. I felt as though I had lost her, that our time together would never be the same. The fact that Steve and the majority of my close friends were working didn't help. I found the pull toward the office as much a function of my hunger for adult company as it was a need for affirmation that I could still step back into my work role and savor some of its rewards.

For Nancy, the social aspects of her work and the status she enjoyed in that arena were hard to let go of. She told me that she felt as though she was in a foreign country—and in a very different time zone—from most of her colleagues. Calling to chat was definitely not an option ("I knew how annoying that could be"), and trying to connect with total strangers in the park proved futile: "Frankly, where we live, most of the women in the park were nannies. I spent most of my time with my mother. Thank God she lived nearby."

There's no question that one of the most important supports during the first few months of your baby's life is other new mothers. You don't need a network, just a couple of women who can provide advice, comfort, and a little perspective on your new life. Your colleagues at work, even those who have children, are guaranteed to hold up the wrong mirror—the one you used before your baby was born. Only another mom or someone who remembers keenly how abnormal the initial months feel has the sense and the sensitivity to say, "Hey, you're never going to get back to normal. You'll just find your footing and begin to find yourself again."

What you may discover is that the new you belongs at home, not at the job you thought you loved. Or you may realize that being home 24/7 with a baby isn't what you're cut out to do. Whether you transition back to work or stay home full-time, your decision will require much soul searching and engender everything from ambivalence to high anxiety. Even if you think it's about your baby and what's best for him, believe me, it's not that simple. As your fourth trimester comes to an end and you emerge from the cocoon of fatigue and confusion that often characterizes this early "altered state," you'll experience a dramatic shift not only in your relationship to your baby but in all your relationships—most important, your relationship to yourself.

Stage 2

❧

Finding Your Footing, Finding Yourself

Months Four Through Twelve

Unlike the first three months, which one mom described as a time of "total caregiving with no return," the four-to-twelve-month period is often the "falling head over heels in love" phase. Looking at photos of Maddie when she was five, six, or eight months old (of which there are several trunkfuls), I'm reminded how her body had a kind of delicious ripeness, like a spanking new pillow, creamy and cool and soft. After her bath, I would put my terry-wrapped beauty on the bed and lie next to her for hours, admiring the formation of her ears or the perfection of her tiny wrinkled toes or the soft sound of her burbling voice.

We had made the transition from a stage when Maddie's relentless neediness elicited a kind of primal pull to soothe, feed, and hold her to a phase choreographed around a much more reciprocal dance. Coming into her room in the morning, I experienced the helpless bliss of watching a frown of frustration melt into a gummy smile. At the sound of my voice, joy animated every fiber of her body; no matter how rough the previous night had been, no matter how wasted I felt when I dragged myself out of bed, her beaming face washed away the fatigue.

As my three-month maternity leave galloped to an end, I experienced moments of sheer panic. I had missed the daily challenges, mental stimulation, and rewards of my job, but the image of handing Maddie over to Ana, the Filipino woman we had hired to care for her, sucked the energy out of me. Ana was young and eager, but I wasn't confident she could handle an emergency. Of course, I couldn't think what that emergency might be, but during her first two weeks on the job, I had to force myself out of our apartment in order to give her some solo time with Maddie. Having longed for a chance to run some errands, even have lunch with a friend, I would speed through my neighborhood like the Road Runner pursued by Wile E. Coyote. When I came in one afternoon to find Ana struggling to give Maddie a bottle of formula that she had neglected to warm, I felt the ceiling begin to crumble. I called Steve at the office, moaning that we would need to find someone with more experience or that I would just have to quit my job to stay home. As always, he managed to put the incident in perspective, to help me out of the emotional weeds.

Most of the working moms I interviewed returned to their jobs three to six months after giving birth. A few—in particular those living in Europe—took longer maternity leaves, but several agreed that it seemed easier to go back to work when their children were infants than it would have been once they were older. At three months, although your hard work and sleepless nights are rewarded by smiles and the occasional well-timed coo, your baby is still too little to play or to produce the range of emotions of a six- or twelve-month-old. As difficult as it was to wrench myself away from Maddie when she was three months old, it was even more so as she approached her first birthday.

The Pull Toward Home

In fact, when Maddie was about ten months old, I began to think about quitting my job as the managing editor of *Good Food* magazine. It just became too painful to pry her fingers off my coat every morning, to fight rush-hour crowds to be home for a couple of hours before her bedtime, to travel out of town for work. I was plagued by questions every working mother faces: Am I doing the right thing? How do I know?

I loved my job, my colleagues, the challenge of getting a magazine launched, but Maddie was hitting a stage when every day brought with it some new feat of developmental magic: a new word, an emerging sense of humor, a clap, an attempt to sing, or the wobbly foreshadowing of her first steps. There just was no way that a tasting of microwavable side dishes could hold a candle to watching Maddie taste vanilla ice cream for the first time.

Countless emotional conversations with Steve and close friends ensued. Several people suggested that I'd go crazy at home, and my accountant warned that we would have to change our lifestyle drastically. But Steve was willing to plan for this dramatic change and was supportive of my decision either way. He also pointed out that it was probably worth trying. "You can always get another job, if that's what you decide you want to do down the road."

I wasn't so sure, but I decided to take the plunge and picked a target date for my departure. My plan was to tell my boss on a Friday, a conversation I was dreading. Alex was an old friend and someone I deeply respected. Her husband, Steve, had been my first boss, and like many "child-free" couples, they had countless surrogate children, including me.

Devoted to her job, Alex had launched the magazine, working eighty-hour weeks, and had hired me when I was six months pregnant the first time. When Molly died, she had given me ample time off, urging me to take as long as I needed to recover—even though our tragedy could not have been more poorly timed. When I announced that I was pregnant again—not long after I returned to work—I vaguely recall that Alex blinked hard a couple of times, but once again she came through with support and enthusiasm. My one consolation as I anticipated telling her my plans was that her work was such a huge part of her life, I knew she would find another second-in-command quickly.

I was so focused on my own agenda that when she called me into her office on the preceding Tuesday, I assumed we were going to look at a layout together or discuss some personnel issue. Instead, she took a long drag on her cigarette, looked me in the eye, and with palpable tension and distress announced that *she* was leaving. I have no memory of exactly what she said, because at that moment I felt as though someone had dropped an anvil on my head. My hands actually went numb. By the end of the day I had been offered the top spot, along with a substantial raise, and the plan I had crafted so carefully seemed hopelessly irrelevant. I felt myself being yanked from home base and placed back on square one.

If there was one thing I had gleaned from my first months of motherhood, it was to expect dramatic shifts in the terrain and to assume that the minute your map begins to make sense, the itinerary is guaranteed to change. To expect to reach some distant destination by cutting a straight path between logical points is unrealistic at best, demoralizing at worst. If I wanted to be an editor in chief, here was my chance, and should the pull toward home make this new opportunity feel hollow or just too hard, then I would revert to Plan A and make a go at freelancing.

As it turned out, the job propelled me along a path that, within a few months, led me to the big leagues. I was hired as the editor in chief of *Parents* when Maddie was a little over one. It was a dream job, an opportunity to have my life and my work come together in a uniquely gratifying way. I would never have been hired had I not held the top spot—even for a brief period—at another magazine.

Managing Work with New Muscles

I can't say I never looked back, nor do I know for sure that freelancing from home would not have held its own satisfactions and, perhaps, fewer stresses, but I know that being a mom made me a better editor. Obviously, I was able to stand in the reader's shoes, to empathize and anticipate her concerns, but I also felt up to practically any challenge flung my way. As a new mom, I'd had my juggling abilities, flexibility, and resourcefulness honed every day of Maddie's first year. The celebration of her birthday had marked the most dramatic year of change in my life; I had developed entirely new muscle groups, tapped into energy reserves I never knew I possessed, discovered new ways of feeling happy and alive even after nine hours at the office.

I often wondered if I had grown a new lobe in my cerebral cortex, because there were parts of my brain that seemed to hum incessantly, even when I was at the office. There was no way to compartmentalize my "mommy" self from my "worker" self, and luckily for me, there was no pressure to do so. If, in the middle of a meeting, I suddenly remembered to remind Ana that we were meeting at the pediatrician's office during my lunch hour, no one rolled her eyes or shot me a dirty look. If I was conspicuously late getting into the office, I didn't have to fabricate a suitable alibi, as fictional mom Kate Reddy does in Allison Pearson's fiercely comic novel *I Don't Know How She Does It:*

> It is possible to get away with being late. . . . The key thing is to offer what my lawyer friend Debra calls a Man's Excuse. Senior managers who would be frankly appalled by the story of a vomiting nocturnal baby or an AWOL nanny (mysteriously, child care, though paid for by both parents, is always deemed to be the female's responsibility) are happy to accept anything to do with the internal combustion engine.
>
> "The car broke down/was broken into."
>
> "You should have seen the"—*fill in scene of mayhem*—"at"—*fill in street.*
>
> Either of these will do very well. Car alarms have been a valuable recent addition to the repertoire of male excuses because, although displaying female symptoms—hair-trigger unpredictability, high-pitched shrieking—they are attached to a Man's Excuse and can be taken to a garage to be fixed.[1]

Like the fictional Kate, my friend Nicole, who has four children, worked in a testosterone-rich environment. She recalled that after she gave birth to her first child, she tried to express milk in a toilet stall and then hid it in the back of the office fridge. But mostly she remembered the indifference of her colleagues. "I wanted to show everyone Isabel's photos, to tell them about her amazing daily accomplishments. But they would be sitting in a meeting, agonizing over something I thought was so insignificant compared to what was happening at home."

Having given birth prematurely and struggled through a series of Job-worthy plagues (sick baby, extended family tragedies, husband who traveled extensively for work), Betsy, who lives in Alabama, found her job exhausting and, at times, infuriating. "I was so aware of all of the time wasted during the day with chatting in the halls, coffee breaks, phone calls," she remembered. "I hated it, because everything seemed manic and unproductive compared to the efficiency with which I had worked a five-hour day at home during the end of my maternity leave." When her son was a few months old, Betsy's feeling of being constantly pulled in different directions led her to a spiritual retreat, where a monastic nun provided support and guidance. "I prayed, wrote out my goals, and talked to a close friend on the long drive home. I had decided to quit, work out of my house, and be with my son. I was firm in my conviction that this was the right thing to do."

Feeling torn between your baby and your job is one of the universals of this—and practically every other—phase of motherhood. But it can feel especially raw and painful if you have no one to share it with, no comrade in arms. I remember how stunned and shaken I was when, just back from my maternity leave, I learned that the receptionist in our office, whose baby had been born around the same time as Maddie, had quit. Apparently, her mother-in-law, who was home caring for the baby, had mistakenly smeared first-aid cream on the baby's gums instead of teething gel. The baby was fine; Mom toppled over the edge. Watching her tearfully collect her belongings and flee, I felt like a hapless soldier deserted in the trenches. We had been the only two women with young babies; now I was the only one—a highly stressed, insecure one.

In a recent poll of working mothers, *Parents* found that 99 percent of them said they felt "stressed some or most of the time."[2] Most of us assume this stress could be alleviated by improved child care or more flextime or a more involved spouse—and all those things would help. But we also need to accept the fact that ambivalence is a fact of life postbaby. And that sometimes the tension we feel between our working selves and our mothering selves can be energizing and creative.

No, I'm not being a Pollyanna. For several moms I interviewed, the gift of the first six months was their awareness of their own creativity, passion, patience, strength, and resourcefulness. Applied to their jobs, these qualities enabled them to switch careers entirely or to bring their work into laserlike focus. Not long after her son was born, Alyce began thinking about her career as a designer. "Once I got past the initial months of feeling exhausted and out of control, I had this great feeling of how amazing it is to do this—to pull off this miracle. It's bigger than I thought! And having done this, I now feel like I can do even bigger things—workwise. I'm not going to fuss around with different projects. I'm ready for something big—another giant challenge. It's like being recharged."

For many women, taking risks seemed to come more naturally once they became moms. "I know I took chances at my job that I would never have considered before I had a baby," an investment banker confessed. "I mean, I wasn't acting irresponsibly, but I was voicing my opinions, advocating for changes in a way I would never have had the chutzpah to do before."

I remember returning to work after my maternity leave and having little patience for small talk or for meetings that seemed a big waste of time. My hours were precious, because the more I could get done at the office, the easier it would be to get home on time and to focus on Maddie when we were together. In her book *Life After Birth*, Kate Figes describes how motherhood made her "more courageous at work." She, too, found the BS of office life hard to tolerate: "I have found that the ubiquitous, spiritual presence of one's own child diminishes the significance of office politics, hierarchy, and the self-importance of people at work."[3]

Prior to having a baby, Erica had maintained a private practice as a psychologist and had entered the corporate world as the developer of a successful seminar series. Wanting to be home as much as possible forced her to think about her skill set—not just her schedule—and make some significant adjustments. "I needed to work, but I had to find a way to work the least number of hours and maximize my income per hour. I think I approached that challenge with a different kind of creativity once Bryce was born. I sat back and evaluated all of my skills, not just those I had utilized in my practice, and began to think about ways I could express myself. Having Bryce pushed me to the next stage of my life."

For Jackie, who put herself through school, set up and ran a physical fitness center with her husband, and cared for her chronically ill mother, working a sixty-hour week had always been part of the fabric of her life. So when she became pregnant with twins, she assumed she would take a few months off and then jump back in with both feet. When we met, her boys were five months old and already wearing twelve-month sizes. Jackie, on the other hand, was back to a buff size 6, and her no-nonsense New York delivery belied a softness I had not seen before. "I know it sounds corny to say this, but I really feel that my life didn't begin until I had them," she said. "Not that I didn't do things before, not that I hadn't accomplished a lot, but having these babies has given me a reason to look at myself in a whole new way." She went on to explain that she was not going back to the gym to work with her husband. "Having them made me realize that I want to be a better person. I just sit and think, 'Am I doing everything I want to do? Am I worthy of these looks that they give me—these looks that say, "You are just the best thing ever!"' I wonder whether I'm good enough to live up to that. It's made me rethink who I want to be."

For some of the women I interviewed, those "You are the best thing ever!" looks made the pull toward home insurmountable. "I never imagined that I would feel as attached as I did," Erica told me. "Even though I am a very attached person, I assumed I would have help and that it would be fine to rush back to work full-time after three months. But it didn't feel that way at all. There was this wall when we were approaching the three-month mark, and I realized I just couldn't go back and work the same number of hours. That surprised me. I never considered how much I would enjoy this space with the baby. No one could have told me what it would be like."

One of my television colleagues—an up-and-coming correspondent who was being groomed for a top spot on a talk show—admitted that she was terrified about compromising her career when she found out she was pregnant. "It wasn't planned. In fact, I had always thought, 'Well, maybe when I'm thirty-five we'll start trying,' so I was convinced I would be back at work in three months, no problem." But the first five weeks of her son's life were really difficult. "I was a wreck, exhausted. I secretly—guiltily—questioned whether I had made a terrible mistake. People kept saying, 'Oh, motherhood is the ultimate gift,' and I was thinking, 'Some gift!' As far as I could tell, it was all take, take, take and no return."

But then, around her son's fourth month, he began sleeping more and she was rewarded regularly with big, heart-melting smiles. "I was smitten. I mean totally bowled over by how much I adored him. Unfortunately, that turning point happened just as I was given a big assignment that sent me to California. I was away for five days, and I felt like I had left my organs at home. I was physically ill being apart from him."

When the network let her maternity leave drift into a kind of limbo land with fewer calls to cover stories and with a marked decrease in on-air appearances, my friend had mixed feelings but was basically relieved. "I still love, love my job, but I also really love being home with him more than I ever thought I would. I do still have fleeting moments of insecurity, because I did pay a price. I was punished—taken off the A-team roster, but unwittingly, the network did me the hugest favor by letting me work part-time. I still have ambitions, but I think this is the greater reward."

Other moms I spoke to voiced the sentiment—sometimes with a tinge of confessional guilt—that they looked forward to their jobs, to the predictable, orderly, confirming routines of their "old life." Sandra, who's a single mom, saw her return to the office as critical to her sense of herself as an independent and highly competent working woman. "I needed to work, financially, but I also needed it for me. I couldn't possibly be home full-time. I know that about myself. Yes, it was hard, and when my maternity leave was up I wished I could have stayed home for six months instead of four, but I really didn't want to give up my career. Later on, when the kids were older and I was involved with a man who made a good living and was willing to support me and my kids, I still could not stay home. I'm not the type."

For my close friend Jane, going back to work was her salvation. Having suffered the pain of postpartum depression, exacerbated by being isolated with a three-month-old, she found that returning to a familiar routine, supportive coworkers, and a job she loved pulled her out of the darkness. "I know a lot of women who suffered some of the feelings I had, but not as prolonged or as intense. They found those early months scary, isolating, lonely. The answer for me was to go back to work. I found that my job centered me."

Living in the moment—as we do when our babies are new—and then very much moment to moment as the months tick by, we are forced to sit back and ask ourselves how this phase in our own development will affect the stages to come. But it's not easy to weigh the short-term gains against the possible long-term outcomes when the number of variables seem infinite and intricate. You can't know when you're staring into your four-month-old's eyes whether he'll be the independent sort, happy to toddle off with his pals in child care, or whether his need for your presence will intensify and make it harder and harder to separate. You can't be certain that the loving nanny you're handing your baby off to will be as vigilant as you, just as you can't expect your child to be a perfect angel as a reward for your deciding to quit your job and stay home full-time.

Help Wanted

Despite the fact that the vast majority of research tells us that child care does not hurt kids—assuming that that care is consistent and nurturing—there isn't a mother alive who doesn't feel guilty and conflicted as she heads out the door. The truth is, you'll never know for sure whether the decisions you make today are the ones that matter the most down the road. All you can do is accept what research and common sense confirm: Being true to yourself is paramount. A child at home with a depressed or frustrated mom is going to suffer more than a child whose mother nurtures herself—through work or other activities—and is, therefore, replenished and ready to give when she's home.[4] Babies need and love their moms, but they certainly don't need to be with them every minute of every day. They also thrive when they have a chance to interact with other loving adults.

Ahhh, but there's the rub. How does one find "other loving adults"— even one other loving adult? Quality, affordable child care ranks with the Holy Grail in terms of accessibility. The parade of potential prospects Steve and I interviewed merges in my memory with that scene from *Mrs. Doubtfire* when Robin Williams impersonates a series of nightmarish baby-sitters in several brilliant vignettes. I seem to recall one woman we spoke to who, like Williams's "candidate," kept repeating, "I am job. I am job."

The first woman we hired had been billed as a "Jamaican Mary Poppins, fabulous with kids," and she was definitely jolly and energetic. But from day one she made me feel like the bumbling apprentice or, worse, like an overly anxious meddler. When I told her I wanted to give Maddie a bath one afternoon, she handed her over, said, "Go ahead then," and headed for the kitchen. I called for her help at one point, and before I could ask a question, Maddie was whisked out of the tub and swaddled into a damp, bug-eyed package. Building teamwork was not a key agenda item for Jeanette. It was her way or no way at all.

One week after she started, I called Steve at his office, weeping and whispering into the phone from our bedroom. I don't remember exactly what had transpired at that moment to reduce me to tears, but I do know I was a wreck, panicked at the thought of having to fire this woman, embarrassed by how intimidated and childish I felt. When Steve reminded me that I had hired and fired dozens of people over the course of my career and that this person worked for me and that I should just tell her what I wanted or get rid of her, I howled that he didn't understand at all and hung up the phone.

In fact, I don't think Steve did understand how different this relationship was from other employer-employee dyads—evident from the complex mix of guilt, worry, gratitude, and unhappiness I experienced every time I handed Maddie over. I needed Jeanette to fulfill the most important job in the universe, nurturing the tiny sun that ruled it, and I worried that her care of Maddie was intimately linked to my making her happy. If I crossed this bossy baby-sitter, would Maddie suffer? Would there ever be a child-care provider who could fill my shoes? Should I just keep my shoes on and stay home?

The happy ending—although the child-care conundrum never really ends—was that I learned the most important lesson in hiring quality child care: I needed someone who was, first and foremost, on my side. We often make the mistake of looking for child care that is all about our baby's needs. We want a surrogate mom, or a group of surrogate moms in a wonderful child-care center. But one of the keys to making this transition from home to work is having someone or a group of someones who are there for *you*. This means a woman who supports working mothers, really believes that you've made the right choice. If your baby is in center-based care, then you want a place that regularly provides information about what your baby has been doing, not because it will necessarily help the baby but because they know you want to be in on her day. They should also welcome your occasional surprise visits. A child-care provider who seems judgmental, arrogant, or so obsequious that she would obviously never tell you the truth is not the person to hire. A center that holds a dim view of parents who question, call regularly, or stop by is not the one for your baby.

In order to forge the kind of partnership that makes everyone happy, it's also critical that you do your part. Don't micromanage. If you're constantly second-guessing what your child-care provider is providing, you're going to drive her nuts—and perhaps out the door. I have to admit that I did watch over Jeanette like a hawk. When she didn't measure the formula powder to the milligram, I swooped in and offered "constructive criticism." Knowing now that an extra tea-spoon of water would hardly have compromised Maddie's nutritional needs, I realize how annoying I must have been. On the other hand, a good child-care provider, one who has had experience not only with newborns but with new moms, knows we're all a little nuts in the beginning and doesn't get defensive.

When Jackie was struggling to care for her twins, she managed to find a highly competent sitter, but her feelings of insecurity during the first few months postpartum were actually heightened by having a lot of help. "Being someone who is used to doing things myself, I found it really hard to have so much hired help. I kept thinking that I should be doing it on my own. It bothered me that this woman we had hired was so possessive with my babies, and I realized that if I kept allowing her to do everything, I was never going to learn what to do. I felt the more I had her around, the more I was postponing being a mom. She was great. She'd say, "Go get your nails done. Get your hair done. Go to the movies," but I found it impossible to really enjoy myself, because I kept thinking, 'This isn't what moms do.'"

When the boys were about four months old, Jackie got rid of all the helpers—including a couple of well-meaning but not-so-helpful rela-tives. "I just told myself, 'I have two kids and I have a lot of things to do in my day and I have to figure out how to make this work for myself.'" Jackie confesses that the first two weeks were total chaos. "But I felt so happy. I was pretty strict with Michael and Peter, and pretty soon they were into a schedule, and that made me feel so good, so proud."

Jackie's experience underscores the importance of working with a child-care provider who bolsters your skills and feelings of accom-plishment, rather than robbing you of a chance to bond and to learn. It's critical to strengthen your partnership by talking about your baby, your expectations regarding his routine, and what you do/don't want a provider to do. It's also imperative that you recognize how critical her job is to your family and show her the respect she merits. If you are consistently late from work or, worse, late with her paycheck, you're effectively saying, "My work is more important than yours."

One of the mistakes I made with Ana, who worked for us for five years, was that I rarely scheduled times during the week to sit with her and talk about Maddie's and Nick's development, any problems that had bubbled up, or to simply see how Ana was doing. Too often, we had these conversations on the fly, as I was rushing in at the end of the day and she was rushing out.

Many child-care centers keep journals of their charges' days, so parents have a sense of what's going on. The more high-tech spaces even have video cameras in place so you can "peek" in during the day. An at-home provider can easily snap some photos or jot down what your baby did while you were out. Showing you the photos or reviewing the journal entries can be a great way to spark a discussion about your beliefs and fears, to air feelings about your work and about hers.

Your goal is not to become your child-care provider's new best friend; after all, you are her boss. But every employer-employee relationship depends on good communication. If you're not clear about her job responsibilities or if she's reluctant to voice a complaint, then you're going to have a hard time working as a team.

One of the catch-22's of this phase is that when you do manage to find a person who clearly loves your baby and to whom your baby clings with reciprocal adoration, you may want to kill her. Kathleen, who lives in California, found a child-care provider who would work part-time and who came highly recommended by a family in their neighborhood. "Our friends couldn't say enough nice things about her, so I was just thrilled," Kathleen recalled. "But within a few days of her coming to work for us, I was insanely jealous. I would come home from work in the middle of the day to spend time with Christian, and I wouldn't want her around. I wanted to be with him alone, not to share him with anyone. I think I wanted her to mess up, because it was so hard to think that she might be able to stand in my shoes."

I can't tell you the number of moms who have confessed their bile-green envy of the provider whom they perceive as a rival. Fear not. You will always be the sun and the moon to your baby. And if you're fortunate enough to find a loving sitter whom your baby adores, count your lucky stars and give her a raise. On the other hand, if your child-care provider is unsympathetic to your feelings or seems to rub it in when your baby bursts into tears as you enter the front door ("Oh, my. She hasn't cried at all until this moment!"), then find a good time and nice way to tell her to zip it!

Choosing to Stay Home

In a perfect world, affordable, high-quality child care would be accessible to all mothers, not just those who choose or need to work. But even if such a subsidized system did exist, it would never eliminate the ambivalence we feel about handing our babies over to another person. No matter how wonderful or well trained that surrogate might be, millions of moms would still choose to stay home full-time. And for good reason. Mothering our children full-time can fulfill dreams and passions, be expansive and rewarding, serenely pleasurable and always exciting. As psychologist Daphne de Marneffe states: "As mothers, we should give ourselves the room, the dignity, to discover what we think and what we want. Each must think through the issues for herself, so that the life she lives is a personal creation rather than a resigned-to reality."[5]

Erica spoke with a kind of rapture about her time with her son, Bryce. Having been "very ambitious and very high up the ladder," she discovered that her fears of falling down that ladder melted away when she just decided to focus on being present with Bryce. "I realized that when I was maniacally rushing around in my career, barely taking care of myself, I had no mental space. Babies give you a kind of relational space—space just to be with the baby. They also give you a different sense of time and some perspective on what you were doing before and where you want to be headed now."

It had taken several months, but Erica had learned to let go of old expectations, to take a breath, and to follow her son's lead. Other mothers, especially those who had been "high achievers" at work, concurred that the key to surviving the first year with their babies had been to stop trying to be a "high achiever" at home. The day-to-day goals of baby care are amorphous at best; notions of clocking the day's activities are usually fruitless and opportunities to prioritize scarce. Katy, who lives in London and works in publishing, found that at times when she felt as though she was "constantly chasing my tail on a treadmill" she would make announcements—loudly. "I'm sure my neighbors thought me daft, but I would say, 'Today I'm just going to sit and watch you play with your toy! Today I'm not going to do the washing up, but I'm going to take extra time giving you a bath!'" Just being aware of all the tiny, precious moments she and her baby spent together helped mitigate feelings of aimlessness and frustration.

Which isn't to say that being home all day with a baby is boring or exhausting or draining. Of course, it's challenging, but I think we often confuse boredom with ambivalence, exhaustion with depression. Feeling pulled in different directions, conflicted about wanting to be with our babies and wanting the kind of validation that, for better or worse, is more easily achieved on the job front can easily sap your energy and drive. Knowing that you want to be home full-time and embracing that choice without apology can be empowering and joyful. Mothers who believe in what they're doing fare much better psychologically and emotionally than those whose ambivalence and resentment spill over into their interactions with their children. "I have never felt more like myself than when I was home with my babies," Nicole told me, adding with visible anger how hard it was to convince everyone from her husband to her friends that she wanted to give up an excellent job with fabulous benefits to be home full-time. "No one could believe that what actually made me happy was just hanging out with my children, playing with them or just watching them together."

In an article she wrote for the *New York Times Magazine* about educated professional women who have rejected the fast track to be home full-time with their children, Lisa Belkin answered the provocative question "Why don't women run the world?" somewhat equivocally: "Maybe it's because they don't want to." In her report, which garnered hundreds of passionate letters to the editor, Belkin cited research and provided persuasive anecdotal material to support the notion that what most of us want is "sanity, balance and a new definition of success." She concludes her piece by pointing out that as more women seek balance and choose to stay home, men are more willing to leave, too. "Looked at that way, this is not the failure of a revolution, but the start of a new one. It is about a door opened but a crack by women that could usher in a new environment for us all." As one of the women she interviewed points out, the answer to the question "Why don't women run the world?" may be that they really do![6]

Make Room for Daddy

If you do decide to rule your at-home world, you may be shocked to discover that your husband still believes he's king. In fact, his share of the child care and the housework is guaranteed to be a fraction of yours.[7] I realize this sounds somewhat sexist and that there are many fathers who do as much of the diaper changing and cooking as their wives, but if Mom is home all day, Dad often assumes she can and should shoulder more of the day-to-day chores. Frankly, even if Mom is working full-time outside the home, she's likely to find more on her to-do list than on his. (The fact that she even *has* a to-do list of child- and home-related chores puts her ahead of most of the men I know.)

When we did a story not long ago for *Good Morning America* about the so-called chore wars, it was easy to find couples for whom this ongoing battle flared up with astonishing intensity. Stacy and Chris, whom we profiled, lived in a small home in a suburban area of Massachusetts with their four children, including ten-month-old twins. Dad, who worked for Pepsi, trucking and stocking soft drinks, admitted that he did far less of the housework, especially since Stacy had quit her job to stay home with their children. During much of the interview, they joked about the chore wars; Stacy even confessed to sometimes refolding laundry that Chris had done, and he acknowledged that he had a tendency to leave his stuff around for Stacy to pick up.

As we talked, I sensed that Stacy's frustration stemmed less from a fantasy about an equitable division of labor and more from her feeling that Chris had no idea how hard she worked all day long. "I've worked full-time out of the house," she said. "I've worked part-time; I've worked two jobs. And I know that what I'm doing now is harder than anything I've ever done in my life, and he doesn't know that." When I asked what Chris might do to show her that he did, in fact, appreciate her hard work, Stacy turned away and in a strained voice replied, "I just wish he would say, 'Oh, the house looks nice today' or—just anything to make me feel like—" She couldn't continue because she had begun to cry. What had started out as a script for a lighthearted sitcom had turned into a far darker drama.

The debate over who's doing what around the house obviously goes much deeper than the layer of dust building up under the couch. But brushing it under the rug—poor pun intended—because "he just doesn't get it" is a cop-out. Moreover, ignoring the who-does-what issue at this stage in your mothering experience is tantamount to setting a timer on a land mine. It may not explode until your baby is older, but you'll hear it ticking every day, if not every night. When I asked Stacy if her resentment ever spilled over to the bedroom, she admitted, "Yes, occasionally it does. I hold out on him."

Ask any couples counselor to name the top threats to marital bliss, and she is sure to include the division of labor at home.[8] We can joke about it, make fun of our husbands' pathetic efforts, complain, nag, or threaten, but at the root of the debate is an understandable desire to feel connected to the person you love most in the world. When our husbands don't do their share or when fatherhood leads to more time on the job or when we feel we're speaking different languages, anger, exasperation, and loneliness pile up in dark corners. The challenge is to bring these feelings out in the open and to explore together, if possible, why they run so deep.

For many of us, the chore wars are, in fact, a battle with ourselves, an internal struggle over how much control we want, how much authority we need in order to feel like good-enough mothers. We're usually much more willing to relinquish the housework than the child care, eager to have a partner in the kitchen washing up after dinner but more competitive when it comes to bonding with the baby. What's really "fair" has to be evaluated not only in the context of your marriage but in terms of what you really want for yourself. If your dream is to be home full-time with your baby but your family depends on your income, you may find yourself putting in a second shift in order to feel as connected as possible with your role as a mom. If mothering 24/7 leaves you drained and unfulfilled, then your resentment of your husband's freedom to "go about his life just like before" (as one mother told me bitterly) is guaranteed to rankle.

Of course, it's incredibly hard to sort out the complex and conflicting feelings of this stage. We're apt to give mixed messages to our husbands because we rarely have the opportunity to sit back and evaluate exactly what we want and what has to change. When Maddie was a baby and Steve and I were both working full-time, it was hard enough to finish a sentence, let alone find the time to contemplate whether or not I liked my life. It was far easier just to plow ahead, joking about or quietly grumbling over who did the laundry more often.

I thought about this recently when I happened to pull out an old video of Maddie's first birthday party. Steve, with disarming humor, provided the voice-over of my day, starting at dawn with the cake (from scratch) preparation; chronicling the arrival of friends and relatives, the obscene pile of gifts (most of them purchased and wrapped by me); and ending at dusk with the cleanup of twenty-five chocolate-covered plates. What's notable is that I'm the star at the stove, the sink, the table, the sink again. At one point I actually comment to my Spielberg wannabe that there are more plates to be loaded into the dishwasher.

The first time I watched this tape, I focused on the fact that I had clearly done everything that day, and the taste of residual resentment began to burn in the back of my throat. But when I watched it again, another theme began to emerge. I heard loud and clear the dozens of compliments Steve lovingly scripted into our home movie. I claimed top billing not simply because I wanted to be the writer, director, and producer of the day but because the cameraman was shining a warm and appreciative light on my efforts.

I don't mean to imply that Steve's appreciation was all I needed then—or now—to feel the chore wars are a myth. (Believe me, there have been innumerable times in our twenty-five years together when a trainload of roses couldn't have righted the unfairness of the child-care imbalance.) But his consistent expressions of gratitude underscored a basic understanding that in order to make the transition to parenthood work, we needed to tune in to each other with renewed concentration and energy. In her seminal book, *The Second Shift,* Arlie Russell Hochschild profiles several couples for whom "the scarcity of gratitude led to a dearth of small gestures of caring."[9] In practically every case the results were increased strain, even estrangement, especially as additional children entered the picture.

Of course, showing gratitude is a two-way street, and for most of the working mothers I interviewed, the closest they would come to throwing their partners a bone was to say, "I guess he's better than a lot of dads I know." It's often the case that we wind up using very different yardsticks to measure our contributions. Mothers tend to compare their husbands with themselves, while fathers often measure their contributions against what their own fathers did at home—a comparison that makes any effort look like a major improvement.[10] I'm convinced that's why Steve's many contributions were often accompanied by a drumroll-and-cymbals announcement of same. "I gave Maddie a bath, and I coaxed her into taking those kiddie vitamins," he would crow, pausing—waiting, I realized, for my grateful response. As one friend said angrily when I mentioned this over lunch, "It's incredible! I might have been up all night with the kids, but when I come into the kitchen, he'll say, 'Aren't you going to thank me? I made pancakes for the kids!' Whoopee! I make three different breakfasts three hundred fifty-five mornings a year!"

The tendency many of us have to keep score during the first years of motherhood seems to me both understandable and forgivable, because it speaks to a desire for symmetry in our relationships. I not only wanted Steve to be as involved in Maddie's care as I was, I wanted him to *feel* the same way about her as I did; I wanted him to experience the same pangs of guilt, to share my anguish at saying good-bye on Monday mornings. But Steve didn't feel the same way I did. Don't get me wrong. I didn't question for a nanosecond his passionate love for Maddie; he would have killed for her. But his fundamental sense of who he was had not undergone a massive shift, whereas mine seemed to lurch and tumble every day.

Several moms shared the sense I had during the first year of Maddie's life, that fatherhood, though profound and thrilling, didn't shake their husbands' basic priorities or expectations. "Initially, I felt as though we were on the same page exactly," Dawn told me. "In fact, Danny was even more gaga over the baby than I was. But once he went back to work and kind of slipped back into our old life, I definitely had moments when I would be thinking, 'What are you doing? Don't you get it?' Like the other night, we were going out and we had promised our sitter that we would be home by nine. So when it was like eight-fifty, I said, 'Hey, we really have to go.' And I knew that he was having a good time and he wanted to stay, but the time is passing and I finally had to say, 'Look, I'm leaving. You can stay if you want.' He said, 'No, no, I'm coming,' but I could tell that he was disappointed to leave, whereas I had been thinking constantly about what was going on at home, whether the baby was okay, what time we had to leave. He was exactly the way he would have acted a year ago."

A mom who went back to work full-time when her son was six months old confided that she felt incredibly resentful of her husband's seeming lack of stress. "I guess it would be worse if we both were miserable," she said with a weak laugh. "But I just don't get how he can stay late at the office night after night and not feel guilty about missing this stage in the baby's life. When I'm stuck at my work, my bones hurt! He apologizes for being late, but I just know we're coming from totally different places. And that makes me feel cut off from him in a way I never anticipated."

One of the paradoxes of the first year is that the baby can bring you together and pull you apart with searing intensity. I never felt closer to Steve than when we would lie together and look at Maddie and whisper to each other, "Isn't she beautiful? Do you believe we *made* her?" But I could also feel as though we were shouting across a canyon when issues of who did what and whose job was more important brought us face-to-face with our fundamental differences. Learning to respect and even embrace those differences took time and patience and, to a certain extent, a willingness to capitulate.

I would love to report that by the time Steve filmed Maddie's first birthday, we had found a fair and loving way to share her care. But the truth is we struggled—sometimes intensely and always differently—with our new roles; we argued and made up, hired more help and sacrificed opportunities at work. Steve's involvement in Maddie's life had increased enormously as her toddlerhood approached, which bolstered his confidence and helped me to loosen the reins a bit. But when her first word was *Da-da*, I can't deny that I experienced a pang of resentment along with joy.

For Steve and me, the challenge to embrace a new definition of *we* mirrored our individual struggles to accept a radically altered sense of ourselves. Maddie's first birthday was a celebration of the longest year ever to whiz by; so much had happened in so little time, yet I could readily recall nights early in her life that I thought would never end and long, exhausting days. As a mother I had come so far, discovered vast reservoirs of energy and hidden strengths. There were even occasions when I experienced what Tibetan Buddhists refer to as my *lungtha*—a feeling of being on the top of my game, a Wind Horse Mama, no longer straining to maintain my seat.

Of course, the year had also forced me to face my share of demons, to accept that I had a long way to go before I would feel totally in balance—at home, at work, in my marriage, and in relation to extended family, friends, colleagues. I had learned that, as Daphne de Marneffe writes in *Maternal Desire,* "motherhood puts women in a different relationship to themselves . . . not as some sort of pale 'shifting of priorities,' but as a new relationship to experience."[11] To survive this first, dramatic year, I had had to let go of the expectation that my days would ever be completely my own; to accept that life with a baby rarely goes as planned, that the tension between the love and the anger we feel toward our babies could bend steel, and that unless we nurture ourselves, we cannot possibly summon the reserves we need to care for them.

Stage 3

❧

Letting Go

The Toddler Years, One and Two

I can't remember the precise moment when I realized that Maddie was no longer a baby, but I do recall the longing I felt throughout her toddler years for those earlier times of sweet surrender, when she could be scooped up on a whim and tucked snugly in the crook of my arm. The first time she walked, I clapped and whooped like a crazed fan, but the tightness in my throat belied my enthusiasm. Even as she teetered stiff-legged toward me, falling into my outstretched arms, I knew she was gradually moving away.

I was right. Not long after she had mastered walking on her own, she would frequently let go of my hand, cock her head slightly to one side, put one hand on her hip, and march off, swinging the other arm with exaggerated vigor. She looked like a huffy maître d', a pint-sized caricature of an adult, which is precisely the impression she was hoping to achieve. I loved her "Mrs. Lady" routine, as Steve dubbed it, but there were moments when Madeleine lost her babyishness so completely that she took my breath away. I would suddenly see her as the little person she was—her own person—separate and different from me.

Separation is painful because, as Judith Viorst notes, it reduces our power and control, makes us feel less needed, less important, and because we worry that separation exposes our children to danger.[1] And though we're engaged in the push-pull dance of independence-dependence throughout our children's lives, the many milestones of years one and two (first words, first steps, first friends) provide dramatic proof that our children can't be controlled or constantly protected. During our children's toddler years we move from holding their hands to holding our breath to occasionally holding our head in our hands.

For some mothers I met, their children's physical independence produced a vigilance that bordered on lunacy. Carol was raising her eighteen-month-old daughter, Amanda, in a rubber apartment. In addition to installing multiple child-safety gates, she had laid mats throughout the living room (the bedrooms were carpeted). Large pieces of foam and what looked like chunks of discarded tires clung aggressively to every edge, corner, finial, and decorative protrusion. The rooms were as snug and safe as a womb. Even so, Mom kept a hawk-like eye on Amanda's every movement. The day I visited she was enjoying a new book, despite Carol's frequent admonitions to watch out for the "sharp corners of the pages."

As easy as it was for me to pass judgment on this mom, to label her behavior over-the-top or neurotic, I also knew that her anxiety reflected other stresses in her life. Carol's dad was very ill, having suffered a stroke, and she was running back and forth to the hospital to visit him. She felt miserable about returning to work, and though money was tight, she clearly wasn't ready to leave her daughter in the hands of a baby-sitter. A first-time mom at thirty-eight, Carol told me she wasn't expecting to have any more kids, so "Amanda is my one and only angel."

What's Behind Separation Anxiety

Whenever we find ourselves holding on too tight, we need to try to figure out what's driving our anxiety. It could be heavy baggage from a childhood trauma or work-related stress or all-too-familiar mommy guilt. I remember how hard it was for me to get Maddie to bed at night when she was about one. Our routine typically took close to an hour and included a couple of books (or one book read three times), a variety of protracted "night-nights" to her 3,500 stuffed animals, songs in the rocking chair, back rubs in her crib—you get the picture.

I was complaining about this to a friend, the mother of three slightly older kids, who nodded sympathetically and said, "But the evenings are the one time during the week when you're together. On some level, you must want to drag it out."

She had a point. Work was extremely demanding, and despite my best intentions, I was never home in time for Maddie's dinner. My complaints about our "bedtime ordeal" belied a guilt-o-meter reading of "high" and a concomitant wish to indulge Maddie's need for one-on-one time. When Maddie begged for another story or lingered in my lap a little too long, I was in no rush to let go. Feeling torn clearly fueled my need to savor our time together; even as I dubbed our routine an ordeal, I was not really interested in cutting it short. Looking back, I think many of my struggles with Maddie and, subsequently, with Nick grew directly from this rocky, ambivalent terrain I stumbled through every day. It was very hard to set limits or to let the kids play by themselves when I unconsciously experienced these "separations" as intrusions on our time together.

There will be countless occasions during this stage of motherhood when your own separation anxiety wrestles with your toddler's natural desire to become more independent. Sometimes the result is a full-fledged tantrum—his or yours. Sometimes it's a far more subtle and insidious series of mixed signals. Just eavesdrop in the hallway of a day-care center, or listen, as I did, to a mom as she bids good-bye to her toddler on the morning of her first music class: "Okay, sweetheart, Mommy's going now."

Suzy picks up a tambourine and starts to shake it.

"Bye-bye, honey," Mom says a little plaintively.

"Bye-bye," Suzy replies, still shaking the tambourine.

"I'll see you very, very soon," Mom says, a question mark nibbling at the edges of her statement. Suzy doesn't seem to hear. "I'm going now, okay?"

"Okay."

"I'll see you later. You have a good time, okay?" Suzy seems to detect a note of uncertainty, and a tiny cloud crosses her brow. "Don't be sad. We'll be together very, very soon," Mom says, then asks for one last hug.

Suzy runs to her mom and bursts into tears. "Mama no go! Mama no go!"

Mom sighs and looks desperately over at the teacher, who helps pry Suzy from Mom's coat. She dashes out, alternately waving, shouting encouragement, and wiping tears away.

This particular scenario brought back vivid memories of my children's toddler years and my tendency to unwittingly undermine their strides toward independence. I can't count the number of times I lingered too long, practically inviting my kids to do their baby-starfish routine, plastering themselves against my legs, as I miserably tried to exit.

Don't get me wrong. I'm not saying that my ambivalence about leaving was the driving emotional force behind my children's separation anxiety. I have no doubt that their feelings of fear and anger were very real. There's no way those desperate cries, those Ironman hugs, weren't a reflection of the pain and panic they experienced before a competent teacher or loving baby-sitter came to the rescue. But hanging around, postponing the inevitable, certainly didn't make parting any sweeter a sorrow.

What did work was letting go of the expectation that saying good-bye, launching one of the kids into a new environment, would ever be easy. Day by day, week by week, month by month, we all struggle with how to reconcile our needs with those of our children. For me, what often worked was shifting the locus of control to the kids. By giving Maddie and Nick an occasional opportunity to lead the dance, I forced myself to step back and see the world from their point of view rather than through the lens of my own ambivalence and guilt.

If you think about your toddler's day-to-day existence, you quickly realize that she has practically no say in your comings and goings. If Mom announces, "I'm going out for a little while, but Grandma will stay with you," there's not much to do except register a complaint as loudly as possible, at which point Mom is likely to say, "But sweetie, you love when Grandma visits" or "But it's only for an hour" or "Okay, okay. Mommy will stay for ten minutes and then go, okay?"

When Maddie was a toddler (and had absolutely no idea what ten minutes or ten hours felt like), I tried to help her gain more of a sense of control by choreographing a very predictable exit routine. We would pick a favorite book or video—one that I knew by heart (rarely a problem, given her insatiable appetite for repetition)—and decide together when I would leave; for example, "at the picture of the smiley truck" or "when Big Bird sneezes." A couple of times I made the mistake of hanging around beyond the sneeze, only to have Maddie say impatiently, "Okay, Mama. Go now."

This approach played out even more dramatically one night when Nick was about two. It was way past his bedtime and we were both exhausted, but he was putting me through the wringer. I would sing a song, pat his terry rump, say good night, and try to exit, only to watch him hurl himself against the crib rail and launch a cry guaranteed to wake the dead. I reentered the fray, but this time I sat down in the rocking chair in the corner of his room and said, "Okay, Nick. You tell me when I can go." You could practically hear the brakes in his brain screeching to a halt. His eyes widened slightly as he slid down onto his belly, and in a voice husky with power, he barked, "GO OUT!" I tried not to skip across the threshold of his room.

No-Win Power Struggles

Of course there were many more times when I simply lowered my horns and pawed the ground, chanting "I will not submit" under my hot breath. Those scenes were not pretty. I recall tiny fingers curled around the base of Maddie's door as I held fast to the doorknob and ordered her to stay in her room for five more minutes of time-out. There was the morning I forcibly stripped off Nick's sopping diaper (he had wanted to open the tabs himself) and then attempted to reason with my outraged, shrieking son for forty-five minutes, only to hear Maddie cry in frustration, "For gosh sakes, Mom, just put the wet diaper back on!" I fished the five-pound (now cold) trophy out of the trash, slapped it on Nick, and watched as, narrow shoulders still heaving, he gingerly removed the tabs, stepped over the soggy diaper, and lay down on the floor so I could put on the clean one.

The story seems sitcom-worthy now, but at the time I was not laughing. I felt stupid and diminished—a loser in more ways than one. As one mom of an eighteen-month-old told me, "I've always been a very competitive person, so I experience our power struggles as a win-lose contest. If I give in, especially after he's been screaming and carrying on, I feel as though I've lost, been beaten down. And I just hate that feeling."

My friend Nancy Samalin, author of several excellent books on discipline, has run parenting seminars for over a decade. She thinks parents *do* lose if they give in only because they're desperate to avoid "the
happiness trap," so named because we get trapped into never letting
our children experience disappointment. Letting a toddler whine you
into submission every time he wants another cookie or caving at the
first pissed-off peep is not what your little tyrant wants. She longs for
limits, because the world is big and highly unpredictable.

According to T. Berry Brazelton, one of the reasons to let your little
guy experience frustration, fury, and the calm after the storm is that
it provides a sense of mastery over anxiety and an inner sense of success.[2] I wish I had known that when Maddie threw her first tantrum—
an experience so shocking that I wanted to run screaming from the
supermarket. Yes, the supermarket—a place where the number of
tantrum-inspiring temptations should qualify Gristedes, Giant, Safe-
way, etc. as additions to the efforts of the International Committee to
Ban Landmines.

As I recall, what set Maddie off was a Ritz cracker. I think it broke.
Or maybe it was just chipped a little. Or maybe it had nothing to do
with the cracker, but in the beat of a nanosecond my characteristically
sweet-tempered daughter morphed into a pint-sized Orc—growling,
spewing, whipping her head back and forth, and kicking the supermarket cart so hard her shoes flew off. I considered throwing them
back at her, but instead I managed to extricate her from the cart, sit on
the floor, and hold her in my lap in the middle of the canned legumes
aisle. Rocking her back and forth, talking softly about anything I
could think up—the history of legumes, perhaps—I waited for the
tornado to pass. When she looked up and asked, "Where does the Jolly
Green Giant live?" I knew she was back.

There are dozens of theories about how to handle tantrums—from
walking away to spanking. Needless to say, I don't subscribe to the
latter; fighting out-of-control behavior with out-of-control behavior
doesn't make a lot of sense. All spanking teaches a child is that a big
person can use his strength to hurt a little person. And I think the former only works if you let your screaming Mimi know you're nearby,
willing to help if you can. Brazelton suggests you actually say, "This
tantrum is your job" and then give your child "the space to resolve his
feelings."[3] That may work at home, where you can say whatever you

want, exit the Tower of Terror, and peek in occasionally to guarantee her safety or to reassure her that you haven't deserted her (trying not to add, "even though I sure as hell wish I could"). But when you're in public, your concern for your child's safety goes head-to-head with feelings of humiliation. You imagine that dozens of your fellow shoppers are rolling their eyes, tsk-tsking their way around you, and labeling your child a spoiled brat, product of a bad mother. And you're probably right. Strangers just love to tell themselves that they would never let their child get away with that kind of behavior—especially those who have never had kids. The best way to deal with judgmental know-nothings is to chant softly to yourself, "I don't know these people. I'll never see them again. I don't give a damn what they think of me."

Some moms have more difficulty with this than others. Lanie describes the day her daughter Sophie, who was "always pretty obstinate," threw a fit in the middle of the street. "She was just mad because she didn't want to be in the stroller, but she was clearly tired. And she didn't want to wear a coat, but it was cold out. So she threw herself down on the sidewalk, and I just knew that we were not going anywhere until we resolved this. Well, actually, until *she* resolved it, because I can't force her when she's like that. And meanwhile our neighbors are passing by, and some of them clearly thought I was indulgent and she was being bratty, but I didn't care. Part of this stage of motherhood for me is knowing that I have to do what's best for my kid. And at that moment I had to just stand there and wait. I can't let what other people think about me add to my stress."

If the "other people" happen to be your own relatives, the scene can become ugly. Judy recalled a visit with her parents one summer that included a full-fledged meltdown by her two-year-old son, Nate. "His tantrums were never easy to handle. And this one was a doozy. He was screaming and kicking the floor and making a hell of a racket, but I was handling it. Or I thought I was handling it, until my mother put her head in the room and said that Nate would just have to stop because he was disturbing the neighbors and it just wouldn't do to have all this noise. That was when *I* lost it," Judy admitted. "I screamed for her to get out and leave us alone, with the same intensity as Nate."

When she reflected on the scene later, Judy realized how deeply rooted her rage had been. "I guess I was reacting to my mother's screwed-up priorities, which have hurt me in countless ways over the years. The fact that she was more concerned about the neighbors than about my needs brought back a lot of feelings I didn't know were still there."

The ways in which you were made to feel secure and loved surface big-time during the toddler phase. Mothers who received inadequate nurturing are far more likely to abuse or neglect their kids than moms who grew up in homes where appropriate responses and loving support were integral to the discipline they received.[4] In an interesting study of moms of toddler boys, researchers found that the ways in which mothers remembered and described their relationships with their own mothers had a profound effect on their current interactions with and feelings about their sons. "The quality of a mother's current representation of her own attachment experiences is related to the way she thinks and feels about her relationship with her child."[5] This was particularly true of mothers who reported close and positive bonds with their moms.

Obviously, our mothers' lives and how we experienced their love shape our interactions with our toddlers. Whether your mother was a positive or a negative role model, a happy or an angry force, authoritarian or liberal, you will consciously or unconsciously make choices every day that reflect her influence. If you were spared the rod, rarely reprimanded, never ridiculed, you may be burdened with far more guilt regarding your own anger when it does bubble up. Women whose mothers' dreams of a career were frustrated by family responsibilities may overcompensate on the job front; young moms whose working mothers were rarely around may swear they'll do it differently. My friend Sandra, whose upbringing included spankings, rolls her eyes during our True Confessions tales of losing control. "Oh, Lord," she will say with a sigh when someone admits to having told her child to shut up. "You are all such wimps."

She's probably right—some of the time. When a toddler is throwing a fit because he's been denied his fifteenth run down the slide, a clear, firm "I know you're mad, but we have to go now" will get you out of the park more quickly than trying to reason with a totally irrational little person. But trying to remember that discipline is a form of teaching, not punishment, is usually much easier said than done.

Ellen, whose two-year-old son Alex had a very hard time separating from her when he started a toddler program, admitted that she was ready to throw in the towel the day he cried so hard he vomited: "I remember I had lunch with a friend afterward and I questioned whether to keep it up. I had been inching my chair closer and closer to the door for weeks. But I thought, 'If this is making him so unhappy, maybe I shouldn't continue.'" As it turned out, her moment of equivocation was rewarded the next week, when she was able to leave without a scene. "The teachers and other parents cheered when I left. It was as if we had won the Notre Dame game!" Ellen recalled with a laugh. "I was surprised by how relieved I felt. Accompanying him to school the next time, I felt as if someone had lifted a trunk off my shoulders. I was *so* happy."

Difficult transitions, handled with patience and the support of a teacher or child-care provider, usually progress from torturous to triumphant. Tantrums, on the other hand, tend to leave you exhausted, angry, guilty, or all of the above. The temptation to hand over the potato chips or to permit another fifteen minutes of TV time can be simply irresistible, as Marianne, the working mother of "a handful" discovered during her eldest son's toddler years: "I had a lot of trouble with Joseph's tantrums when they first happened," Marianne told me. "I just found it really hard not to give in, because the one cookie or small toy seemed minor compared to how upset he got. But after talking to other moms and reading about tantrums, I realized I wasn't doing him any favors by giving in. I didn't want him to learn that if he yelled and screamed, he would get what he wanted every time."

For most of the mothers I interviewed, the challenge of this preverbal, short-fuse period was anticipating when the world would cause that fuse to short out. "Jesse's tantrums seemed totally random to me," Jane recalled. "He would flip out—screaming and crying—and I would usually haul him out of the store or the playground. One time I dragged him onto the bus and then realized that we were only two blocks away. I think I was so focused on getting him home that I lost touch with where we were."

You don't have to be Übermom to know that a two-year-old who is hungry, tired, not feeling well, or frustrated can't handle a question like "Would you like macaroni, peanut butter, or chicken soup for dinner?" Too many choices may cause him to short-circuit, and he's likely to express his feelings of overload by biting, hitting, kicking, or pulling the hair of anyone who crosses his path. All of the books on toddlers will tell you that the trick is to anticipate when the overload button is about to start flashing and to use time-out *before* your child has a fit—not as punishment. But the reality is, you probably won't be prescient enough to steer clear of emotional land mines. When the explosion happens, don't add to your misery by telling yourself that you should have seen it coming.

When Twos Are Terrible

It takes enormous energy, self-control, compassion, creativity, and wisdom to get through a day with a toddler, yet we all hold on to unrealistic expectations of seamless transitions, hours of independent play, moments of crystal-clear communication. But that's just not possible. The "Terrible Twos" were so named not because these years are unrelentingly awful but because the intensely joyful highs are offset by the inevitable and often painful lows. If you're in a good mood, if you're rested, well fed, energized, and calm, then almost anything your toddler chucks your way will bounce right off. Better yet, you'll be able to ride through the storm and show your little guy the rainbow on the other side. But if you've had a bad day, a sleepless night, no chance for a decent meal or a phone call to a friend, no opportunity to talk to an adult or glance at the newspaper or make your own bed, then your toddler's psychotic reaction to being denied access to your jewelry box may make you want to do something really ugly. It's a little like that scene in *Annie Hall,* when Woody Allen and Diane Keaton are first in love. They're preparing a lobster dinner, but the lobsters escape and Allen and Keaton laugh and shriek their way around the kitchen, obviously having fun and sharing a memorable moment in their relationship. Later in the film, Allen—now dating the wrong woman—reenacts the exact same scene, but the date doesn't get it. She doesn't think the skittering crustaceans are the least bit amusing, and she's clearly not connecting with Allen. I remember countless times when the same routine with Maddie or Nick that had been fun or funny the day before was an unbearable burden on a day when I was too tired or grumpy to play the scene the way the kids wanted. I was the wrong date.

For Katherine, who became pregnant with her second child when her first was still in diapers, the challenge of meeting her toddler's demands "with this other one dangling from a sling in front of you" was particularly tough—physically and emotionally. "I just find it extremely hard to accommodate very acceptable bits of behavior. I took Julie out for her birthday to the museum of natural history, and what might not have bothered me before the baby came along was unbelievably irritating. She wanted to touch everything in the shop or would not get into the stroller. All of those are perfectly easy to deal with if you only have one, but that's a luxury I don't have. I have a baby and a toddler. So that's the thing I find hardest—that impatience with Julie, which just makes me so sad."

One mother of an "off-the-wall" toddler confessed that she often throws a tantrum along with her two-year-old. "I find myself screaming and sometimes crying. It's as though he's contagious or something." A toddler's mood *can* be contagious. In *Motherhood as Metamorphosis,* psychologist Joyce Block describes the phenomenon of mothers who "join their toddler's world" so completely that they experience tantrums and the other normal out-of-control times as their own: "Surely, when all of these experiences occur, there is a confusion of identities, a loss of distance, or what some psychologists might call a blurring of boundaries."[6]

More than once I was dragged down into the emotional abyss along with my hysterical child. One particularly miserable afternoon comes to mind when I was suffering from the flu. Steve was away on business, and both kids had been cooped up in the house for two days. I was balancing Nick on one hip, trying to get a snack for Maddie, and ignoring their incessant whining as well as the knot in my stomach caused by that incessant whining. Nick's eyes fixed like a laser on a package of chocolate chips. "Candy!" he demanded. "No candy now," I countered, bracing for the explosion. "CANDY!" he screamed. I handed Maddie a graham cracker and offered one to Nick, who batted it onto the floor and then swatted me in the face. I didn't even think. I just whacked him back, smacking his hand with enough force to make a noise that turned Maddie to stone and upped the volume of Nick's shrieks. "You hit Nick!" Maddie gasped, eyes wide with disbelief. As I kissed Nick's hand and mixed my own tears with his, I prayed that I would never, ever, lose control like that again, that I would find a way to keep my anger in check.

I never hit Nick or Maddie again, but believe me, there were plenty of times during their early years when I understood completely how loving parents wind up losing control. My rage had nothing to do with how much I knew about child development or the right way to use time-out or the other discipline techniques touted in the pages of *Parents* magazine each month. The depth of my anger was a reflection of the depth of my love. And I often had as little control over my tears of frustration and anger as I did over my tears of joy and laughter. In a wonderful, funny essay about maternal anger, the writer Anne Lamott alludes to the painful irony of loving our supremely frustrating children: "Some of us wanted children—and what they give is so rich, you can hardly bear it. At the same time, if you need to yell, children are going to give you something to yell about. There's no reasoning with them. If you get into a disagreement with a regular person, you slog through it; listen to the other person's position, needs, problems; and somehow you arrive at something that is maybe not perfect, but you don't actually feel like smacking them. But because we are so tired sometimes, when a disagreement starts with our child, we can only flail miserably through time and space and holes in between; and then we blow our top."[7]

Research shows that rates of depression are twice as high among women with toddlers as they are for other mothers.[8] In her book *The Sacrificial Mother,* Carin Rubinstein hypothesizes that depression is the cost of self-sacrifice, of constantly giving, giving, giving—time, attention, empathy, understanding—with very little "payback."[9] Certainly, the emotional drain of sacrificing so much can take its toll, but so can the frustration and anger. When your toddler hurls his bowl of sauced macaroni off the table—the macaroni you cooked just the way he likes it—murderous thoughts may flash though your mind. But you don't act on those thoughts. You may not even give them voice; instead, you turn your rage inward, where it sits like a lead weight on your chest. Dragging around a lead apron is exhausting. It's also a fairly apt description of what it feels like to be depressed.

Giving yourself permission to walk out of the room, close the door, scream, punch a pillow, or simply exhale not only enables you to gain some control, but it models exactly the kind of behavior your child is trying to master. When you say, "I'm very angry right now. I need to be alone so I can calm down," your toddler may not understand a single word you've said, but he'll absorb fully the benefits a self-imposed time-out can provide.

Give Yourself (and Your Toddler) a Break

Modeling the importance of boundaries, carving out a little Mom time in the middle of the day can be particularly tough during the toddler years. Marianne, the mother of twins, described herself as "Magnet Mom." Within minutes of entering the door after work, she has "one kid wrapped around my left leg, the other pulling on my right." Her escape time is the seventy-five minutes she spends commuting. "It's the one hour I have to read the paper, maybe close my eyes without anyone demanding something of me."

I remember how important it was to have a six-minute reentry routine at the end of my workday. I would greet Maddie briefly and then announce I was going to change into my play clothes. She rarely protested because I never equivocated. I needed to stand in my closet, slowly peel off my suit and panty hose, and then, just as gradually, trade my work uniform for something soft and forgiving. Often I turned out the light and spent the last minute breathing deeply in the dark. By the time I joined her in the living room, I was much better prepared to plunge into our evening routine.

And you need all the adrenaline you can pump through your veins when you're mothering a toddler. I had forgotten how exhilarating and exhausting it can be to follow a two-year-old as she gallops, leaps, dances, and dives through her day when my friend Jackie happened to drop by with her twin boys. Once sprung from their double stroller, they ricocheted off the furniture like human pinballs. Michael charged up and down a small series of steps with the focus of a kamikaze trainee, while Peter, still a little wobbly on his feet, made a beeline for a bowl of nuts I had forgotten to move. "How do you do this every day?" I asked Jackie, who used to be a personal trainer. She shrugged and laughed, just as Michael dove into her arms from a chair. "Thank God I'm in good physical shape," she replied, lifting thirty pounds of boy into the air.

I complimented Jackie on her expertise as a "spotter," ready to help if absolutely necessary but willing to let her boys tumble and fumble their way through our living room. When Michael missed his mark, clunking his head on the floor, I expected Jackie to rush in and make a big fuss over his spill. But she just trilled, "Oopsie, doopsie," set him on his feet, and watched him run.

I failed spotting. I tended to hover, helicopter-like, on the perimeters of Maddie or Nick's play, poised to swoop in and help out. As much as I may have saved them from frustration, I often deprived them of the supreme satisfaction of mastering a task or practicing a skill. I learned this the hard way one morning when Nick was a little over two. Maddie and I were watching him struggle to put on his socks. "Look at Nicko's ears," Madeleine whispered. "They're red like crayons." She was right. Nick's efforts had sent a flush from his cheeks to his ears, which glowed like little taillights on either side of his furrowed brow. The temptation to rush over and align the heel properly was so great, I had to take a couple of deep breaths and look away. As his frustration burned hotter, I couldn't stand it, and as sweetly as possible, I said, "Honey, turn your socks around first." This proved about as helpful as dousing burning embers with gasoline, and the explosion that followed included hurled socks, large tears, and an outraged cry of "No, Mama! Don't talk! I do it!"

According to a study conducted in the late eighties, toddlers are told "No!" every nine minutes.[10] All the important daily decisions are made by grown-ups, who often misinterpret cues or fail to understand their toddler's limited language. Your little guy desperately yearns to do and try and test and do again. Experiencing frustration just makes the victory that much sweeter. As a wise psychologist once told me when I was about to rescue Maddie from under a chair (she had crawled in, sat up, and couldn't figure out how to get back out), "Tell her what to do. But leave her to her own devices for a minute." I got down to her eye level, and told her to bow down and then crawl back out. She looked a little panicky at first, but suddenly she got it: Like a pint-sized yoga master, she touched her head to the floor, snaked her way out, and flashed me a triumphant smile.

Think Empowerment, Not Punishment

Recognizing your toddler's competence and resilience can be incredibly liberating. It enables you to rethink many of the separations that can feel punitive and cruel. Take sleeping. If the message to your toddler is "I know you can put yourself to sleep" rather than "I hate to do this, but it's for your own good," the emphasis shifts from your willpower to your child's competence. Bedtime becomes a chance to help him overcome his fears, to learn to soothe himself, to relax. Obviously, this doesn't happen in one night, but a change in your attitude is the critical first step.

Some arenas may prove more challenging than others. It's very hard to back off and let your toddler lead the way when it comes to food, which is why most mothers of toddlers report that feeding is second only to bedtime in terms of frustration and stress.[11] We all come with buttons installed many moons ago by our well-meaning but inexperienced parents, so if food and eating were highly charged issues in your family, then you may also have a host of relatives turning up the volume on the "he eats like a bird" refrain. I actually found what I thought was an ancient grocery list not long ago, which read as follows: "Three raisins; eight ounces milk; four grape halves; two bites toast; two cups bathwater; one M&M; one-third breadstick; one-half teaspoon toothpaste." I couldn't imagine why I had saved this bizarre scrap of paper, but then it hit me: It was a list of what Nicholas had eaten one Sunday, prompted by my aunt remarking that he looked "scrawny."

In fact, Nick was a very healthy eater. But like most toddlers, he was too busy practicing walking to sit still in his high chair. And he was definitely too intent on mastering the use of a spoon and a cup to let me shovel applesauce into his mouth. I fed him as one would a parking meter—running around with bags of Cheerios or slices of banana, which I slipped into his mouth more or less according to his mood.

I knew from Maddie's toddler years that Nick's diminished appetite was normal and not life-threatening. (There are very, very few middle-class children in this country who suffer from malnutrition—even if they seem to subsist only on plain noodles.) I had also learned the value of taking the long view. Rather than obsess over a day when your toddler has eaten nothing but goldfish crackers and apple juice, keep track of an entire week's worth of grazing. You will undoubtedly discover—as countless studies have corroborated—that children will eat when they're hungry. Your job is to offer plenty of healthy options, not to force your toddler to clean his plate.

"Take the long view" should become your mantra during the toddler years. Challenges that throw you off balance or keep you up at night may, within a couple of months, seem like minor blips on the radar screen. Problems that seem overwhelming and scary often resolve themselves. My friend Jane was uncharacteristically worried when her eighteen-month-old daughter was speech-delayed. "Her language skills are way behind where Jesse was at her age," she told me one night over dinner. "She has probably a dozen words max in her vocabulary, and when she does say a new word, it then goes underground for weeks."

Jane's distress was no doubt exacerbated by the fact that she holds an advanced degree in conversation. Before the introduction of call waiting, I often asked the operator to verify whether Jane's phone had been busy for two hours because it was off the hook. "The line appears to be in use" was the inevitable diagnosis.

It took a visit to a speech therapist, who reassured Jane that her daughter's slight delay would have no serious repercussions down the road, and a few months of backing off and getting a break herself (she and her husband took a much-needed vacation together), to help both mother and daughter move past this particular roadblock. Now, two years later, Jane is more likely to laugh with pride as Julia prattles on than she is to recall the days when she feared she would never speak. She's also quick to point out how vastly different her two children are and how much joy she derives from learning to nurture their unique skills. "It's just amazing to me how Julia expresses herself—she's very different from Jesse—but they're each so, so wonderful."

Stop Comparing

Putting your child's progress in the right perspective is particularly tough during these early years of dramatic growth. I recall a particularly low moment in my journey through motherhood when a woman in the adjacent supermarket line asked innocently enough, "And how old is *your* little boy?" For a variety of reasons, I lied. "He just turned one," I responded, when in truth, Nick was approaching fourteen months. But I had been eavesdropping in the checkout line long enough to learn that my interviewer's son was about to celebrate his first birthday and to overhear at least a dozen perfectly articulated words coming from his mouth. In fact, it was right after he had pointed to a tiny shoe and said, "Sneaker off, Ma" that Ma had popped the question.

Nicholas's vocabulary at the time consisted of three words— actually three syllables: *ma,* used variously for "milk," "mine," "more," "Maddie," and "Mama"; *da,* meaning "Dad," "that," and "there"; and *na,* referring to bananas and his favorite word: *no. Sneaker* was definitely not part of his verbal repertoire.

So, rightly or wrongly, I took Mother of Boy Genius's question as a competitive challenge, a gauntlet signaling the start of a familiar duel. It's a competition you will experience many times during the toddler years, and you may, like me, find it both irritating and irresistible. When, at a fairly early age, Maddie moved from a wobbly walk to a stiff-legged jog, I loved to show her off at our local playground. If someone asked her age, my response was guaranteed to elicit an incredulous "Wow! She's running already! My daughter is three months older, and she can't walk by herself at all."

The problem with making comparisons is that they're grounded in the specious notion that an auspicious start guarantees a successful future. But as each and every book on child development will tell you, there is no magic age at which your toddler should be doing *anything.* Children develop at very different rates, so if Nick seemed a bit dilatory in the language arena or if Maddie outtoddled her peers at the playground, these differences were sure to fade over time. Believe me, by the age of five, Nick could talk us all under the table.

What makes comparisons particularly insidious is not only the insecurity and anxiety they produce but the antipathy they often generate among other mothers. Andrea, who had moved from a city apartment to a posh suburb, was stunned when she called a woman in her neighborhood to arrange a play date. "Our sons were practically the same age, so I thought it would be nice to get them together. But she starts to cross-examine me about the kinds of toys Jonathan enjoyed, the activities he preferred, whether or not he was talking a lot, that kind of thing. Then she actually says to me, 'Well, I think Pete's a little ahead of your son developmentally, so perhaps we should wait a year or so.' Do you believe that?"

Given the intense pressure so many of us feel to provide our children with the very best stimulation at the earliest possible age, it didn't surprise me that a mom would actually want to edit her toddler's Rolodex. But as I pointed out to Andrea, it was the other mother's loss. Alienation is the last thing you need at a time when there's no such thing as too much reassurance. This is especially true if you are grappling with the challenge of balancing work and family and worrying—as the vast majority of moms do—that you are cheating your kids and yourself out of precious hours together. Finding a circle of sympathetic coworkers, relatives, or friends is critical during the roller-coaster toddler years. If you don't have someone's hand to grab as you careen around an unexpected turn, you may wind up screaming in the dark alone.

"I definitely look for mothers who are like-minded," Lanie concurred when I asked her about how motherhood had affected her friendships. "But it's not so much a question of who's working or who used to work as it is their parenting style that causes problems. For example, my daughter Sophie doesn't understand the concept of sharing. I mean, what two-year-old does? So she'll grab a toy from another kid, or he'll take something of hers. I believe you need to trust them to work out a certain amount on their own. But I have a very good friend, who I always felt was on the same wavelength. I was so happy when we had kids at the same time, but I can't stand the way she is with Sophie. She hovers over them and jumps in, and I don't think it's good for Sophie, which has made getting together very tense and difficult."

We all have a natural desire to seek out our tribe, a sorority of kindred moms who tacitly or explicitly validate the choices we've made.

The trick is to avoid getting so entrenched in our thinking about "those other mothers" that we limit our own options. This is true throughout motherhood, as we're often forced to radically reprioritize, to reconsider our choices, to question ourselves. But the sheer volume and intensity of changes that take place during the toddler years make the territory particularly tricky to navigate.

Pulled in Different Directions

"I just don't feel as though I'm doing anything well right now," Marianne, the mother of three under three, confessed. "If I won the lottery, I would get a part-time job. But that's not an option. And it's important for me to have something besides being a mother and wife. On the weekends the nanny goes home and it's really hard. I look forward to Monday. But I can't take on extra projects, stay late, because I'm needed at home. And I want to be home with the kids. So I just feel like I'm not doing as well as I could at work, and not as well at home."

Working-mom guilt percolates on high during the toddler years not only because you imagine you're missing all those firsts—steps, words, revelations—but because one- and two-year-olds are so much fun to be with. "I never, ever imagined I could love someone the way I love Alex," my friend Ellen said recently. "And I certainly never dreamed I would have the patience, or derive so much pleasure from just hanging out together." The challenge for Ellen—as for practically every mom I interviewed—was to learn to be fully present when she was with her son. Staying attuned to his needs, filtering out the "work noises" in her head, letting herself just "be here now" spelled the difference between feeling torn in two and being more integrated.

Some of the sweetest memories I have of Nick's toddler years are the summer evenings when, vacationing in the Adirondacks, I would give him a bath and then carry him outside to sit on my lap under the darkening sky. I would tell him stories or sing as we watched the stars come out. Away from the phone, the dinner dishes, the noisy glow of the house, I would sit, wrapped in the quiet of the night, Nick enveloped in a blanket, and experience a transcendent joy. These moments were particularly special in the context of Nick's toddler years, when he muscled through his days with characteristic Taurus intensity. He was a passionate, high-energy charmer, but his eagerness to catch up with "Mimi" (his nickname for Maddie) allowed little time for sitting quietly on Mom's lap.

One of the pleasures of this stage is an older toddler's increased ability to engage in pretend play. When Maddie was close to three she would regularly act out vignettes inspired by her favorite Disney heroines. I recall hours of playing the prince to her eyelash-batting Sleeping Beauty or pretending not to notice the tsunami of tub water washed on the bathroom floor by my shy Little Mermaid. Her dress-up games also included scenarios of heart-stopping realism. One Sunday morning she chose as her prop an old briefcase, into which she stuffed pieces of construction paper and assorted envelopes before announcing, "I going to work now, sweetie." Shoving her pudgy hands into my gloves, she added in a voice dripping with pity and remorse, "And I out to dinner. And I not coming back until later tomorrow late." As she stepped into a pair of my shoes and clattered down the hallway, I felt the pinch of hers. "I call you later!" she sang out. The pinch, the sting, the heartache, as she disappeared into the coat closet.

I absolutely adored my job at that time. Even if I could have afforded to stay home full-time, I knew I wanted to work, but the struggle to find a balance, to divide the pie into adequate portions of time and attention, meant someone—usually me—was last to be served. In *Reinventing Ourselves After Motherhood,* Susan Lewis uses her own journey from corporate lawyer to at-home mom as a window into the lives of dozens of former career women who chose to stay home. Some "had no idea how hard they'd fall in love and how consuming it would be." Others found that inadequate child care, their spouse's work, and "the jigsaw puzzle craziness of life" made it just too damn hard to do it all.[12]

The pull in two directions usually goes well beyond the issue of "not enough time to do everything." Yes, there's that, just as there is the undeniable fact that most businesses in this country have failed mothers by paying them less than their male counterparts, by offering minimal opportunities for flextime, and by rarely providing child-care support. Many mothers I interviewed described the emotional dissonance they felt between their home and work environments. Hope, an attorney who specialized in divorce law, explained: "I was very good at matrimonial law, but I don't think I'll ever go back to that kind of work. I just don't have the anger and the adversarial feelings I used to have before Juliette was born."

With notably few exceptions, the working women I spoke to reported that for them their children's toddler years were plagued by stress and self-doubt. "When she was a baby, I didn't really have a problem going back to work," one mother of a sixteen-month-old told me. "I had an excellent baby-sitter, an elderly Hispanic woman, whom I trusted completely. But now that my daughter is walking and talking, I realize that she's pronouncing certain words with a Spanish accent or that she seems to know a lot of television theme songs, and it's getting me crazy. I just feel I should be there during these formative years."

I used to feel a throb of guilt and envy whenever our caregiver called to report some major milestone in Maddie's day. But I realized that as much as I regretted not being there, video camera loaded and rolling, to capture her very first solo step, she was thrilled to show off the minute I got home. And when Steve arrived, she happily obliged again—and again and again. Eager for the emotional boost our praise provided, Maddie couldn't have cared less whether our applause came at first or at last.

When I think of her taking those first halting steps, I remember the way her eyes would fix on mine, how she would stagger drunkenly into my outstretched arms, then immediately push away to try again. She still needed me, but her walking signaled her independence so dramatically that, along with her hand, I was forced to let go of an image of myself, to accept this exciting separateness as central to the toddler years.

Along with her independence came the anxiety born of her awareness that I was a separate person. Like all toddlers, she went through a phase when her play consisted of little, darting trips away from me, followed quickly by a return to the safety of my presence. She wanted my full attention so badly that she would put her hands on my cheeks and direct my head her way. Or she would imperiously bark an order at me, only to reject my help. Her confusion about her place in the world paralleled my own at times. I wanted to be there for her, but I also valued my space at my job, with Steve, and with my friends. Anticipating her entrance into preschool and her reliance on other adults and on her peers for emotional support, I experienced an intense need to connect with her babyness and, at the same time, to find a way to let her fly. It was probably no coincidence that one of our favorite games during Maddie's toddler years was "birdie in the nest," which involved creating a comfortable nest of couch pillows and then sending my little bird around the living room in search of food. The best part, of course, was when she would come flying back into my arms.

Stage 4

‹∞›

Trying to Do It All

The Preschool Years, Three to Six

I've never met a three-year-old I didn't like. Yes, there are moments when they throw tantrums that rival toddler tornadoes or they dig in their heels with ferocious determination or they wear you out with whining, but more often they greet the day with a kind of wide-eyed, breathless, "Isn't the world fantastic!" charm. Glancing through family photo albums, I always pause long and longingly over images of the kids as preschoolers. There's Nick, arms outstretched, running naked through a lawn sprinkler, or Maddie, dressed to the nines in some crazy scarf-based getup, or each of them in turn engrossed in a book I remember reading over and over again. I see their heads thrown back in laughter or their arms wrapped in a love grip around my neck or their bashful bow in some preschool curtain call, and I recall this phase as particularly rich in emotion, learning, and laughs.

I loved just hanging out with the kids when they were three, four, and five. Their speech was rife with colorful malapropisms ("Look, Mom! A croissant moon!" my petite gourmande declared one evening), their imaginations wild and free, their feelings deep and open ("You're my sweetie, baby Mama," Nick would croon as he kissed me good night six or seven times). But as is often the case during this phase of our kids' lives, the constant demands of work, school, and extracurricular schedules made "just hanging out" a rarity.

Looking back, I see myself cast in the hackneyed role of a well-dressed juggler on a tightrope—the prototypical working mom with a preschooler, newborn, busy spouse, messy house, and little ability to delegate. I walked a fine emotional line between pride/joy/confidence and self-doubt/guilt/resentment. I seemed to be doing it all, but I regularly questioned whether I was doing it all rather badly. When my work suffered or a home emergency kept me from the office altogether, I felt guilty for letting my staff down; when Maddie's preschool outing rolled around and, despite several well-stationed Post-its reading "PACK LUNCH FOR SCHOOL!," I forgot, I handed over the hastily purchased brown bag of a bagel and juice as though it contained atomic waste. The teachers rarely seemed to care, and Maddie certainly didn't, but it was one of countless experiences that made me wonder if there wasn't some better way.

What I couldn't see until years later was how much of my guilt was a direct result of my own brutally unrealistic expectations. After many years of working under the delusion that there are really thirty-six hours in a day, I have developed a mathematical formula for maternal guilt. It looks like this:

$$\frac{(UX) \text{ job} + \text{spouse} + \text{child(ren)} + \text{extended family} + \text{friends} + \text{extras}}{18 \text{ hours}} = \text{GUILT}$$

The mysterious UX factor stands for "unrealistic expectations." Add up the hours one devotes to work (in or out of the home); to a child or children; to one's marriage, friends, and extended family; and to any "extras," like volunteer work or religious observance or fitness. Divide those hours by 18 hours. (I'm assuming a twenty-four-hour day and allowing six hours for sleep. Only Martha Stewart can survive on four—and look what happened to her!) Now multiply that fraction by UX—unrealistic expectations, the pernicious Perfect Mom Meets Martha fantasy—and you inevitably wind up with guilt to the tenth power. Reduce the UX factor by redefining what you mean by "doing it all" or, better yet, by what you mean by "all," and you stand a much better chance of reducing the guilt.

This formula applies to all mothers most of the time, but it's especially relevant when our kids are preschoolers and, despite their newfound independence and time away from home, highly needy. During this phase of motherhood, one adds to the jobs of caregiver,

playmate, and disciplinarian the talents of professor, coach, social secretary, short-order cook, wardrobe consultant, negotiator, and shrink.
It helps if you can bake, sew, sing, act, draw, and wrestle a screaming
thirty-pound dervish into a booster seat. But you can't possibly do all
of these things perfectly. You can't even do them half as well as your
neighbor, who boasts an immaculate house, well-tended garden, and
exciting social life. "How does she manage a job, kids, church choir,
and dress the way she does?" you ask yourself whenever you're on the
ledge. If your answer is "She's just better organized than I am" or "If I
only got up a little earlier, I could do more" or "She's a much better
cook," then you're stepping right into a trap baited with BS and guaranteed to bite you in the ego.

The novel *I Don't Know How She Does It* is a portrait of a mom dancing as fast as she can to succeed at home and on the job. The opening
scene finds her "hitting mince pies. No, let us be quite clear about
this, I am *distressing* mince pies, an altogether more demanding and
subtle process." Why is the heroine, Kate Reddy, removing the little
pies from their foil wrappers and altering "their blameless floury
faces"? Because her child's preschool has sent home a note asking parents to contribute "appropriate festive refreshments" at the upcoming
Christmas party. As Kate wryly explains: "Notes from school are written in code, a code buried so cunningly in the text that it could only
be deciphered at Bletchley Park or by guilty women in the advanced
stages of sleep deprivation." She adds that when a school solicits refreshments from parents, they mean mothers are expected to bring in
something baked from scratch—"definitely not something bought by
a lazy cheat in a supermarket."[1]

Like dozens of other vignettes, this passage had me weeping tears
of laughter and self-recognition. I immediately conjured the evening
Maddie phoned me at the office to announce that she couldn't bring
the three dozen oatmeal cookies I had miraculously remembered to
bake for snack day because the theme for that particular Wednesday
was Sweden. "We have to be making something from there," she said
firmly.

"Like what?" I asked, stopping short of barking, "Herring? A
delightful smorgasbord for twenty-three?"

"I don't know, Mama," she said softly, anxiety building in her reedy
voice. "But we *have* to."

"Okay, sweetheart," I relented. "I'll figure something out."

It was, of course, pouring rain when I left the office, and past closing time at the gourmet food store in our neighborhood. I was forced to dash from one late-night deli to another in search of Ry-Krisps and flavored cream cheese. I spent at least two hours spreading the latter without shattering the former and another half hour convincing Maddie that this was a genuine Swedish treat.

Why, you may ask, did I not tell Maddie that oatmeal cookies were a national Swedish dish? Or, better yet, just say that Swedish Day was next month and that tomorrow was, in fact, High Fiber Day at her Montessori school? For one thing, Maddie had reached the point in her development when following the rules and worshipping one's teacher (in her case, a lovely SWEDISH woman named Kirsten) were paramount. I had reached a point in my development when proving to myself and to my preschool daughter that Mama could do anything was paramount, that Mama would never let her down, that even though Mama had had to work late two nights that week, she would make it up to her by racing around to find Ry-Krisps for Swedish Day.

That's why I bothered to bake cookies, to join the PTA, to throw elaborate, themed birthday parties. I remember one particularly miserable night, when I sat in my living room, the digital clock numbers spinning toward midnight, glancing despairingly at the large green towel and wire coat hangers in my lap—the vain makings of a Little Mermaid costume for Maddie's fifth Halloween. Maybe it was God's idea of a joke, but as I flipped through the late-night TV offerings, I was lucky enough to happen upon the second act of *Gone With the Wind*. Minutes later, I was brought to tears—not by the death of dear little Bonnie but by that scene in which Mammy manages to transform Mrs. O'Hara's velvet portieres into a gorgeous green dress. When Scarlett flounced into Rhett's cell, the tasseled tiebacks now a flattering belt, the curtain fringe flirtatiously accentuating one shoulder, I threw down the towel, stomped the wire coat hanger into the rug, and, like a petulant southern belle, stormed out of the room. I think I bought some crappy costume the next day, and Maddie survived; in fact, she was probably delighted to run into several similarly Kmart-clad Little Mermaids trick-or-treating around our neighborhood.

Unrealistic expectations and the guilt they provoke are fed by the self-defeating thinking that we "should" be doing something we can't or don't want to do. Or that we "should never" do any of the things captured in one of my all-time favorite cartoons by Roz Chast entitled "Bad Mom Cards—Collect the Entire Set!" It includes "#23: Lucy L—Told friend 'funny' story about kid and had a laugh at kid's expense" and "#61: Deborah Z—Has never even *tried* to make Play-Doh from scratch" or "#89: Becky O—While on phone, told child to *SHUT THE HELL UP* or she would brain her."[2]

Perfect-Mommy Myths

I've met hundreds of mothers with children of varying ages who suffer from the perfect-mom fantasy, but it seems to cling with punishing tenacity during our children's preschool years. Having survived their babyhood and coursed the rapids of the toddler years, we march into this period fully expecting our honed muscles and accumulated wisdom to guide us through. But as our children enter preschool or attend more out-of-home activities or as we ramp up our own extra-familial lives, the pressure to keep it all together can exact a high toll.

Not long ago I worked on a segment for *Good Morning America* about parent coaches, women primarily, with very little professional training, who "coach" other moms over the phone on how to deal with the many stresses of their lives. Buffi, the coachee in our story, was a beautiful young mom with two small children; a helpful husband; a large, spanking-clean home; and a part-time job. Her sister, who lived nearby and had a baby of her own, watched the kids when Buffi was at work. Buffi spoke to her own mom regularly and seemed to have a network of friends, yet she was willing to shell out close to three hundred dollars per month to talk to a stranger about how to be a better mom.

"The first time I decided to call Peggy as a parent coach, it made me feel that I wasn't a good parent," Buffi confessed. "There's definitely a stigma to asking for help, because you're obviously doing something wrong. But I needed help. And I thought, 'Well, I ask for help with my business.' I have my own company and a lot of people who help me run that business, so I just kind of put that idea to work in my home life."

When I asked her what she felt she needed help with, the perfect-mommy fantasy reared its ugly head: "I felt really out of balance and unhappy. I would say that my kids come first—always—but I wasn't doing that. I was putting the dishes first. I was putting the laundry first. And I was putting anything, everything on my to-do list, first." Buffi's to-do list included extensive volunteer hours for her daughter's Brownie troop, her son's preschool soccer league, her church. She was also knee-deep—literally—in an ambitious children's garden project, and she had an ailing grandmother whom she promised to visit regularly but rarely could. Then there were the dishes to wash, the house to clean, the business to attend to.

So when her preschool son, Zach, needed her attention after dinner, Buffi would tell him to wait until she finished the dishes, or if he wanted to play before she had vacuumed the living room, he was told, "Just give me a minute." But a minute often became a half hour—an eternity to an eager four-year-old—and by the time Buffi had hung up her apron and joined Zach on the living room floor, "he would be cranky and our time together wouldn't be much fun."

Buffi's coach, Peggy, suggested that she either put the dishes on hold or put Zach to work. In fact, most preschoolers are willing and able to load a dishwasher or dry nonbreakables or put pots and pans away. They love handheld vacuums and other tools of the housekeeping trade. Most of all, they want to hang out with you, to walk in your footsteps, wear your apron, try on adult roles by performing adult tasks.

Buffi's dilemma reminded me of an evening when Maddie was Zach's age and I had forty-five minutes to prepare dinner for six relatives, four of whom always arrived fifteen minutes early. When Maddie asked to help, I came up with the brilliant assignment of decorating the napkins before setting the table. Maddie took great pride in her table-setting prowess, so she eagerly laid out the place mats, the flatware, and even the glasses before setting busily to work with her markers. The subsequent thirty minutes were filled with cooking, chatting, and a little singing as we pursued our parallel paths. Though I could see only the back of her head, bent with determination over her work, I loved having her nearby while I hurled pots and pans around the kitchen. I was humming happily to myself when I heard Steve come into the kitchen and ask, an audible edge to his voice, "Maddie, honey, what are you doing?"

"Oh, I'm doing decorating, Dad," she said brightly.

"Does Mama know you're doing decorating?"

"Yes! She told me to."

I was afraid to look, but look I did. And there, all over my brand-new French linen place mats, were the fruits (and flowers, stick figures, and squiggles) of Maddie's labors. A large pile of paper napkins sat in virginal splendor to her left.

"Maddie!" I gasped before realizing from the look on her face that I was about to ruin a perfectly wonderful quality-time moment. "Oh, sweetie," I recovered. "Those look beautiful."

Of course, there were many more occasions when the lack of quantity time overwhelmed any attempts at quality. We had to get to school and to work by eight-thirty; friends were meeting us in the park at three; we had tickets to a Raffi concert and couldn't be late; we had a doctor's appointment—all meaningless assignations to a preschooler engrossed in a puzzle or happily splashing in the tub. I often felt pulled between the seemingly conflicting desires to provide the kids (and me) with some kind of predictable schedule and to permit them to just "be here now." A local art class that seemed the ideal alternative to Saturday-morning cartoons would, on the succeeding Saturday, suddenly conflict with Maddie's discovery of the joys of leggings and her passionate need to try on several pair before heading out the door. I learned to build in an extra hour for the legging parade, even to let go of the need to force her to the art class, but my latitude came at a price. I felt frustrated and annoyed by what I saw as unnecessary dawdling, and I wondered if I was being too indulgent.

On far too many occasions I *was* too indulgent, an exemplar of the parenting-by-guilt syndrome that drives mothers (in particular, the overwhelmed who overthink) to cave, delay, or back down altogether.[3] In her book *Spoiling Childhood: How Well-Meaning Parents Are Giving Children Too Much—But Not What They Need,* Diane Ehrensaft describes parents who are pulled in two directions and forced to "run in both directions at once trying to fix the problem—too much for themselves, too much for the children." Ehrensaft labels this "the most pernicious peril of parenting," and among her prescriptions for a way out is to "let go of the fantasy of living *with* our children in favor of a more realistic notion of ministering *to* our children in ways appropriate to their ages and stages. But we also have to have the requisite time to do this."[4]

Time Matters

One of the mistakes I made with Maddie was to confuse a calendar choked with classes, concerts, and culture with "quality time." Standing on line during my lunch hour to buy tickets to a children's concert may have allayed my guilt about working late that day, but by the time the event rolled around, we probably would have had just as much fun hanging around in our PJ's and going out for breakfast at McDonald's.

By the time Nick hit the preschool years, I was better able to reconcile my need to fill his day with activities and his need to hang out with no agenda. We were doing just that one early fall night during a spell of Indian summer. Frozen yogurts in hand, we sat on the front stoop of our Brooklyn house, watching the neighbors pass by. When our friend's teenage son whizzed past on his Rollerblades, Nick blurted out excitedly, "You know what, Mom? When it snows later, later, later, later, later, later, later, then we can go ice-skating." Then he added, "Remember when we goed to that ice ring yesterday? The blue one. And I felled down? And the boy that had the red hat felled down, too?"

I did remember, even though the incident dated back more than a year. It was amazing the details he supplied and the sequence of events he described in his rudimentary way. For Nick, time was more compressed; the past entered the present with startling clarity, and the future was now. His "yesterday" and "tomorrow" were painted with a broad brush, because he lived mostly within the canvas of "today." My "soon" was his "now," unless, of course, I wanted him to do something "now." Then he seemed to grasp the power of "soon" all too well. His sense of the future was limited to wishing for a recurrence of something enjoyable (like the "ice ring"), and when it came to clocks, they weren't much more than useful props in the game of playing grownup. He would glance down at his favorite fashion accessory, a big plastic watch, and ask, "Know what time it is now? Eighteen-thirty!"

Having learned the value of routines and the uselessness of trying to hurry along a dawdler when Maddie was a preschooler, I was wise enough to build plenty of markers into Nick's days. If we had to get out the door by 8 a.m., I actually set a timer and put him in charge of telling me when it went off. And when something unexpected squeezed our time together even more, I tried to abbreviate certain rituals rather than eliminate them altogether.

Of course, preschoolers are never pressed for time; they may pick up on your anxiety when you're rushing them out the door, but they don't understand why or what's making you so upset. In that sense, they remind us daily of a lesson that I too often forget: Stop thinking about tomorrow. Seize the present and really enjoy it—even if "it" is basically nothing. Yes, that sounds incredibly corny, but it's far wiser than trying to cram soccer, art classes, music lessons, and preschool into your child's life at a time when it's often just as satisfying to sit on the stoop and watch the world go by.

In our goal-oriented, fast-paced lives, there is often little room for activities that don't seem to have a specified outcome attached to them. We take our preschooler to a swimming lesson, because it's clear the aim is to make him comfortable in the water and, perhaps, to teach him to paddle across the pool on his own. But when we just hang out with children, we are actually doing a lot more than we realize. Spend five minutes with a three- or four-year-old, and you're sure to be barraged by off-the-wall questions ("Who turned off the stars, Mama?"), treated to keen observations about nature ("Look! The tree is dancing!"), or brutally honest appraisals of your appearance ("Why do you have hair up your nose?"). Everything from how you answer these questions to the ways you touch or look at your child while you do so boosts his confidence, builds his vocabulary, teaches him valuable social skills, and, of course, strengthens your relationship. In that sense, "just hanging out" is rarely a waste of time; it's often the richest experience in an overscheduled week.

Keep in mind that you can *choose* to fill up your child's schedule with good-for-them activities, but make very certain that you're doing so because that's what they enjoy, not because your neighbor's kid is being groomed for a peewee triathlon or because you loved ballet when you were three. Buffi admitted that part of what drove her to stretch herself to the limit was the sense that all the other moms in her neighborhood were doing just that. "In my mother's day, there was no way your kid would be taking music and dance at the same time. You'd be lucky if you could dance once a year or maybe once in five years! Nowadays, everybody's signed up for a multitude of events. And mothers are keeping their children busy all the time. I feel like there's such a pressure to be the perfect mom. And what that means is defined by everybody other than me."

Just as insidious as trying to keep up with the Joneses is the tendency to compare all that you *don't* do with your children with what your own mom did with you. "My mother didn't work," Karen, who has four siblings, recalled. "Her whole life was devoted to taking care of us." A saleswoman for a major insurance company, Karen was bemoaning the fact that she never had time to bake cookies or go on class trips with her four-year-old. "What kinds of things did your mother do with you when you were really little?" I asked. Karen paused and recounted a couple of sweet memories—paper dolls, those cookies again. Then I handed her a piece of paper and asked her to write down everything she did with her daughter. When she started on the other side, I took the paper away. Her list included everything from movies to make-believe tea parties to weekend nature walks.

Why, then, did Karen feel she fell short—of her mother, of some idealized image of a mother, of her friends who she believed were infinitely better mothers? I am not a psychologist, nor did I know Karen well enough to really probe, but I sensed that her unhappiness was due not to a lack of quality time with her daughter but to a deep and nagging sense of doubt that no matter what she did, it was never going to be enough. What she couldn't see was that her daughter's increased independence, her often willful expression of what she did and did not like, had absolutely nothing to do with how many activities Karen could list on a page. Her four-year-old frequently yelled, "You're the worstest mommy in the whole world!" not because Karen was anything of the kind but because, at that particular moment, she was frustrated and pissed off.

One of the realities of this stage of motherhood is that we can't fulfill our children's every need. Nor should we want to. As difficult and painful as it is to make our preschoolers unhappy, it's far worse to indulge their every request. A child who is told no may rant and rave, but when she calms down, she's been given an invaluable gift—the experience of knowing she can handle frustration, weather an emotional storm, and wander back into her mother's loving arms.

Getting into the "Right" Preschool

As our children venture out into the world, the struggle to make certain we're providing only the best can bring out the worst in even the most reasonable parents. Take the preschool feeding frenzy typical in many cities across the country. The much ballyhooed story of former Citigroup securities analyst Jack B. Grubman and his boss, Sanford I. Weill, is *the* case in point. At the center of the scandal was one of Manhattan's most elite preschools, the Ninety-second Street Y Nursery School. Grubman, the father of two-year-old twins, was so desperate to get his kids into the Y that he sent an incriminating e-mail to Weill, suggesting a swap: Grubman would recommend AT&T stock if Weill would recommend Grubman's twins for coveted spots at the Y. The girls were admitted around the same time Citigroup donated $1 million to the preschool.

The scandal touched a nerve and ignited a media blitz full of outrage at the absurdity of the preschool-admissions race. Can-you-top-this stories emerged: the parents who hired help to sit by the phone and hit "redial" in order to get through to the admissions office the day tour appointments are scheduled (it can take the better part of a day); the mother who joined a local congregation when she was pregnant in order to better her child's chances of getting into the church preschool; the search for some kind of six-degrees-of-separation connection to anyone and everyone affiliated with a coveted school. My friend Nancy, who was head of the board of trustees at an exclusive Manhattan school, used to joke about the number of "old friends" she heard from ("people I have never met in my life") who came out of the woodwork every year just when applications were due.

In many parts of the country the pressure doesn't build until kindergarten, but it's the same emotional dance. Suddenly you feel as though your child's future is at stake and, if you're not careful, that your future is somehow tied up in the kindergarten decision. One mom I spoke to described how the headmistress of her child's church-based preschool held a meeting with all the parents during which "she lectured us about not talking amongst ourselves, not sharing which schools we were applying to with our friends." She described how she agonized over whether to defy the headmistress and confide in her close friend about their children's applications or "be a good girl and keep it to myself." Needless to say, the infantilizing of the parents only exacerbated their tendency to overidentify with their kids—to feel (and occasionally act) like kindergartners themselves.

"We were all acting like panicked children," this mom confessed. "I mean, there was so much pressure to get our kids into these schools. And we shared the very real fear that they might not get in anywhere. And then what?" It feels pretty miserable to have little control over, no real purchase on, a decision that may have a lasting impact on your child's future. Even if you swear not to get swept up in the hysteria or if you're lucky enough to live in a community with a plethora of options or no options at all—and, therefore, no call to agonize—you're likely to feel as though you've lost your footing. For the first years of your child's life, *you* held the reins, pulled the strings, cut a path through his little world.

When your child enters preschool or kindergarten for the first time, you're made acutely aware of a larger threshold and a much more competitive arena. Suddenly, the fear that your child may wind up in a mediocre preschool or kindergarten is linked to the belief that nursery school is the first step in the long march toward college and a lucrative career. In cities like New York, parents talk openly about the fact that the right preschool is considered a feeder to the right kindergarten and a leg up to a prestigious private school, then to an Ivy League college, and, ultimately, to a rewarding career.

If you're reading this and thinking, "Oh, for God's sake! Who cares what preschool my child goes to, as long as she's happy and enjoys her day," hold that thought. It's true that the most important factor in your child's early school experience is the quality of her interactions with her teachers and her peers. Yes, it's great if the preschool offers music or movement or math readiness or plenty of opportunities for verbal expression, but physical or cognitive readiness may be less important than emotional readiness. Pushing your child to be toilet-trained or to recite the alphabet on cue may guarantee her entry into preschool, but it won't promise a happy experience. What may matter more is her ability to listen to the children around her, to stop when asked to, to share, take turns, follow simple directions.[5]

Emotional readiness—how she gets along with her pals and with her teachers—is going to have the greatest impact on her early school experiences, so if she needs another year in a less formal environment, or if the preschool teacher suggests she repeat a year before moving on to kindergarten, don't panic. Ask about the social skills the school is hoping your child will develop and then find ways to work on those skills. Play dates, role playing, and lots of praise when she demonstrates those skills can make a huge difference in a very short time. In fact, giving your child an extra year, during which you pull back and evaluate your options, along with her strengths, is far better than allowing your own panic to turn "quality" time into "high-achievement" time, card games into flash-card drills, or opportunities to just hang out together into additional pressure to clog the calendar with educational activities.

Of course, some of us don't have the luxury of waiting an additional year. We want our kids enrolled in preschool because we need a half day or more to ourselves. "The mornings Joel goes to his tumbling class are heaven," Helen confessed. "For the first time in three years, I have two hours to myself. The other day I barely braked as I dropped him off!" Helen was laughing, but several mothers who worked full-time confessed with far less complacence how much they longed for Mondays to roll around after a weekend with their preschool kids. Sally, who has two boys, three and almost five, described her office as "the one oasis of calm—even on the most hectic days." In *The Bitch in the House,* a collection of essays by a group of wise and brutally honest women, Kristin van Ogtrop contrasts her work and home life in "Attila the Honey I'm Home":

Here are a few things people have said about me at the office:

- "You're unflappable."
- "Are you ever in a bad mood?"
- "You command respect as soon as you walk into a room."
- "Your straightforward, no-nonsense style gets things done."
- "You're good at finessing situations so people don't boil over."

Here are things people—OK, the members of my family—have said about me at home:

- "Mommy is always grumpy."
- "Why are you so tense?"
- "You just need to relax."
- "You don't need to yell!"
- "You're too mean to live in this house and I want you to go back to work for the rest of your life!"

This last one is my favorite. It's also the saddest, because it captures such a painful truth: too often I'm a better mother at work than I am at home.[6]

There is no question that I often found my office a welcome respite after a long weekend of nonstop child care. As torn as I was to leave Maddie with her sitter Monday mornings, I needed to exercise different muscles, to connect with other parts of myself. When our child-care arrangement became problematic, I began to look for a preschool program, even though Maddie's late-September birthday meant she could easily have waited a year. In fact, I somewhat guiltily enrolled her in a wonderful local program the summer before she turned three in order to get her used to going in the fall.

Weathering a Tough Transition

The first week was agony. Maddie clung to my legs and begged me not to go, so I stayed. Most of the other parents departed unscathed, but there was one mom—dressed in a business suit like me—who became my comrade in the trenches. Her son, Freddie, was having a tough time separating; in fact, he made Maddie's reaction to my imminent departure seem tame. Freddie's mom and I kept glancing at the clock as we tried the "one last story/one more game" trick that sometimes facilitated our exit. But a whole week went by with only minor progress. Then, the Monday of Maddie's second week, she ran happily into the classroom, while poor Freddie continued to cling and cry. I felt a strange ambivalence about leaving this mom—still a relative stranger—behind. I admit to relishing a tiny taste of triumph, coupled with relief, at not being the last, along with a twinge of guilt as I dashed out the door.

When Jackie's twins entered preschool, she was shocked to watch her typically gregarious son Michael metamorphose into a hysterical mess every morning. "It was so bad, I had to sit in the classroom for a week. Then I gradually moved my chair into the hall and sat there all morning. Eventually, I moved the chair down the hall toward the front door. And then outside. It took him three weeks, but he finally was able to join the class and not run out every five minutes to see if I was still standing guard." Jackie described feeling alternately angry and embarrassed. "It was hard being the only mom in that hallway. I felt really stupid, like I had done something wrong."

It struck me then, as it does now, that our sense of personal success or failure is so intimately linked to how our children do in this new arena. Here we were, accomplished women (Freddie's mom was a VP at a major financial institution; Jackie runs her own business), whose egos were bolstered daily by our professional accomplishments, yet we suffered a gnawing sense of failure when our children lagged a bit in school.

For any mom with a child just starting in school there's the hope that he will be a successful ambassador, a bright tribute to our success as parents. When a teacher calls to say our child has bitten a playmate or kicked a teacher or failed to participate in circle time, the pulse quickens, the stomach drops, and the mind lurches toward an explanation that usually starts with "I."

When Maddie came home one day with a note from her teacher that read, "Please make sure Madeleine wears underpants under her skirt tomorrow," and I realized that she had gone bare-assed to preschool, I was inordinately embarrassed. (Maddie didn't care at all.) By the time Nick was going to the same wonderful school, I had learned to let go of the need to see my kids as billboards—at least when it came to what they wore. Like a mom I know whose preschooler's wild clothing preferences led her to pin a note on her daughter that said, "Outfit is not a reflection of the taste of the management," I had lightened up considerably when it came to wardrobe. I even let them shop for school clothes, praying that we would wind up with items that didn't glow in the dark and that blended well with spaghetti sauce and grape juice. One memorable year Maddie set her heart on an Elton John–style neon-pink jacket with gold, heart-shaped buttons and a Nehru collar. It wasn't until she had worn it six times that I discovered the "dry clean only" tag. And I must confess that Steve and I did push back the morning Nick came down to breakfast in a dress. He insisted that boys wore dresses to class all the time. Steve said no way. Nick said yes. Steve said not in his lifetime. So I suggested he wear it during breakfast and at home but not in school. Nick grudgingly toed the line.

But, of course, appearance is easy. Bad behavior, back talk, even a particularly impish imaginary friend can turn the preschool years into a time when we're forced to question everything from our own parenting skills to the school we've chosen to match our child's personality. The first time Steve and I met with Maddie's pre-K teacher to discuss her first six months of school, I felt, well, like a nervous prekindergartner. Maybe it was the awkward little chairs or the agitated rustle of the gerbil in his cage or the elevated temperature of the classroom, but I couldn't shake the feeling that I was being evaluated, too. As Maddie's poised, soft-spoken teacher ran through a litany of her strengths, I kept waiting for a *but*. None came. "Maddie can be really stubborn at times—especially when it comes to cleaning up," I probed. "Does she do that at school?"

"Oh, no," Kirsten said with a smile. "You see, I think a lot of Madeleine's stubbornness, her intensity at times, her ability to stick to something, is a reflection of her determination. And that's a quality we want to channel, not eliminate."

"She's also really shy and quiet around new people," Steve volunteered. "Does she get along with the other kids?"

"Maddie is a keen observer," her teacher replied. "She watches and waits before making a move. But that's why she's such a talented artist. I would guess she'll be a great painter someday."

So, Maddie's stubbornness was perseverance; her shyness, artistic genius! Steve and I left rubbing the kinks out of our lower backs and glowing with pride. We marveled at how this wise, experienced teacher had seen things in Madeleine we had somehow missed.

Of course, all she had done was reframe Maddie's behavior, change the key of her temperamental tunes from minor to major, so that we could listen more appreciatively. She had also fostered a feeling of teamwork between me and Steve—a much needed sense that we were on the same page. I say "much needed" because the difficult patches during Maddie's preschool years had rarely, if ever, made us feel like a team. More often, her obstinacy or whining or begging or all of the above drove Steve out of the room and me up the wall. I felt he was copping out; he thought I was trying too hard. Then there were times when Steve would cave ("What's the big deal?"), casting me as the proverbial "bad cop," or I would criticize how loud and "retro" he sounded when he disciplined Maddie.

Your Versus His Parenting Style

No doubt some of our disagreements over discipline harked back to the "expert/dumb apprentice" trap (see page 53). I was not only more involved in Maddie's day-to-day life, but my job as editor in chief of *Parents* magazine made me something of an expert—at least in the eyes of several million moms. That said, I was hardly a pro when it came to setting limits, and I certainly didn't want to go it alone. Unfortunately, the one question I failed to ask myself was whether I was truly willing to work alongside Steve in the discipline arena or if I just wanted him to do it my way.

Among the many wise advisers I turned to for help in this regard was Ron Taffel, psychologist, teacher, and author of many excellent books on child rearing. Unfortunately, Ron had not yet written the book I needed then—*Why Parents Disagree and What You Can Do About It,*[7] but I recall a conversation during which he asked me how often I left Maddie and Steve alone together. The pause that followed said it all. I stammered some embarrassingly low number as I realized how much control I managed to exert over their limited one-on-one time.

That night Steve and I talked about my need to let go and his need to step up to the plate more often. We each aired some of the frustrations we were experiencing with Maddie—and with each other—and while I can't claim to have crossed over into a happy land of mutual respect and understanding, we definitely made progress.

A few weeks later Maddie came into the kitchen and announced that she and Steve were going "on a babenture."

"Where to?" I asked excitedly.

"We're going to visit Eddie Rosenmalt's house!" she cheerily replied. "Who's Eddie Rosenmalt?"

"You know, Mom. The president from the olden, olden days," she replied, her voice dripping with condescension.

"Oh, *that* Eddie Rosenmalt!" I said as solemnly as possible, recalling that Steve had mentioned a visit to Theodore Roosevelt's house, Sagamore Hill, on Long Island. "That sounds like a great plan."

As I began to wonder what Maddie, then three, could possibly get out of a long car ride to a historic museum, I stopped myself. Since our conversation about discipline, Steve and I had tried several times to orchestrate some Dad-Maddie adventures, but most of our suggestions for solo time with Dad had met with the same response: "I want Mom to come." Even if I told Maddie that she could choose between seeing a movie with Steve and watching me fold the laundry, *The Little Mermaid* lost out to the Big Laundress.

For reasons I dared not question, "Eddie Rosenmalt's house" did the trick, so as Steve dashed out the door with nothing more in tow than his wallet and Maddie's Teddy bear ("He's named like Eddie Rosenmalt, Mom!"), I kept my mouth shut.

"Steve should have taken a couple of juice boxes, some crackers, a sweater for Maddie, and an umbrella," I told my mother after they had left. "But I didn't say a word."

"They'll be fine," she assured me. "As long as he isn't doing anything life-threatening, leave them alone."

Steve and Maddie's "babentures" definitely helped forge a bond between them. Their outings bolstered Steve's confidence in himself and mine in him. But the challenges of sharing the day-to-day child-care load, of forming a united front when it came to discipline, of being equally involved in Maddie's life persisted. Looking back, I tend to attribute my larger load to the exigencies of Steve's work life. He worked longer hours, couldn't run out for teacher conferences or pediatrician appointments as readily as I could. But I know I'm being disingenuous.

I think a big part of my unwillingness to let go of Maddie's care related directly to the guilt I experienced when I worried that she was getting too little too late during a hectic week. If Steve was unable to pick up the emotional slack, to be home more, or to intuit my anxiety, I turned up the volume on my expert dial, overcompensating for my absence. Feeling frustrated or conflicted went hand in hand with feeling unsupported; I sent Steve decidedly mixed messages because I was so mixed up myself. Yes, I wanted him to help more with Maddie, but no, I wanted to be Übermom, jumping into her life with both feet and pushing Steve to the sidelines.

I wish I could say that I saw this clearly and initiated a heartfelt conversation about our parenting roles, our fears and hopes regarding Maddie's care, but the truth is, we kind of muddled through her first three years, falling easily into the paradigm of Mom-as-primary-caregiver, Dad-as-primarily-helper—until Nick came along. Then we were forced to adopt the one-on-one defense that got us through family time: Steve would attend to Maddie's needs while I cared for Nick, or I would pass Nick to Steve so Maddie could have a little of my exclusive attention.

Having Another Baby

Wanting Steve to have more one-on-one time with Maddie was definitely *not* one of the reasons I wanted to have another baby. If anything, I worried that the increased load would topple us. And although I'm sure Maddie's greater independence elicited an unconscious desire to replace aspects of my earlier bond with her, consciously I thought more about the potential negative impact another child would have on her life. Having grown up with a sister and brother who were eight and twelve years older, respectively, I knew how hard it could be to grow up the baby. But I had no idea what sibling rivalry felt like, because my position as the much-doted-on youngest was never usurped. Steve, the eldest of four, knew all too well what it was like to have a (or three) younger rivals vying for Mom and Dad's attention. Privately, we talked about planning and timing but were not yet ready to try for a second when a kind of conspiracy seemed to emerge. It was a little like those odd times in life when a song gets stuck in your head, the tune running relentlessly through your mind, and suddenly the guy next to you on the bus or the store cashier or the colleague in the adjoining cubicle starts whistling the same damn song. "What a strange coincidence," you think; "they couldn't have *heard* the song running through my mind, but . . ."

No sooner had I started thinking about a second than a flyer from a local diaper service arrived in the mail, promising "double the diapers delivered in half the time." Not long afterward, a friend from college who had a three-year-old called to announce excitedly, "I'm pregnant!" And the grand finale was a call from Madeleine to my office, which opened with "I want a baby sister, Mama!"

"What?" I countered, thinking perhaps she was in the middle of lunch and had peanut butter stuck to the roof of her mouth. Maybe she said, "I have a gravy blister" or "I have a crazy wish." But her tinkly voice rang loud and clear the second time: "I want a baby sister!"

I feigned peanut butter on the roof of my mouth, mumbled something incoherent, and changed the subject. What—or who—had put the notion into her head? After all, Maddie was just three, innocent about what a sibling would mean to her—not to mention to me and Steve. I quickly started compiling a list of suspects: my mother, or our baby-sitter, a definite nosy Nora, could have put Madeleine up to it.

As it turned out, Maddie's request had been prompted by a visit to a friend's house, where Caroline, the new baby sister, commanded center stage. "You should have seen Madeleine," Caroline's mom reported. "She was so gentle and sweet with the baby. They looked adorable together."

That night I was acutely aware of our time with Maddie. She didn't bring up a baby sister as she prattled on about her day in preschool. And she clearly basked in the two-on-one attention we gave her after dinner. I remember listening to Steve sing "Let It Be" "one last time" before Maddie released him from around her little finger. I considered the hold she had on our hearts, the vast regions of our lives she had mapped out, and I wondered how we could expect her to share that territory with some tiny intruder. But as the idea of expanding our family took hold, I realized that as the lone navigator, Maddie carried all our baggage, brooking those times when our lack of experience forced us into choppy waters. At least another sibling could deflect some of the attention (both healthy and unhealthy) that Madeleine bore alone.

These feelings were echoed recently by a mom I interviewed during the last trimester of her second pregnancy. Having grown up an only child, Hope had always assumed she and her husband, Jeff, would stop after one. "Jeff is the middle child but frankly always wished he was an only. And I was an only child. But as Juliette approached two, I began to feel a kind of sadness that I had experienced when I was growing up. I began to realize that being an only child wasn't the best thing for me and might not be the best thing for her. I didn't want her to be alone, to feel sad, as I had at times."

Many of the mothers of preschoolers I spoke to about their decision to have another baby expressed a longing for the baby years. "I miss the baby smell," one mom said. Several others said they craved a baby "to snuggle." A fifty-year-old friend who has four children and is well past the point of seriously considering a fifth nonetheless experiences a pang whenever she sees a newborn in its mother's arms. "I just loved that phase," she told me. "There's still a part of me that would have more—if I could." Another woman, whose eldest started preschool a year ago, talked about the long stretches of time when her four-year-old is in their church nursery school. "I'm not as central in his life, and that definitely gets to me."

For Hope, who had experienced the first few months of her daughter's life as "totally traumatic," longing for a baby was not front and center. "A lot of friends talked about sadness when their kids went to a big-girl bed," she said. "Or when they started to walk. I never felt that way. I didn't long for a baby to cuddle. If anything, I enjoy Juliette much more now. She's so companionable, so much fun. I'm really happy to hang out with her." I wondered if the thought of sacrificing some of that time made her feel guilty. Without any defensiveness, Hope replied, "I don't feel guilty, because I've been able to spend a lot of time with Juliette; I've given her a lot. I'm really not concerned about having enough time or love for her. Maybe I will once the baby comes; maybe it will be different. But right now, I'm more excited. And so is she. She's 'given birth' to a number of dolls this summer!"

I admired Hope's attitude, recalling the guilt that gnawed at me (maybe that's why I had heartburn the second time around!) throughout my pregnancy with Nick. Countless nights I lay awake, playing the same unconstructive tape in my head: "I hardly have enough time with Maddie now. How will I be able to divide my hours between them? How can we expect her to just move over and welcome some little stranger into the family? We're about to change her life forever—and she didn't even have a chance to vote on the decision . . ."

To make matters worse, when I was about eight months pregnant with Nick I took Maddie to visit my best friend, who had given birth to my beautiful goddaughter, Isabel. The plan was to let Maddie spend some time with a one-month-old, to hold her and learn a little about what newborns are like.

Our visit could not have gone better. Madeleine held Izzie tenderly, cooing and singing to her like a little angel. I had tears in my eyes when I crooned, "Oh, honey, you're going to be such a wonderful big sister!" Flashing a beatific smile, Maddie promptly replied, "You are, too, Mama." Then I made the mistake of saying, "Oh, but, Maddie, sweetheart, I'm going to be the baby's *mama*." An excruciating pause followed, during which I could sense the tiny wheels of her mind spinning around before she said softly, "But you're *my* mama."

Ice pick to the heart! My desperate attempt to explain that I would be mom to Maddie and to her baby brother just rewound the guilt tape; in fact, by that point in my pregnancy, I had added a few choice tracks: "We aren't ready." "Our already hectic lives will spiral out of control." "Maddie's going to metamorphose from the sweet, loving center of our universe to a cold and distant planet." "Our devoted baby-sitter will experience overload and quit." And, worst of all, "Nick is doomed to get short shrift, the leftovers of our attention and love."

The truth was that Nicholas's slice of the quality-time pie was often served fast-food style, and with a few Maddie-sized bites taken out of it. This was less of a problem when he was a baby, because I was able to focus as much, if not more, on Maddie's demands for attention and one-on-one time as I was on Nick's basic baby needs. But as he entered the toddler years and struggled to keep up with the family parade, I sensed that he suffered when we all marched off to work and school and he couldn't "come too."

Speaking recently to a young mom who lives in Alabama with her three young boys, I was reminded of how difficult it was during the kids' toddler years to balance Maddie's need for independence and protected turf with Nick's quest to keep up with and grab as much of that turf as possible. When Cathy's five-year-old son, Ford, started kindergarten, his parents' focus was, understandably, on the adjustment he would be making to a new school and to the rules, routines, and even a fairly strict dress code that came with it. "Ford had no problem whatsoever," Cathy reported. "But what we were totally taken aback by was

Jack, my middle son. Up until then he and Ford had gone to the same morning program, and whatever his big brother did, Jack did. So he really experienced a crisis having to let go of his brother and having to stay home." Cathy and her husband enrolled Jack in a gymnastics class, hoping that would give him something special to look forward to, but he wouldn't go near the mat until "his big brother showed him. Then he jumped in and loved it." As long as his sibling was along for the ride, Jack was a happy camper.

Running to keep up with Maddie definitely made Nick quick and bright and so eager to try everything himself that "Me do it!" became his slogan long before it ever had with Maddie. More important, the guilt and anxiety I had anticipated when I was pregnant with Nick were mitigated by the sense that Maddie had some company when I was stuck unexpectedly at the office or desperate for a little solo time with Steve. And I definitely didn't experience the same kind of guilt pangs about leaving Nick at home that I remember suffering when Maddie was a baby. For one thing, I was a little older and wiser. (Make that older and a little wiser.) For another, I knew that Maddie's presence mollified Nick's fears of separation. She kept a protective eye on Nicko, even when she exclaimed, "He's so annoyish!" One night Steve and I were out for dinner, having left a sweet young woman babysitting for us for the first time. Around their bedtime, I phoned to see how she had fared with Nick, who was notoriously crib-averse.

"How did it go with Nick?"

"Oh, just fine," she reported. "Maddie's in his crib with him now, reading books. She told me she knew the ones he likes best."

"And did he eat any dinner?"

"Yep. Maddie fed him and he seemed to love it." She laughed and added, "To be perfectly honest, Mrs. Murphy, she's hardly let me touch him. She even jumped into the tub with him, although I know you said she didn't need a bath."

Sibling Rivalry

Don't get me wrong. Maddie wasn't always the model baby-sitter's helper. She had more than once "jumped into the tub" with Nick, her mood and motives closer to Ursula's than to the Little Mermaid's.

And although she never physically harmed Nick when he was a newborn, she indulged in those boa-constrictor hugs that jealous siblings euphemistically call "loving my baby." "I'm just loving my baby, Mama," Maddie would say with feigned indignation as I pried her fingers from around his neck.

I did find—as you will when that second bundle of joy arrives—that whatever you give the first won't be enough. Your eldest is hard-wired to complain that you spend too much time with the baby or that you "never did that with me!" I used to get into ridiculous arguments with Maddie about how much I rocked her to sleep when she was a newborn compared with the time I spent rocking Nick in the same chair, until my wise friend and colleague Nancy Samalin (I highly recommend her book about siblings entitled *Loving Each One Best*) suggested I try a different tack. "Why don't you just say, 'I bet you wish I still rocked you in this chair' and see how she responds."

As Nancy had predicted, Maddie sadly and shyly concurred that she wanted to be rocked, too. So of course I obliged, and as she curled onto my lap, I encouraged her to indulge in another rivalry buster. This one I call "Throw the baby off the train and other demonic fantasies."

"I bet you wish we could lock Nick in a closet and throw away the key," I said.

Maddie hesitated, not certain how to respond. Then a glimmer of a smile gathered around the edges of her face. "Yeah. Or we could put him in the washing machine," she suggested.

"Or throw him way, way up into the sky?"

"Or all the way to the moon! Or flush him down the toilet!" she shrieked, dissolving into giggles that definitely flushed much of the tension from her small shoulders. I felt a little guilty devising increasingly ghoulish ends for my sweetly sleeping newborn son, but I knew our words would never hurt him as much as his sister's envy and potential rage. I also knew that assuring Maddie she would grow to love Nick was about as likely to change her present feelings as trying to persuade Rush Limbaugh to vote Democratic.

To get a taste of what your eldest is expected to swallow, imagine how you would feel if your husband came home one day with a new woman on his arm and announced, "Darling, this is my new wife, Joanne. She's going to be living here with us from now on. I know you're going to love her as much as I do." It's not quite the same, of course, but it's critically important to lose the unrealistic expectations we all harbor that harmony will reign when, in fact, it's much more likely that your eldest child will yell "I hate the baby!" at some point in the early months. Even if she never voices her negative feelings, she needs to know you're willing to hear them, to acknowledge how hard it is to accommodate a new little person in one's life.

Several moms with new siblings in the nest talked about the difficulty of being the target of their firstborn's rage. "He doesn't get angry at the baby," Jordan reported when her second child was about a month old. "He's actually very sweet and gentle with her. But he's furious with me." Deborah, who had two sons, including a preschooler, when her daughter was born, said that her middle child told her regularly, "You're not a fun mommy anymore." The first time he said it Deborah laughed, "but it also stung a little."

Child-development experts will tell you that it's normal and healthy for your preschooler to direct his rage toward Mom, but it's not much fun to have your characteristically compliant firstborn scream "I hate you!" and refuse to do as he's told. As guilt-ridden as you may feel, it's critical to understand how important respecting routines and enforcing limits can be at this time of upheaval and transition. While it may be tempting to compensate for the sacrifices your eldest has had to make by bending the rules or by tolerating excessive verbal abuse, you'll be doing no one any favors. What your preschooler needs more than ever is to know that you still have the energy and love necessary to keep his world as predictable and safe as it was before his little brother or sister came along.

Weathering Emotional Storms

Even if you're raising just one—or if you have not yet expanded your family—the preschool years are sure to promise passionate shifts in your family's emotional climate. You may find, as I did, that the twos were not nearly as "terrible" as the threes. Perhaps because we're conditioned to expect the worst during the toddler years, it's that much harder to accept a three-year-old's meltdown or a four-year-old's obstinacy. "I thought this was supposed to be over by now!" a young mom said to me recently as we waited to board a plane and she struggled to hold on to her preschool-age son's hand. He was big, so his screaming and whining did seem slightly regressive. But it had been a long day for him, and his desire to get the hell out of this long, boring line of cranky grown-ups was more than understandable.

Some moms told me that their toddler's meltdowns barely registered on the Richter scale of annoyance, while the whining or "why-ing" of their four-year-old shattered their patience in minutes. Hope, whose daughter Juliette was highly verbal even as a toddler, found that as her chatty daughter's vocabulary increased, so did her ability to push Hope's buttons. "We'll be driving in the car, and suddenly Juliette will yell, 'Say it, Mama! Say it!' So I'll ask, 'Say what, honey?' And then she'll repeat, "What you just said. Say it!' And as she gets more and more insistent, we engage in this Abbott and Costello routine. It just drives me crazy. And I think she knows that."

When Nick was about four, Steve came home from work one night laughing over an encounter he had had with a homeless man who camped out regularly near the ATM at our local bank. "Tonight he asked me for a dollar," Steve said, shaking his head. "When I didn't give him the buck, he asked for fifty cents, then twenty-five, then a dime, a penny, and, finally, a prayer. When he got to the prayer, I gave him the dollar!"

Living with Nick when he was four and five was a little like living with that homeless man. His negotiations rivaled Johnnie Cochran's in terms of sheer tenacity. I knew that his willingness to go to the mat for an extra cookie underscored his realization that words were powerful tools to get what you want. And that he would keep trying in the hope that just the right sequence of words would crack the code and open the door to more candy or another turn on the slide or one more book before lights-out. Sometimes he wore me down or made me laugh and basically charmed the treat out of me, but just as often he wound up ticking me off.

During the kids' preschool years, I understood more than ever why parents often resort to the "because I told you so" school of discipline or to spanking. There were days when a short time-out worked so well, I was ready to nominate myself to the T. Berry Brazelton Hall of Fame. If the planets were aligned just right, natural consequences made sense even to the child with arms crossed angrily across his chest. But much more often, nothing kept the kids from fighting or got them to clean up their toys. I felt like I was constantly forced to rewrite the Murphy Family Rule Book (don't think for a second that such a document actually existed), knowing full well that the key chapter, "When 'No' Means "No,'" was missing.

I consulted all the books about setting limits, had long and informed discussions with the many experts on *Parents* magazine's advisory board, even purchased a special time-out chair, which Maddie found so appealing that she sat in it as often as possible. What I really longed for was an authority hovering in the wings to discipline the kids for me. She would know exactly when to stick to the rule book and when to bend those rules to accommodate a bad day. Her better judgment would be decidedly better than mine.

What I learned is that setting up a framework in the context of your family and, most important, with your child's unique personality in mind is key. If your preschooler reacts to being alone like Haley Joel Osment in *The Sixth Sense,* then banishing him to his room for a time-out isn't going to work. Gathering him onto your lap and holding him close until he calms down may be a lot more effective. I found that taking away Maddie's Barbies or some coveted toy until she had calmed down worked better than time-outs. And because Maddie was very verbal, I could also explain what I was doing. Rewards were very successful with Nick, but given his tenacious negotiating skills, the most important disciplinary step I took was inspired by an article we ran in *Parents.* The mom who wrote it had successfully altered her whole approach to discipline by turning her decisions over to a "higher power." This slightly New Agey approach enabled her to say to her kids, "Look, that's the decision. It's out of my hands." Her mind-set shifted totally; she was able to stick to her guns, to make no mean no, because she told herself that she was simply following orders.

Of course, I'm sure that this kind of thinking contributes to the popularity of Bible-wielding "experts" who advocate "benevolent dictatorships" at home and a kind of authoritarianism that inevitably includes a spare-the-rod-spoil-the-child attitude toward spanking. To parents who are desperately searching for an excuse to play hardball with their kids, the appeal of this kind of rigid discipline is understandable. As much as I despise this approach, I can see why it holds such sway. Telling yourself that a spanking is the only way to make your child obey (and getting the short-term result you're after) is much more satisfying than anticipating when your preschooler is going to pitch a fit or get into trouble and redirecting him. It takes time, extraordinary patience, physical strength, and emotional fortitude to discipline effectively. No one has all those skills at her disposal at one time; and few of us can call upon the skills we do have while waiting on line at the supermarket or under the righteous eyes of judgmental relatives.

Mothers spank their kids for countless reasons, including cultural differences. If you grew up in a family where a swat on the rear end was the way your mother got you to behave and it didn't seem to do you any harm, then it's natural and certainly easy to justify doing the same with your children. (Of course, you should also ask yourself if you "turned out okay" *because* of the spanking or *despite* it.) Study after study confirms that corporal punishment is one of the least effective modes of controlling a young child's behavior;[8] all it teaches is that a big person can use her superior strength to hurt a little person. And that's not a lesson you should rush to instill.

At the same time, when your child has reached an age when questioning Mom's authority is a big part of his moving away, it's tempting to use one's physical "bigness" to assert that authority. Cathy, whose five-year-old had recently started kindergarten when I spoke to her from her home in Alabama, marveled at how often Ford would come home and question what she or her husband told him. "All day long he'll say, 'How do you know?' Or ask us why, why, why. It's not only annoying at times, but it's clear that I'm not the all-knowing person I once was in his eyes. Now he's learning things from other people. He's learning that there are other authorities—his teacher, Miss Lucy, for example. And it just irritates me when he says, 'How do you know?'"

My friend Ellen, a Yale graduate and one of the smartest women I know, recalled how surprised she was by the "gaps in my education" she had to face when her son turned five. "He'll ask me about dinosaurs or the stars or something he's learning about in school, and I'll have no idea! I'm no longer able to answer all his questions." A book lover like his mom, Alex enjoyed going to the library to learn more about a particular subject, and their visits enabled Ellen to teach him about doing research and discovering answers together. Other mothers talked about the gift of the Internet—how much fun it was to sit with their preschooler on their lap and find the answer to a question about the world that might have stumped the queen of Mensa. "The problem I have," Jane confessed, "is that Jesse is so much more adept at the computer than I am, I sometimes wind up feeling even stupider than when he posed the question we were hoping to answer!"

Oedipal Wreck

When Cathy's son fell in love with his teacher, the wonderful Miss Lucy, Cathy was forced to face an adjustment most mothers make when their children enter kindergarten. Although her son had been attending day care and then full-time family care since he was a baby, the first day of "real school" caught Cathy totally off guard. "I didn't think it would be a big deal to send him to kindergarten. But when I got to my office the day I dropped him off for the first time, I decided to e-mail some friends about the morning. I was recapping how he dressed himself in his little uniform and ate breakfast and got ready for school. And as I was finishing my e-mail, I started bawling. So it was definitely more of a big thing for me than it was for him."

Whether you e-mail friends or keep a journal or pick up the phone and talk to someone, the milestone moment of sending your child through the doors to "big school" should not be brushed aside. I always knew when one of my colleagues had a five-year-old, because the first day of public school inevitably included mothers standing red-eyed and distracted at the elevators or sudden confessions of how hard it had been to say good-bye. "She went up the stairs to the door and she looked so tiny," Gail, an editor at *Parents,* told me the day she dropped off her youngest daughter. "I just couldn't believe she was going into that building alone!"

If it's your youngest child—the last sparrow in the nest—who is winging her way to school, then the first days of kindergarten can be particularly tough. Sandi, who lives in Oklahoma and has worked throughout her kids' lives, recalled a moment when she stopped dead in her tracks after dropping off her youngest son. "I experienced this oh-my-God sense that this was it. I always thought we would have another one, and I wish I would have known earlier that he would be the last. It was very, very hard to see him go."

When your child's orientation shifts from one universe to another, you may discover that you're no longer the sun and the moon in his galaxy. Mothers of sons may find that the passionate attention they enjoyed during the aptly named Oedipal phase is suddenly beamed on a competing planet—Miss Lucy or another adored teacher or a new-found pal. My close friend Patty wrote a wonderful essay entitled "Oedipus Wreck" in which she chronicled her son Matt's relationship with his kindergarten friend Gus.[9] When I asked her recently to remind me what had happened, she actually sighed (Matt is now four-teen) before smilingly retelling the story of his first few months in kindergarten. "At first—during the honeymoon period—he brought home drawings and collages and cards, lovingly inscribed 'TO MOM.' He told me I was beautiful and wanted to hang out with me con-stantly. Then one day each and every piece of artwork was dedicated 'TO GUS.'" According to Patty, Matt talked incessantly of Gus: after school, before bed, first thing in the morning. "When we went on this amazing vacation over the Christmas break, Matt spent hours shop-ping for Gus. He filled his knapsack with things from the hotel for Gus—soap, little shampoos. He searched the beaches looking for the perfect seashells for Gus and insisted we buy gum and candy in the airport for him." But the coup de grâce came on the plane ride home, when Patty, hoping to be thrown a tiny bone, asked Matt what he had enjoyed the most on his vacation. "Thinking about Gus," he replied wistfully.

Patty laughed recalling that period in her relationship with Matt, but she admitted to feeling at the time "a sense of real loss, a feeling that part of me had been displaced."

Most child-development experts agree that while Freud may have been wrong about many aspects of our psychosexual development, he was definitely onto something when he first described the Oedi-pal complex. The preschool years are unquestionably colored by the deeply purple passions children express toward one or the other parent but rarely to both in equal measure. Although there are exceptions, most boys fall in love with their moms; girls with their dads. As Kerry, a young mom from Missouri, recalled, "My son was my snuggle bunny. He would come in and snuggle in the morning, and that was how we'd get our day going. Just anywhere Mommy went, that's where he would go, too—he even loved grocery shopping. My husband would say, 'Do you want to go to the *hardware* store?' and he was like, 'Well, no, I'll stay home with Mom.' He talked about marrying me when he grew up and was very upset when his brother told him, 'It's against the law to marry your mom.' After that, he would ask me, 'Am I going to have to leave you?'"

I, somewhat guiltily, loved Nick's Oedipal stage. What wasn't to love? He laughed at all my knock-knock jokes, claimed my tuneless rendition of "Over the Rainbow" surpassed Judy Garland's, paused in the middle of a game to place his pudgy palms on my cheeks, lock his dark brown eyes with mine, and coo, "Ooooh, you're my lovey, dovey, honey Mama." One night, after I had invented a bedtime story about a royal chef who created for his beloved princess a necklace of edible jewels, Nick's eyes widened with excitement. "You know what, Mama?" he whispered. "When I'm growed up, I'm gonna make you a special, special cake. And it's gonna be tall and really, really big, and it's gonna have raspberries on it. And you know what?"

"What, honey?"

"When you cut it open, it's gonna glow in the dark."

But the gift that took the cake, so to speak, was unwrapped the Christmas of his fifth year. It consisted of a cardboard toilet-paper roll stuck in a blob of clay and topped by a rounded canopy of more clay that hung down just enough to make its phallic shape unmistakable. Below the cardboard shaft, stuck in the clay, were two large gold buttons, while from the top (or tip) of the canopy shot several colorful feathers. "Wow! Nick! This is beautiful," I gasped, trying not to make eye contact with Steve. "What is it?"

"It's a tree, Mama."

"A very happy tree," Steve added as he unwrapped his gift. "And what's this, big guy?" Steve held in his hands what looked like a clay turd skewered by four Popsicle sticks.

"Oh, that's a horse, Dad," Nick explained. Then, pointing to a tiny Lego man glued to one side, "And that's you falling off the horse."

Letting Go Again

Of course, just as my mother was predicting that Nick's Oedipal passions would cost him years of psychoanalysis, he entered first grade, took one look at the adorable assistant teacher, and decided she could do no wrong. The year was punctuated with "Guess what Miss Thompson did today" accounts of golden afternoons, special games, even an excited announcement that he had invited her to dinner. "I think I'll make my black-pepper fettuccine," he said with a sigh as I tucked him in one night. And he did!

Countless moms have told me similar "Oedipus wreck" stories of being displaced by a teacher or "best, best, best friend" or by Dad, who suddenly rules Olympus. Kerry's "snuggle bunny" turned six, discovered soccer and the joys of hanging with the guys. "Now he really wants to be with his dad more. In fact, just this past weekend they were going off to the soccer game and they didn't even invite me along. Not that I wanted to go, but . . ." Her voice trailed off, but I didn't really need to ask her to complete the thought. Then she added with a little too much energy, "But I thought, 'Wow! I have this whole afternoon to myself. With nothing planned.' I guess I was happy and yet sad about it."

Happy and sad describes the universal ambivalence moms experience when the child who wouldn't go near "the big swings" a year ago dares his pal to "race to the moon," or when a child whose voice rarely exceeded a whisper performs in the preschool show, or when all the kindergartners line up for graduation.

By the time Maddie turned five, Nick was a toddler, stumbling his way into her world with increasing intrusiveness. I have a vivid memory of him running after his big sister on a farm where we vacationed, his little toddler legs too short and uncoordinated to propel him down the hill at her breakneck speed. "Mimi! Mimi!" he bleated as he stumbled after her. "Wait me! Me go, too!"

I sat on our porch, wanting Maddie to wait, wanting Nick to wait, too—to stop growing up and away. Just that week Maddie had been trying on clothes from the preceding summer, greeting Popsicle-stained

T's and patched denim shorts like long-lost friends. Wrestling to button a beloved blouse, she moaned, "It shrunk, Mom!"

"No, honey," I said, laughing. "You grew!"

They were both like the proverbial weeds, especially Maddie, whose sinewy legs seemed to get longer by the minute. Nick, too, was lengthening out, losing those rolls of sweet toddler flesh and the baby smell I wished I could bottle. I sensed that he would be our last child, and that conferred a certain poignancy on the many milestones we celebrated. I often held on a little too tightly, babied him a bit more than I should have, indulged my own need to drag out the little-kid years as long as possible. In fact, it took a visit to a chiropractor toward the end of Nick's preschool years (and his suggestion that the painful stiffness in my hip and shoulder could be "due to lifting a heavy weight") for me to admit that I carried Nick around quite a bit. When he naturally asked, "How old is he?" I lied. His raised eyebrows confirmed what I already knew: At three (he was actually closer to five), Nicholas was certainly able to walk by himself. The question was whether I was willing to put him down.

It certainly should not have required a trip to a chiropractor to force me to face my ambivalence about this phase of Nick's development. At five, he was a joy to be around—funny, loving, curious, boundlessly energetic, achingly sweet. Sometimes when I would lift him up or, yes, carry him, he would mold himself to my body the way he had as an infant, even though his long legs hung down well past my waist and his bony arms felt more boylike than babyish. Still, I knew that his forays into a wider world would include longer separations, more time away from me, and would require of us a very different way of relating.

The changes I anticipated would be due to more than his increased physical separateness. The way Nick thought about me had developed along with his ability to communicate how he was feeling. Just a few years before, he would throw a fit because I couldn't read his mind; now he could express what he wanted using the hundreds of words in his ballooning vocabulary. But letting Nick do that, not trying to read his mind, was a challenge because it ran smack up against my desire to be needed, to maintain my place as the center of his universe. When he insisted on making his own snack, teaching me a card game, calling from a pal's house to ask if he could spend the night, it was more difficult than ever to celebrate these strides, not experience them as marginalizing my importance in his life.

The key for me—and for many mothers of preschoolers—was to stay connected to or to develop other roles that were meaningful and gratifying. For some that meant a return to work at the time their children entered kindergarten. For others, their children's increased separateness signaled a chance to connect with their husbands more often. But for all of us, the preschool years should include plenty of time to step back and take note of the fact that had it not been for our constant, caring presence in our children's lives up until now, they would not be ready and able to move ahead with confidence, to take risks, to develop friendships, and to learn.

Stage 5

∽

Reading the Compass
to God-Knows-Where

Years Six to Ten

The "expert" take on this period in a mother's life is that her child is now more independent and self-reliant, and although that can bring up issues of separation, it's basically good news. Also, because the scary adolescent era seems miles away, and the stormy toddler years are long gone, moms breathe a sigh of relief, perhaps indulge in a little more introspection, confident that not much is supposed to happen between ages six and ten. Hmm. I found this period in my kids' lives one of the fullest and most challenging, especially once they started "real school."

Yes, confidence runs high during this phase. You pick up a baby album and stare at your face—a puffy mask of exhaustion—and remember how terrified and overwhelmed you felt "back then." Or you filter the toddler years through the lens of experience and know you could handle a tantrum today with Buddha-like calm. But because your children are gone more of the day, learning and growing in a world you're not privy to, you may feel, as I did, that time is slipping away or that the few hours you spend together in the evenings must be choreographed with Disneyesque wit and whimsy.

The hectic pace of our lives during Maddie and Nick's early school years regularly forced the "Is this worth it?" question front and center. I loved my work, but as the demands of my job ramped up, the schedule of school activities, after-school activities, weekend activities, and social activities moved into high gear as well. I felt pulled in more directions than ever, acutely aware that my hold on the kids, my control over their lives, was the most tenuous it had ever been.

Because Maddie attended a Montessori school, where five-, six-, and seven-year-old children were grouped together, I didn't have the major adjustment to "real school" that many of my friends experienced. But I shot at least a dozen photos of her in a new red plaid dress, her smile as full of promise as the shiny notebooks in her shiny backpack. I saved all of them, even the last, which is slightly out of focus, because Maddie turned at the last moment to greet her friend Susanna. Then, as I shouted good-bye, they dashed hand in hand through the entrance, talking and laughing and leaving me in the proverbial dust. It hit me then: This was it. She had crossed the threshold into days more often defined by friends and schoolwork, favorite teachers and after-school activities, than by my comings and goings.

My friend Nicole described her twins' entry into first grade as triumphant: "Claire looked so confident and grown up at her little desk, and Theo practically skipped into school that first day. He just couldn't wait." But for her the day was tinged with a deep sense of loss. "I cried the minute I left the building. And I've been crying all morning. I know these first few weeks are going to be awful."

It is awful at first, because you not only miss the hand holding on the way to school, the good-bye hugs and kisses, the opportunities to connect with your child, but you lose contact with a group of mothers, the ones who linger and chat outside the classroom. All through the kids' preschool years, there were mothers I didn't know very well but who, nonetheless, provided a loose network of support that I relied on practically every day. I could double-check a school-calendar question, commiserate about earache season, ask for the name of a reliable weekend baby-sitter, or verify some claim Nick had made about needing a hermit crab "because every, every, everybody has one, Mom." Plans for play dates or news of a great kid-friendly show or complaints about holiday overload flowed along the corridors festooned with droopy collages and colorful handprints. Even if I was rushing off to work, I could catch a glimpse of what was happening in the classroom or check in with the kids' teachers. And on mornings that featured tears or tantrums, I was welcome to linger a little longer or to peer anxiously through the one-way glass to make certain all was well.

With the Kids at School, Where Am I?

Most important, when our kids enter first grade, spending a full day or more in activities we are rarely privy to, we lose a certain version of ourselves. They're on their own and so are we. Handling this shift from the pitcher's mound to left field is one of the central challenges of this phase of motherhood.

"Meaghan's school was literally next door," my friend Patty recalled recently. "There was only a fence separating their outdoor play area and our garden." Patty would listen for Meaghan's voice, picking out her daughter's laughter from that of the other chirruping six-year-olds. One day she decided to peek over, but as she climbed up on a ladder, she lost her balance and fell. "I was fine, but it took an actual blow to the head to make me realize that the fence was a perfect metaphor for the increased separateness of our lives. We were still close, but there was more and more of her life I really knew nothing about. I could try to listen in, to catch a glimpse of what she was up to, but actually, what she said to her friends at school, what they did together minute by minute, was none of my business."

Feeling excluded from your child's school day, cut off from what she may be thinking or feeling, and less involved in her increasingly ornate life, can make you wonder, "What am I doing with my life?" Nicole, who had been happy to work very few hours at her part-time job, consciously chose to ramp up her work schedule. "I know they're moving into a stage when they just aren't going to need me in the same way. I need to develop my own interests, my own life, so when that time comes I don't feel I've invested my whole sense of who I am in my kids."

Josie, an executive I've known for many years, telephoned just months after receiving a major promotion to a position she had coveted for over fifteen years. Her voice was so low, I had to ask her to speak up: "I have to see you. I'm going through this terribly tough time, rethinking my life." I knew what she would say. As a single mom, she was lucky to have an involved ex-husband who assumed more than his share of the parenting load, but she had convinced herself that this new job would promise better times ahead. She could work really hard, make a lot of money (her ex-husband was unemployed), and "earn" more time with her kids. "But you know what?" she said. "It doesn't work that way. There's this diminishing window of opportunity. They are only six and eight; it's not like we're talking about college applications, but every day I see how much less influence I have, how much less they need me. And so all of a sudden I'm like wanting to connect and be with them in a way that I really feel kind of desperate about." She began to cry.

Contributing to Josie's sense of desperation was the fact that one of her kids was struggling in school. "Lizzie for the first time this year had a not-perfect report card, and one of the issues was her homework. I rarely get home in time to thoroughly check her homework. And although our baby-sitter says she makes sure Lizzie does it, that's not the same. I was just ignoring that."

The Complacency Trap

Because this stage is comparatively problem-free, it's often tough to remain vigilant, to fight the tendency to ignore blips on the screen. If your child has been happily skipping off to school, developing friendships, sleeping and eating well, enabling you to live your life in a way that just wasn't possible a year or two ago, it's natural to breathe a sigh of relief. But then when problems do arise, as they inevitably will, it's sometimes hard to accept them, to really listen to what's behind the whining or complaining. I learned this one night when Maddie was finishing third grade. It was well past her bedtime, and I had been singing, telling stories, and urging her to "just close your eyes" for over an hour. Tired and resentful that my eight-year-old was acting like her five-year-old brother, I grudgingly agreed to sing her favorite lullaby one last time, but my monotone, double-time rendition met with a whiny plea to "sing it slower."

"No, Maddie," I whined back. "I'm going to bed now and you are, too. We're both overtired." As I started down the hall, I could hear her climbing out of bed, trailing softly behind me.

"I'm afraid of ghosts," she said hesitatingly, testing the skeptical maternal waters. I would probably have lost it then and there had I not taken a deep breath and a closer look at her worried eyebrows. In lieu of another lousy lullaby, I suggested we go to the kitchen for a midnight snack. It took a bowl of cereal and about six minutes to chase away the "ghosts," which turned out to be understandable anxiety about starting a new school in the fall.

As Maddie ran through a litany of worries ("The teachers won't be nice," "I'll miss my friends," "I won't know where the bathrooms are"), I had to resist the expedient path, to refrain from leaping in with a host of cheery solutions just because I wanted to crawl into bed—not to mention avoid discussing an alternative school. With my emotional earplugs removed, I was able to really listen, and as the clock struck eleven, I urged her to list three things she might do the first week to make it a successful year. As she struggled to come up with optimistic possibilities, her small shoulders began to relax, and a few minutes later she took my hand and we walked back upstairs.

Voltaire once said, "The road to the heart is the ear." This tender bit of wisdom is never more apt than during the school years, when we may be tempted to rush in and pick up the pieces or simply sweep them under the rug in an effort to get through the day. But as important as it is when they're toddlers to let our kids solve their own problems, to work through frustration and weather minor storms, it's even more critical when their primary developmental task is to validate the motto "I can do it!"

"I Can Do It Myself"

The good news is that school-age children are actually amazingly competent and their eagerness to be good at things, to satisfy what Erik Erikson called "a sense of industry," makes them enthusiastic helpers.[1] The question is whether you have the patience to let them help. "I'm constantly jumping in to take over Michael's cleanup efforts," one mom of a six-year-old confessed. "I just go nuts when it takes him forty-five minutes to put his dinosaur collection away while his clothes are scattered all over the floor. And frankly, it's just easier to do it myself." I recall the challenge was often how to steer my kids clear of certain chores without dampening their enthusiasm. Highly attractive jobs like vacuuming, cooking, and mopping inevitably led to vacuum bags emptied on the rug, kitchen counters covered in slime, large puddles on wood floors—in other words, to more chores.

Looking back, however, I would take an eager five-year-old over a reluctant teenager as a chore warrior any day. They may not be as fastidious, or as facile with a dustpan, but the earlier they're taught that chores are a family responsibility, the better. Once kids hit the preteen years or, worse, their teens, the chances of getting them to put away their clothes (which are bigger and more abundant by a factor of five) are close to nil.

I definitely lost in the clothing department. Left to their own devices, my now-teenage children inhabit rooms that run the gamut from mild chaos to health department violation, but when it comes to kitchen crew, I wisely started early. When Nick was five, I gave him a pasta maker for Christmas. A couple of birthdays later he received a waffle iron, and by the time he turned ten, his batterie de cuisine rivaled many a chef's.

Tools were key. This is an age when a mini vacuum cleaner, old-fashioned eggbeater, or bottle brush can make KP duty highly appealing. The genius who first introduced those child-sized shopping carts should win a spot in the Supermarket Hall of Fame. It was at our local Gristedes that I learned the fine art of enabling my kids to strut their stuff a little, to try on adult roles, without patronizing or overmanaging their efforts. I remember taking Nick to the supermarket when he was about six and the kid-sized carts had just made their appearance. Armed with a short list from me and a long list of items he insisted we *needed,* he spent a thrilling half hour loading up with boxes of macaroni and cheese, doughnut holes, a bag of marshmallows, and, as I recall, a Superman coloring book. When I told him it was time to go, he wanted to pay for his stuff himself, so I handed over a twenty-dollar bill and trailed behind. I watched as he tenderly unloaded each item, glancing with awe and respect at the sullen teen behind the counter. I had to bite the inside of my cheek to avoid smiling too broadly as he crossed his little arms and waited to pay. Despite my best efforts to remain incognito, the cashier looked over his tousled hair to ask, "Are you together?"

I hesitated. "Well," I whispered back, "he's pretending to be on his own."

Needless to say, my whisper ricocheted like a shout down a canyon and my suave shopper lost his cool completely. "Mom! Don't tell!" he barked, a combination of humiliation and frustration bringing tears to his eyes.

"Okay, okay, Nick," I countered as calmly as possible. "Give the girl your money for your stuff."

"I know, Mom!" he said, clearly trembling on the brink. "Just let me do it!"

When Your Kids Can't

Handling your child's budding competence, being willing to let go a little—even if the results aren't up to your standards—is one thing. Helping your child appreciate and accept that there's often a disconnect between what we think we can do and what we're really about is another. One of my fellow editors at *Parents* had a basketball-obsessed eight-year-old who was not only small for his age but decidedly uncoordinated. "He'll just never, ever be the next Shaquille O'Neal," she would say with a sigh as she described his elaborate fantasies of filling his idol's size-22 Nikes. "I don't know whether to burst his bubble or nurture the illusion that he's creating for himself. I know he's going to get a rude wake-up call when he gets into junior high and is suddenly playing with kids twice his size."

One of the most difficult aspects of this stage of motherhood is accepting the fact that we can't be there to make it all better when our children stumble at school or when they simply lack certain skills. Katie, the mom of a dyslexic boy, described the agony of watching her bright, outgoing six-year-old struggle over one page of homework for hours each night. "It was just grueling. Every night we'd sit down to do these homework projects with him. And he would cry and just get hysterical. And I'd cry, too. It was crushing." Katie, who lives in an affluent suburb of Boulder, Colorado, enrolled her son in an innovative, experimental program to treat learning disorders. In addition to shelling out close to twenty-five hundred dollars, she supervised a series of prescribed daily exercises, took him for monthly checkups, and paid additional money for a tutor. It was clear that she would have tried just about anything to ease her son's burden, to boost his flagging self-esteem.

As mothers, we want to help a child who is in obvious pain, whose problem is fixable, and we should. But sometimes our motivations are less altruistic and more narcissistic, and our desire to provide the best veers dangerously into the neighborhood of "Whose life is it anyway?" The mother who holds her child back because he's not ready for first grade may have only the best of intentions, but there are countless others who retain their children simply to give them a better shot at quarterbacking the high school football team or leading the pack early on. As Diane Ehrensaft writes in *Spoiling Childhood*: "Their dream is to see their advanced, well-sized six-year-old shining in a class of more immature, less developed five-year-olds. From kindergarten success will come the confidence for first-grade excellence, and from there an assurance of a Harvard acceptance. In either case—the parents who protect or the parents who push—the voluntary holding back of their children is centered around the cult of success we've created for our children."[2]

Seeing the world through our children's eyes is one of motherhood's great gifts; living vicariously through our kids is a trap that's set at this phase and baited throughout the school years. A *Family Circle* reader once wrote me for help with her "sideline rage," and her short letter spoke volumes about the challenge Jung so beautifully articulated when he said, "The most powerful element in a child's life is the unrealized dream of the parent." This mother, who lived on the West Coast, described losing control at her nine-year-old's soccer matches. "I was a really good athlete as a kid," she explained, "but in those pre–Title IX days, I had very few opportunities to participate in organized sports. Now my daughter is in a competitive soccer league, and although I swore I would never be one of those ugly sideline moms, I find that I'm always yelling angrily at the ref or giving my daughter a hard time after the game. She actually started to cry the last time I criticized her. I felt terrible."

If you're thinking to yourself, "I would never, ever do that to my child," accept the fact that our own unrealized ambitions, fear of failure, frustrations, and anxieties inevitably creep out of even the most well-defended caves. We tell ourselves that we push, prod, nudge, and nag because we "only want the best" for our children or because we "know she could do better" or "we don't want him to limit his options." But the truth may be that we're actually doing it for ourselves.

Knowing when to push and when to coddle is particularly difficult at this stage; there seems to be a lot at stake, yet there's also plenty of time ahead to adjust the course. Kerry, who lives in Missouri, talked about the frustration of knowing her son could do better. "Austin's a very jovial 'people person,'" she explained. "His motto is basically 'Details are not important as long as you're having fun and the job gets done.' So he'll put in the least amount of effort. I know he could do better. And sometimes I realize that it bothers me because he reminds me of myself. He'll go to clean his room, and the next thing you know he'll be reading something he found under his bed. And he'll forget about the room. I used to do that exact thing! His strengths are his weaknesses. And at school it can be a problem. He gets B's, which I know could be A's. Yet I don't want to pressure him too much. He has this wonderful personality, and I know in the long run that is going to lead him further than a report card."

Kerry's appreciation for her son's unique personality, her recognition that while he might get only B's on his report card, he would probably have lots of friends and, she hoped, lots of fun in school, was refreshingly healthy. I've met so many mothers (and fathers) who simply can't step back. Their clashes over homework or violin practice or sports betray their own need to have a child who "does them proud"; ironically, such tensions only serve to undermine their children's motivation.

The other reason to avoid the "Whose life is it anyway?" trap is that the world of school and outside activities holds challenges all children need to face in order to grow. We can't protect them 24/7, and we shouldn't try. Life is rarely perfect—even when you're in second grade; children can be cruel. When we send our first-graders off, we know from experience that they'll face a host of social challenges involving friends and bullies, secret clubs and cliques. As difficult as it is to picture one's first-grader struggling to form a row of tidy "O's" in his composition book, it's even more heartbreaking to imagine him the last-picked player on the softball team or the picked-on kid at the playground. Even worse may be the image of one's home angel as the school devil, bossing or bullying his way around the classroom.

"The first time Danny's teacher called me to say he had been bullying this kid in his class, I literally felt sick to my stomach," Kimberly recalled. "It was so much worse than being told he was the victim. I was angry and humiliated, and I really didn't know who to turn to. No one has a lot of sympathy for the bully, and they definitely blame the bully's parents. So in addition to feeling worried about Danny, I felt isolated and victimized."

Kimberly, whose son was enrolled in a private school in Boston, was wise enough to see beyond the misbehavior to "not get hung up on who had started it." She stood by Danny's side, even as she established clear rules and consequences for his misbehavior. "The hardest part was trying not to blame myself for the way he was acting. I kept reminding myself that Danny was his own person, and that he'd work this out. I knew he wasn't a mean kid. He really wasn't." Kimberly turned to the head of the school, who was reassuring, but it was clear that other parents had been talking about Danny, which really hurt. "I just wish someone had had the decency to call me directly," she told me bitterly.

Unfortunately, the school years are often punctuated by poor judgment; what you call ebullience, your child's teacher considers "acting out." A quiet child with a gift for music is overlooked as simply "very shy." Reconciling what you see as your child's strengths or limitations with the images others have of her is a tough challenge, especially as teachers and coaches wield increasing power in our families' lives. In some ways, this is the flip side of the denial coin—the antithesis of the tendency we often have to inflate our children's talents as a defense against accepting their normal or even their subpar skill set. But, just as it's important to avoid living through our kids by pushing them too aggressively in one direction or another, it's equally critical to stand by their side—especially when academic or social pressures intensify.

When Carla's very active son was labeled a "behavior problem" by his teacher—an elderly martinet—she found herself constantly reprimanding him to "get in line, to show the teacher more respect." She dreaded picking him up after school because inevitably the teacher would be there, arms crossed, shaking her head as she reported another "unfortunate incident" she claimed Andy had initiated. "I would always question him or chew him out in front of the teacher, because I was so intimidated by her and embarrassed that my son was making trouble," Carla recalled. "It got so bad, I went to a counselor for advice. And she pointed out that poor Andy had no ally. Here he was struggling in school, in a class that was obviously a lousy fit, and then he'd get yelled at by me or by his dad." After meeting privately with the teacher to talk about specific behavior areas Andy needed to work on, and to share what Carla considered some of Andy's strengths, she took a totally different tack. "I decided to stand by Andy's side as much as possible. I stopped reprimanding him in front of others— which I realize I was doing because I didn't want them to see me as a wimp, as a bad mother. And I really listened to his side of the story as much as possible."

According to Carla, the year improved enormously—even though the teacher continued to pick on her son—because he knew he could trust his mom to try to help him work things out. More important, he got through the year recognizing that sometimes teachers don't like certain kids and that there are ways to make a bad situation better. "I think he felt really proud of himself at the end of school," Carla said. "He knew he had done the best he could under really tough circumstances, because we kept reminding him of his strengths, not focusing on his weaknesses—like that bitch!"

Perfectionists and Pessimists

Even in first, second, and third grades, school can be stressful, and while children may keep it together in the classroom, what happens at home is another matter. What has become known chez Murphy as "the Night of the Cursed Ovals" began one evening when Maddie, then seven, wanted to draw a mermaid. No, not just any mermaid, but one with a perfectly ovoid face. Twenty-three ovals later, Maddie's face was blotchy with frustration; despite my repeated reassurances that her ovals were just perfect, she insisted they were "all wrong!" Each and every time I insisted that she was a "wonderful artist," she countered with "No, I'm not! I stink!"

As she started on her twenty-fourth attempt, I announced it was time for bed, then dragged my sobbing perfectionist to her room. We were not a pretty sight. When she had finally calmed down enough to tolerate a bedtime story, I told Maddie about a time when I had rehearsed and rehearsed my one and only line in the third-grade play, only to trip as I made my big entrance, falling on my not-so-big rear end.

"You fell?" Maddie asked incredulously.

"Yes, and the entire class laughed at me."

"What did you do?

"I kind of croaked out my line and ran offstage."

"Did you cry?"

"Yes, I did. But you know what? I did better the next night, when we did the play again. Everybody makes mistakes, sweetheart."

Sometimes life *does* imitate an episode from *Seventh Heaven*. The next morning before school Maddie quietly produced a wonderful mermaid, starting, I should add, with an imperfect oval. No doubt a good night's sleep and some breakfast smoothed the way, as did the knowledge that I fell on my ass occasionally. But what Maddie brought to the drawing table was only half the story. My take-away from "the Night of the Cursed Ovals" was a promise to let go of the need to label Maddie "the best artist in the family." She knew that was baloney. I also swore I would resist the urge to jump in and do the drawing (or math problem or Lego construction) for her. And I would make a concerted effort to model the kind of thinking that leads to solutions, not sleeplessness. I realized that morning, as I blamed myself for "always losing my keys" and complained that my outfit wasn't right, that I had to keep a sharp eye on my own tendency to seek perfection, to criticize my work or my cooking or my clothing in a way that was only marginally more mature than Maddie's "I stink!"

Some of the most interesting research on children's motivation and self-esteem comes from work on optimism pioneered by Dr. Martin Seligman. In *The Optimistic Child,* Seligman describes how a child's "explanatory style" is the key to her self-esteem:

When a child does badly, she asks herself "Why?" There are always three aspects to the answer she comes up with: *who* is to blame, *how long* will it last, and *how much of her life* will be undermined. The distinctions among these three are crucial because the first question— blaming the self versus the world—governs the feeling side of self-esteem. The second and third questions—how permanent is the cause and how pervasive is the cause—govern what she will *do* to respond to failure. Feeling bad about the self does not directly cause failure. The belief that problems will last forever and undermine every-thing, in contrast, directly causes your child to stop trying. Giving up leads to more failure, which then goes on to undermine feelings of self-esteem.[3]

Whether you're an optimist or a pessimist depends on your ex-planatory style. A pessimistic person feels victimized by setbacks. She sees them as an extension of some flaw in herself, one that dooms her to a life filled with problems. More important, she's not motivated to do something about her lot in life, because she sees negative events and situations as unchangeable.

We all know pessimists—friends or relatives who become paralyzed by minor crises, who constantly complain that "work is hell" or that the cold they've had all winter "is never going away." I find "setting-sun mind," as a Buddhist friend calls it, exhausting to be around and, frankly, a bore. But what's really problematic is how easily pessimistic thinking rubs off on children. This is especially true during the early school years, when they're developing new skills every day and mea-suring themselves against their peers. A child who believes he stinks or who consistently blames his "dumb teacher" for his problems or who announces emphatically that "no one likes him" needs to learn how to dispute his negative thinking. But he can't do that if his mom is constantly blaming herself for the problems in her life.

When I was working full-time at *Parents,* I realized that I often came home and did what Steve called a "brain dump" on whomever happened to be around. As much as I loved my job, there were days when all I wanted to do was close my office door and scream. But of course, I didn't. Like a child who holds it together at school only to lose it the minute she gets home, I put on my best editor-in-chief armor at work only to let it clatter to the floor the minute I stepped through the threshold at home. Sometimes I grumbled about my boss, but more often I blamed myself for the frustrations I experienced.

One night over dinner I was complaining about how behind I felt. "I'll never, ever catch up, because I'm always letting people interrupt me. Today I did the stupidest thing—" I started, when Maddie inter-rupted me.

"You're not stupid, Mama," she said. "I think you're smart!"

I looked at her, my fork poised in midair, realizing how irresponsible I was being, how self-indulgent and "stupid" to model the kind of nowhere thinking that all too easily infects small children with big ears. I swallowed my pessimism and remorse and quickly recanted: "You're right, sweetheart," I replied. "I am smart. And so are you." (I was reminded of that vignette recently when I came upon a cartoon in *The New Yorker* in which a mother is saying to her small son, "Why are you special? Because I'm your mommy and I'm special.")

If you tend to blame yourself unfairly, to see the glass as half empty more than half the time, then devote the other half of that time to really questioning your own explanatory style. As Seligman wisely suggests, "To beat pessimism, your own opinion of yourself needs to become the target of skepticism. Don't blindly accept your own insults. Take a step back and consider them with an open mind. If they turn out to be true, fine. Then you need to work on changing the aspects of yourself or your world that bring discontent. You may find that your beliefs about yourself aren't true, that they tend to be catastrophizations—interpretations of bad events in extremely permanent and pervasive terms. If this is so, you need to correct them."[4]

Taking a Child's-Eye View of Yourself

Ironically, one of the best ways to change your perception of yourself for the sake of your kids is to try to see yourself through their eyes. I'm not talking about simply modeling the behaviors we want our children to emulate; of course, that's critical at every stage of their development. But one of the pleasures of this stage of motherhood is that, even as their world expands to include other adult authority figures, six- and seven-year-olds tend toward mother worship. One of my favorite photos of Nick, age six, was taken with my mother, then eighty-five. They're in bathing suits, and Nick is on her lap, looking into her face as she tells him something. He's smiling, totally engrossed in the story or joke or song she's reciting, and as he locks eyes with her he rests his hand on her bony chest, just over her heart.

There's something about that touch—gentle, absentminded, yet totally connected—that draws me back to my kids' early school years, when one of them would say something that stopped me dead in my tracks. They were tuned in to a higher-level frequency, better able to grasp what was going on around them and to articulate their thoughts with the subtlety of a sledgehammer. On at least one occasion Nick's tendency to hold up a mirror to my life, to point out in his affectionate, slightly avuncular way that I was missing the point entirely, had a radical impact on how I saw myself.

It was toward the end of a day during which I had run frantically on a squeaky wheel to nowhere, feeling a little like the kids' gerbil, that Nick treated me to a critical *It's a Wonderful Life* moment. I was keeping him company as he took a bath, sitting with my back to the bathroom wall, rewriting one of several to-do lists I had read and refolded so many times it was falling apart. I was not a happy camper as I stewed over my lack of productivity. When an audible sigh escaped my lips, Nick asked, "What's the matter, Mom?"

"Oh, nothing, honey," I lied. "I'm just frustrated because I didn't get anything done today."

"That's not true," he countered energetically. "You did lots of stuff."

"Like what?"

Looking at me as though I had forgotten his birthday, he said, "Don't you remember, Mom? You found Lego Man's hair."

"Lego Man's hair?" I asked, stalling for time. Then it came to me: the fifteen-minute search on hands and knees under his bed and behind his chair and in his sneakers for a yellow, lentil-sized Lego piece. When I found it, Nick rejoiced like some crazed archaeologist celebrating the discovery of the Rosetta stone.

I was still with the Lego excavation when Nick added, "And you made us macaroni and cheese even though you think it's yuck." True. I'm convinced that the orange cheese powder you mix with milk and a pound of butter is a not-too-distant relative of Agent Orange.

"And now you're helping me take a bath, but you don't have to 'cause I'm bigger than yesterday."

At that moment I felt as though I was soaking in a warm bath myself. My image, as reflected in my son's eyes, was decidedly brighter than the frustrated, frowning face I'd seen in the bathroom mirror earlier. Like George Bailey in *It's a Wonderful Life,* I had been given an opportunity to see how different Nick's day would have been had I not taken the time to provide these seemingly random caring gestures.

The problem was I never bothered to put "Find Lego Man's hair" on my daily agenda. I didn't think twice about treating the kids to a side dish I happened to loathe, and I certainly never gave myself credit for keeping Nick company, even though, as he pointed out, he had learned how to swim when he was five. The countless acts of kindness that filled my day and pushed everything else sideways never made it onto my to-do list. Inspired by my little sage to take another look at that list, I tore it up and started over, this time including everything I had actually done that day; then, with a satisfied grin, I crossed off the top twenty to-dos, starting with "Find Lego Man's hair."

In the home movie of our lives as moms, it's the big events—the birthday parties, trips to Disney World, tickets to the Big Game—that dominate. But our kids have this amazing ability to pause on a single frame, to zoom in on a moment and to hold it in their hearts for a very long time. The *Barney* show is remembered not because of the fabulous orchestra seats you waited four hours on line to get but because your six-year-old cracked a joke that made you laugh so hard you cried. The vacation that cost a month's wages fades to black quickly, but the afternoon you put dinner on hold in order to show your eight-year-old how to fly a kite is permanently stored on his hard drive. When we take the time to give ourselves credit for all of these minor miracles, to filter even the most desultory day through our children's more appreciative lens, we experience less guilt, more patience, and certainly a much deserved feeling of pride.

You're in the Wrong Movie

There's another important reason to take stock of your accomplishments, however fleeting they may seem. It helps avoid what I call "the wrong-movie syndrome." When Nick and Maddie were in preschool and second grade, respectively, I used to torture myself (and Steve) with a near-obsessive wish to have dinner as a family every night. I would promise to leave my office promptly at six, pretend that the commute would take a mere forty minutes (true only on Labor Day,

July Fourth, and Yom Kippur), race in the door, and attempt to throw some kind of meal on the table in twelve minutes while two ravenous children circled my legs and whimpered. Steve would stagger in soon after, and we would wolf down our now cold food with forced cheer.

I was complaining once again about our lack of a civilized routine, about the lack of warm family-dinner memories the kids would have, let alone the steep shrink bills I felt sure would result, when Steve put his hands on my shoulders, looked me in the face, and said, "You're in the wrong movie!"

"What do you mean?" I asked defensively.

"You're remembering your own childhood dinners, holding up as the ideal the way *your* family bonded. But our family is different, and the kids will have lots of warm memories—not necessarily of their daily dinners with us but of our bedtime reading and of the long vacations we take together, of the trips we've already taken with them."

He was right. My father, an obstetrician-gynecologist, left the house before breakfast but returned home every night at 6 p.m. sharp (unless he was in the delivery room). Dinners at seven were sacrosanct; no one but my father was allowed to answer the phone while we ate and conversed and bonded. But when it came to longer holidays and vacations there were very few. Because Papa could never venture far from home, we rarely spent weekends off the island of Manhattan. Summers were spent on Cape Cod, but my father was only there for a fraction of the time. Extended family vacations during other times of the year were just not possible.

In contrast, Maddie took her first trip to Florida when she was three months old, and just about every year Steve and I make a point of socking aside enough to pay for at least one family vacation. Our children spent summers in the Adirondacks, traveled to Florida, visited relatives in California, and experienced countless weekend excursions long before anyone in my immediate family ever had. Which is not to say that their memories were guaranteed to be brighter than mine. I certainly didn't feel deprived. But their movies would be different from mine, and part of the joy of parenthood rests in directing your own film, finding your own ways to be there for (and with) your kids, and accepting the ways in which you can't.

The Entitlement Trap

As wonderful as it had been for Nick to show me the light that night in the tub, I can't say it happened very often during their early school years. My children were sweet and loving, relatively well behaved and appreciative—most of the time—but the bitter taste of feeling taken for granted, underappreciated, and overworked often burned at the back of my throat. There were many mornings when my resentment and anger spilled over as I raced around the house before work, picking up discarded clothes, tidying the kitchen, cajoling the kids into their coats, barking out a familiar checklist: "Do you guys have your lunches? How about the permission slip for Miss Katz? Did you remember your math workbook today?" Or I'd find myself at day's end an exhausted player in "The Witching Hour," a nightly one-act drama that featured hackneyed dialogue about not being a maid and the kids' needing to do their fair share. But my concern went well beyond chores.

Like many baby-boomer parents, Steve and I had been eager to provide the kids with all kinds of opportunities, from private school to piano lessons to day camp. We applauded every accomplishment, framed countless crayon creations, boasted about their many talents, but we demanded very little on the responsibility front. What worried me during this stage of motherhood was that too much giving, praising, doing for our children might sabotage their need to learn from their mistakes, to suffer a bit of pain in order to gain perspective on themselves and their place in the world. As psychologist Dan Kindlon, author of *Too Much of a Good Thing: Raising Children of Character in an Indulgent Age,* wisely notes: "Money can't protect our kids from the discomforts of maturation, and it can't buy them character."[5]

Experts like Kindlon, Diane Ehrensaft, Ron Taffel, and David Elkind have written persuasively about the insidious effect overindulgence has on our children. When—with the best of intentions—we give too much and expect too little, we run the paradoxical risk of jeopardizing our kids' happiness. I say "paradoxical" because it is often a desire to make our children happy, to avoid disappointing them, that drives our behavior at this stage. I've heard many moms sing the same tune when it comes to discipline and demands during their children's early school years: "He's in school and at sports so much these days, I hardly ever see him, so I don't want our limited time to consist of nagging and whining, which is what often happens."

At the same time, among mothers of school-age kids there's a universal dread that they're raising a brat. I'll never forget the media frenzy that followed Mayor Rudolph Giuliani's 1994 inaugural address, when his son, Andrew, then seven, stood in front of the podium, giggling, squirming, and mugging for the cameras. His obnoxious behavior sent a vicarious shudder of embarrassment across the nation; it became *the* watercooler moment, inciting heated conversations, outraged newspaper editorials, *Saturday Night Live* skits, and radio commentary about everything from Donna and Rudy's lax disciplinary skills to the sorry character of today's kids. One *New York Newsday* reader went so far as to say that the young Giuliani's behavior made her question his dad's ability to govern: "I personally voted for the mayor, but now I have misgivings about his ability to fight abusive behavior in a city of millions, when he cannot do that in his own family of four."[6]

I doubt I would go so far as to label a seven-year-old who acts out at his father's inauguration "abusive," but I would agree that highly public displays of bratty behavior are only marginally better than bamboo under the fingernails. As upsetting as it can be to stand on line with a screaming toddler, it's doubly disturbing when the screaming child is double the age—or at least old enough to know better. I cringed far less often when Maddie and Nick were small and their frustrations sometimes led to ugly scenes in supermarket aisles or toy stores than I did when they publicly sassed me—as my Texas-born mother would have labeled their back talk. It's a lot easier to admonish a preschooler to use her "indoor voice" than it is to tell your nine-year-old to lose the Valley Girl question mark at the end of her sentences.

A colleague at work complained recently about her nine-year-old, "I mean, I can't say anything without getting some kind of attitude. It's so much worse than when she was little." My friend Jane simply dubbed her son's third-grade year the "Hello, duh!" era.

Claire, a social worker who lives in Washington, D.C., described her petite fifth-grade daughter as capable of throwing her fifty-five pounds around like a mini sumo wrestler. "She'll look at me, rolling her eyes, her hands on her hips, and say, 'Like weren't you ever a kid, Mom?'" She also has signs posted on her bedroom door that read, BEWARE! KEEP OUT! HOUSE NOT COMPLETED BEYOND THIS POINT!

The signs are a clue to what's going on during the early school years, when children are "not completed" and must struggle to figure out what kind of person they want to be. They are still children but exposed much earlier than we were to adult messages. The result is often described by psychologists as a pressure to grow up too fast,[7] to join the world of "kinderadults."[8] As one writer described today's "under-twelves": "They are a generation that has been raised to challenge and doubt authority, to take little at face value—in short, to enter the world of maturity long before they are mature."[9]

When your eight-year-old parades around in a cropped-off T, her jeans hugging her undeveloped hips, or when your nine-year-old mouths off about his teacher "the idiot," you may face for the first time the uneasy realization that the boundary between your adult world and theirs is increasingly blurred. When that happens, it's critical to stop and think about the ways we may unconsciously contribute to this erosion by actually condoning pseudoadult behavior. After all, it's fun to be able to see movies with your nine-year-old that a year or two ago would have gone over his head; it's nice to shop with an eight-year-old girl who actually enjoys helping you pick out a hip wardrobe. But it's definitely no fun for children to feel that their mom is on their level, that they share equal power in the relationship. As Dan Kindlon warns: "The desire to form a close bond with our children should not come at the expense of not being able to set an unyielding limit or rule when a child needs it."[10]

It should also not come at the expense of asking our children to take on increased responsibilities. One of the healthiest ways to gratify a school-ager's natural desire to be treated like a "big kid" is not to let her dress the part but to expect her to walk the walk. I remember being somewhat amazed by and at first highly skeptical of a stay-at-home mother I met through the kids' school who had three children, a highly successful husband, a huge house, a car and driver, hot-and-cold-running help—but who insisted that her children do their own laundry. "But don't you guys have someone who does the laundry for you?" I asked, knowing full well that they employed a full-time clean-ing woman, a nanny, and a personal secretary.

"We don't *need* Zach to wash his own clothes, if that's what you mean," the mom replied. "But we think he should know how to do laundry or cook a meal or clean up a house."

I suddenly realized that my children might be able to program the VCR with their eyes closed, but there was no way they knew the dif-ference between "presoak" and "rinse cycle." I didn't feel they were spoiled, but I did worry that a paralyzing sense of entitlement was a risk for my children—as it is for any upper-middle-class child.

A few days later I was talking to a friend who had moved with her husband and sons, then six and eight, to a classy suburb. I asked Amy what she worried about when it came to mothering school-age boys. Very quickly she came to the issue of entitlement. "I'm really strug-gling to teach the kids the values I just took for granted growing up in a family where we just didn't have much. We live on the border of one of the most affluent areas in our state, but we're not rich. We chose to stretch at this time because the community has a superb school sys-tem, but the fact is, we're kind of the bottom tier when it comes to wealth. During school breaks, everyone is off to Hawaii or Europe. We can't afford to do that. We don't live in a huge home where everyone is talking about the decorator and the landscape architect and the staff. But I've learned to deal with it over the years, I've learned to accept that it's really not the most important thing in life, and that's what I want to teach to my kids. So when Noah came to me and asked, 'Why can't we have a pool?' I started to say, 'Well, we don't have room for a pool,' but then I added that we were very lucky to have what we do, including a lot of love in our house. I told him we should be grateful for everything we do have. Of course, he just kind of rolled his eyes!"

There's no question that the "When I was a kid, I had to walk six miles in the snow to school" homily doesn't fly far with the Play-Station crowd. Being the best, having the most, knowing the latest, and owning the biggest are intimately linked to a third- or fourth-grader's new sense of vulnerability and their mortal fear of being singled out as different or inadequate by their peers. Kids this age tend to be lousy losers ("Do over!"). They often stretch the truth ("My dad is the best tennis player anywhere"), and they constantly compare ("Why don't we have . . ."). What's tricky is how easy it is to get sucked into the keeping-up-with-the-Joneses game. Often it's not a question of what car the Joneses drive that drives you crazy; it's a more insidious form of competition that rattles our confidence.

Peer Pressure Among Parents

A couple of years ago my friend Kate called to vent. "I need your advice," she said in a tense voice. "Hunter was invited over to a friend's house this afternoon, and when he got home, he announced that the kid's mother had taken them to see the movie *South Park*."

"Isn't that rated R?" I asked, trying not to fan the flames.

"Yes! And Hunter knows he's not allowed to see anything but PG-13 films. But I don't blame him. I called this mom and I told her how upset I was. Would you believe, she goes on and on about how it really wasn't that bad, that most of the humor went over the boys' heads. She made me feel like a jerk."

I commiserated, sharing a similar experience I had had with the mother of one of Maddie's friends, who left the girls (then nine) alone while she ran a bunch of errands. Kate and I wallowed happily in our warm puddle of righteous indignation before I guiltily conceded that the shoe had occasionally been on the other foot. I recalled the time I gave a small group of Nick's classmates sodas and corn chips while they watched some mindless TV show, only to have a mother call to inform me tersely that her son *never* drank soda and *only* watched television for half an hour a week and then "strictly educational programs."

Although my initial reaction was to label this woman an overly educated, uptight health-food terrorist, the sense that my lax ways with sugar, sodium, and satellite TV ranked me "Mother, Second Class" stung. I felt the same need to prove I was right and she was wrong that my kids felt around their peers. But the difference between this self-doubt and the clouds that rolled in occasionally during Nick and Maddie's toddler years was that it rumbled in the background of my life practically all the time. Hardly a day went by when some issue—whether it was appropriate clothing or bedtime or media choices—didn't make me question my mothering style. And there were few certainties. Sure, I could call like-minded friends (or those with more than three kids) for reassurance that gorging on Fritos once in a while was fine, but the pressure to do the right thing, particularly when it came to the kids' moral development, made the stakes feel very high. *South Park* might be an obvious no-no, but what about certain prime-time sitcoms that seemed to feature primarily sexual humor? How long could I hold out on the video-game front, avoiding the ubiquitous kill-and-maim contests—and were they really going to affect Nick in the long run? How many after-school opportunities did Maddie need to keep her happy and to boost her blossoming skills? Wasn't it more important to have some family time?

I've heard countless moms sing the self-doubt blues, but the tune has a slightly more urgent rhythm as the preteen years approach. "Right now I feel very comfortable because I still feel I'm in control of my kids' lives," Amy told me. "I feel like I still make the rules and they'll listen. But I look ahead and feel terrified of what I hear about drugs and sex and drinking. I worry about losing control of them, and sometimes that makes me question little stuff like whether they should play with toy guns or see a certain movie or stay up late."

For me the key to avoiding peer pressure and minimizing self-doubt was to clarify as much as possible the issues I felt most strongly about and then to discuss with Steve the rules we considered nonnegotiable. I hate toy guns of any kind, so Nick learned early that even water pistols were not allowed. (I relented only when he went to sleep-away camp, which held an annual event in which water weaponry of all kinds—balloons, hoses, and big, bad water guns—was a must.) My friend Nicole established an admirable no-TV-on-school-nights law that her four children are rarely permitted to break. When they return from a friend's house with provocative pronouncements ("Ariel can watch as much TV as she wants!"), Nicole shrugs and emits a little derisive "Pfff!" as only the French can. Another friend utilizes an extremely powerful weapon in the "But so-and-so's mom lets him" battles: She just says, "Hmmm," and goes on with whatever she's doing.

Obviously, you can't shrug off or "hmmm" your way through every challenge to your authority, but you can choose to discuss more fully only those dilemmas that merit a more thoughtful response. Otherwise, it's perfectly okay to say, "Look, I'm sorry you're frustrated and upset with me. But on school nights, there's one hour of television and reading before bed. We can read together or not, that's up to you." If your child screams, "I hate you! I'm never going to speak to you again!" or "You ruin everything!" or "I don't care!" take comfort in the fact that, while you may be up all night feeling guilty, your child will undoubtedly sleep like a rock and wake up happy and loving.

Values That Last

One of the mistakes we all make is to avoid taking the time to really think through what we want our families to stand for. We don't stop to ask what values we hope our school-age children understand now in order to practice them later. Teaching our kids to make good decisions when the stakes are really high is much easier if they've had practice stating their beliefs and standing firm on non-life-and-death stuff. But the only way they learn to do that is to have us model and articulate the values we believe are most important.

Of course, teaching good values isn't something we can do in five easy steps, despite the promise of parenting-magazine headlines. You can rely on lectures, literature, or the litany of your particular faith to instill a sense of right and wrong, but unless you demonstrate caring, compassionate behavior, your kids won't absorb much. Even then you're usually left wondering if your children understand the importance of education or the gift of friendship or the importance of hard work. At an age when the "gimmes" can hit with a ferocious tenacity, it's often difficult to see past their obsession with stuff to the stuff inside.

I learned this one stifling summer day when the kids were about six and nine and had insisted on dragging me through a local street fair in search of hideous plastic toys they didn't need and fried foods that promised a future of occluded arteries. All I wanted to do was find a spot of shade, as far from the claustrophobic crush as possible. But as we neared the end of the throng, Nick shouted, "Look, Maddie! There's a jumpy thing! Can we go on it, Mama?"

Having already spent a small fortune on big nothings for the kids, I was loath to give in. "Oh, come on, guys," I sighed wearily. "I really want to go home now."

"Just one ride, Mom?" Maddie implored. "Please?"

I relented, worrying as I often did that I was giving in way too much, the perennial pushover. The dreaded word "spoiled" floated in the back of my headachy brain as they darted off toward what looked like a monstrous cherry tomato. Inside the Moonwalk, as it was billed, shoeless bouncers were free to leap and somersault for five frenzied minutes.

I stood on tiptoe alongside a group of anxious parents, all of us struggling to catch a glimpse of our kids as they hurtled past the grimy plastic windows. A small boy, no more than two, sat rigidly in the middle of the inflated floor, tears of terror streaming down his face. Projectile preschoolers, oblivious to this lone casualty, landed precariously close to him. Suddenly I saw Nick leap toward the little guy, fend off the bigger Moonwalkers, and grab his hand. Then, spotting Nick, Maddie came struggling over, too, taking the child's other hand and gently guiding him out to his grateful mother, who disappeared into the crowd. Pride pushed my headache to a back burner.

A few months later I wrote about this incident in my editor's column for *Parents* magazine, noting that "we never know if the messages of love and caring are getting through to our children until moments like these." A week or so after the magazine hit the newsstand, I received a long letter from the mother of the hapless Moonwalker, who happened to be a *Parents* reader. I don't remember her exact words, but she made my maternal pride-o-meter spike once more as she explained how grateful and impressed she had been by Maddie and Nick's generosity and compassion.

There's no doubt that my feelings were in direct proportion to my concern that I was failing to provide the kids with opportunities to give back. Yes, we would collect and distribute gifts for homeless children around the holidays, visit my housebound ninety-five-year-old aunt, make presents for assorted relatives and friends, but like Amy, whose kids were surrounded by affluence, I was keenly aware of the too-much-of-a-good-thing syndrome.

In *Too Much of a Good Thing,* Dan Kindlon describes "the holy trinity of child care": time, limits, and caring, or TLC. "Time—just being there for our kids, being around, being present, being available, spending time with our kids. Limits—being able to say no, incur our children's wrath, and push them to do things that are often difficult for them to do. And caring—taking an active interest in our children's lives, being willing to listen to what's on their minds and participate in their activities, even if they're not inherently interesting to us."[11]

Clearly, this definition of TLC should inform every stage of motherhood, but the last bit—the directive to show an interest in our kids' activities—has particular bearing on one of the many challenges of the early school years. This is the time of life when your child is likely to become infatuated with something you're just as likely to find excruciatingly dull. It could be bugs or basketball or Britney Spears. It will involve hours of cataloging of inventory, mind-numbing recitation of stats, and a seemingly insatiable appetite for more. Why kids this age collect is intimately connected with their effort to define who they are and what provides them with a sense of mastery or control. Your response to their passions can send important messages about respect, motivation, and the value of finding something in life that really lights your fire.

If you can't connect with your seven-year-old on the nuances of Nintendo, then it's critical to find some common ground, some way of opening up *your* life to him. One mom I met at a party recently described how cut off from her son's life she felt when his obsession with baseball became all-consuming. "I just couldn't get into it," she admitted. "I tried for a while, but all the stats about so-and-so's batting average or the team's latest trade made me want to throw myself down the stairs." Then she discovered that her son loved to garden. "I was very fussy about my flowers. I didn't want James to mess with the plants too much, but I realized that I had been handed a wonderful opportunity. The first time he yanked out a seedling, instead of a weed, I just took a really deep breath and showed him again what to look for. We've had one of the best summers in years planning and planting—and now waiting—for our vegetable garden to bear fruit. He swears he'll actually eat the broccoli!"

If you're the mother of more than one child, the challenge of connecting one-on-one is even greater, but the rewards may be more. Mary, who has four kids, recalled a trip she took with her then nine-year-old son: "There is one train ride I took with Peter to New York

City that I'll never forget. It was the dearest trip. I wrote every detail down. He'd share his headphones; he'd put them on me and say, 'Mom, listen to Will Smith.' He drew this Chinese symbol on my arm in pen that meant 'good woman.' Everything was about *us*."

The fun and sense of intimacy Mary experienced with her son was mirrored in the smiles flashed by several moms when I asked about this period in their mothering years. Many of them commented on how "entertaining," "funny," "energetic," "interesting," "passionate," "insightful" their kids were at this age. "They're just a blast to be with," Amy told me, her eyes bright with thoughts of her two boys, six and nine. "I love, love spending time with them. We always take our vacation as a family because Andy and I don't want to be apart from the kids."

"William makes me laugh every day. Just the way he expresses himself is so wonderful," Laurie kvelled when I asked her about her seven-year-old son. "Last weekend Jim and I took him to a party. He was a real gentleman all night, and as we were leaving the band started playing this song that had been our wedding song. So we started dancing out in the parking lot. William was walking with my sister, and he turned to her and said, 'It appears my parents are having a romantic moment.' We just cracked up!"

My friend Jane also felt that "latency is the best." Not only did she enjoy hanging out with her son, traveling with him, talking about the books he was reading or the friends he was making at school, but she discovered how proud she was to meet the parents of his friends and introduce herself by saying, "Hi! I'm Jesse's mom." Being the mom of this exuberant, bright, funny boy was a big part of how she defined herself. But as his ninth birthday approached, Jane experienced a deep and familiar sorrow. "My mom died when I was nine," she said. "So I do find that I look at Jesse and remember how it felt; I just can't help reliving that pain, even as I recognize how blessed I am to have my health and the promise of many more years as his mom. That's something my mother never experienced."

Our tendency to reexperience our childhoods and project our memories of the school years onto our kids intensifies during this stage in part because the memories are so much more accessible and vivid. Many of us can't recall much about our preschool-through-kindergarten years, but I'm certain you could rattle off the names of your second-, third-, fourth-, or fifth-grade teachers. More important, you can summon the thoughts and feelings, the joys and pain, that characterized your relationships with your own parents and siblings; trace how those relationships shaped who you are now; and consciously decide to mother your children in ways that re-create, recast, or reject the mothering you received.

Sometimes the ghosts that haunt our relationships with our kids are benign. We welcome, even strive to rekindle—through holiday rituals, family stories, "in" jokes—the positive connections we felt with our parents and siblings. Just as often, we remember painful times, when our parents' sins of omission or our siblings' cruelty left darker shadows that trigger complicated reactions to our own kids' behavior. There's a reason we refer to skeletons in the closet, and even more cause to leave them there. But it's far better to take advantage of this relatively easy phase in our children's development to work on our own issues than to wait until the preteen or adolescent years, when life gets, well, decidedly more interesting.

Sibling Rivalry Redux

In part because we can recall our own family dynamics with greater clarity, sibling rivalry can be particularly painful during this period. For one thing, the battles are uglier; even if your kids skirmished occasionally during the preschool years, you could separate, distract, even comfort two warring preschoolers. But when their weapons of ego destruction include emotional missiles aimed with unforgiving precision, then your reaction is likely to flip from mildly irritated to irate. Those ghosts reappear, your stomach drops, and as your nine-year-old sneers and calls his slightly pudgy younger sister "a fat cow," you consider clocking him with a lamp.

I'll never forget interviewing a young boy for a *Good Morning America* segment we were doing on couch-potato kids. According to his parents, Derek was caught in a vicious cycle of gaining weight and then finding exercise harder to do. He was suffering socially, and they were really worried. But when the interview began, Derek maintained that he wasn't teased very much at school. "But your mom and dad mentioned that you're often the last picked for teams, " I probed.

"No, I get picked first," he said, without a trace of concern.

"But do the kids at school tease you?" I asked.

"No, not really," he insisted.

At this point I began to panic. The segment we had pitched on the "lonely, stressful life of a couch-potato kid" seemed pretty conflict-free—not the kind of heart-wrenching scenario you fly across the country to shoot.

Then I asked if his sisters ever teased him.

"Yes," he said so softly I had to ask him to repeat his answer.

"What do they call you?"

"They call me 'fatty,'" he whispered as the floodgates opened and the tears streamed down his freckled cheeks. He cried so hard we stopped the cameras.

In some ways emotional bullying is the worst, but physical brawls aren't much fun, either. Constance, who lives in the United Kingdom with two sons very close in age, described their fighting as "pretty constant," "very physical," and seemingly more intense by the month. "The days when there isn't a major flare-up are wonderful days!" she remarked. "I don't know if they were two girls whether it would be as physical. It's just hitting, slapping, hair pulling, screaming, and you learn very early on to distinguish between the screams that are serious and those that are attention-grabbing."

Even so, we agreed that it's often hard to tell. I remember taking the stairs of our house three at a time when Maddie's shrieks of "Ni-i-i-c-k! Stop!" propelled me to her rescue. I blasted into their room, expecting to find a bloody lip or bared knuckles only to discover the kids seated three feet apart on the floor, glaring at each other. Asked what had made her scream like a banshee, Maddie responded, "Nick was humming. And it's really annoying!" And she was serious. Breathing often qualified as throwing the gauntlet; even looking askance at the other could elicit a reaction worthy of an enraged rhino.

When Nick reached second grade and Maddie was struggling with preteen hell, their battles took a decidedly meaner turn. Nick was more easily bruised by Maddie's finely honed barbs. There were fewer physical fights, but the pain they inflicted on each other was sharper, more lasting. Their battles made me heartsick because as much as I knew I needed to let go, I held on to the fantasy that they would be loyal and loving friends.

Around that time, Nancy Samalin published *Loving Each One Best: A Caring and Practical Approach to Raising Siblings.* Her basic message was simple: The goal in settling sibling disputes is to solve a problem, not to force kids to love each other.[12] As she wisely advised me when I asked her about Maddie and Nick, "You can't legislate love. You can only encourage cooperation."

How you choose to do that depends in large measure on the ages of your kids, the ways you discipline in general, and your goals. If you're expecting happy, loving interactions all the time, you're bound to be disappointed. But if you want them to figure out a way to share the remote control or to stay out of each other's toys or to stop calling each other names, then you need to treat their relationship like any other discipline challenge: Here are the rules, here are the consequences—and don't tell me who started it.

The other thing to avoid at all costs is the *F* word. "No fair!" is the clarion cry of all sibling battles during the school years. And they're right. You can never be fair. You can never cut the chocolate cake into pieces that are exactly the same size and frosted with equal generosity. Even if you give Big Sister a gift that's exactly the same as that of her darling sibling, one of them is bound to detect a microscopic variation. "They watch to the millimeter what each one is getting," Amy told me, laughing despite the fact that her sons' rivalry drove her nuts. "You can never be fair. Never. Ever."

We can't be fair, because our kids don't want to be seen as exactly the same. They want to be treated differently, loved for who they are, indulged in the kind of attention a slightly larger piece of chocolate cake promises to confer—but obviously does not. So refrain from buying matching outfits or the same toys in slighter different sizes. Dole out equal praise for very unequal kids and unique skill sets and you're apt to hear "That's not fair!" far less often.

The other key to surviving sibling battles is to recognize how impossible it is to remain completely impartial. Unless you grew up an only child—and even then, there were probably plenty of other people vying for your mom's attention—you're likely to relive the irritations, anger, and sometimes deep pain of your own family rivalries. I'll never forget the visceral response I had one morning when Nick was about five and he came into my room to show me a pathetic pack of magic cards that Maddie had "sold" him.

"Maddie sold those to you, honey?" I asked, swallowing hard against a distinctly nasty taste. "For how much?"

"Eight dollars," Nick answered brightly.

"Eight dollars! That's your allowance for four months—not to mention that those cards aren't worth more than eight cents!" Before I could stop myself, I charged into Maddie's room, wrestling with such intense feelings of outrage and hurt that my eyes were watering.

"Maddie, how could you make Nick pay you eight dollars for those lousy magic cards!" I shouted. "I am really upset and disappointed."

"But, Mom, it was a game. Look, we're playing store." Maddie was visibly stunned by my anger, and I watched her lip tremble as she pointed to a pile of Monopoly money, a calculator, and a cardboard "cash register" arranged on her bed.

"Oh, sweetheart," I said, sighing miserably. "I misunderstood. I'm very sorry." As I hugged her I felt suddenly depleted. How could I explain to my eight-year-old that what she had just witnessed was the result of years of being suckered into "deals" proffered by my older siblings—bargains that inevitably resulted in my getting the short end of the stick. My antennae shot straight up whenever I thought Nick was being taken advantage of, just as Steve, the eldest of four, admits he often sides with Maddie when Nick invades her privacy.

Disciplining as a Team

One of my favorite Charles Addams cartoons depicts a father and his clone of a son, dressed exactly alike, sporting the same eyeglasses, looking back in surprise at a mother/daughter team, also mirror images of each other. They, in turn, are looking back in surprise at the dad and his pint-sized twin. During this phase of our kids' lives, we're often as shocked by their Mini-Me-ness as we are by their independence. Someone comments that your son "has his dad's charm" or that your daughter is "a math whiz like her mom," and you begin to see the good and the not-so-good qualities in your spouse shaping your child's personality in critical ways.

One mom complained that the chore wars in her house were much worse now that her boys had reached the age when "sitting around with Dad, telling fart jokes and getting chips all over the rug, is a regular riot." Although her husband gave lip service to the idea of keeping the house tidy, he clearly found the boys'-club camaraderie irresistible. "It's not just the mess they make that bothers me," she confessed. "I think he's setting a really bad example in terms of showing me some respect."

Steve would often admonish me to stand by him when one of the kids drove him over the edge. Having reprimanded Maddie one night for talking back to him, he paced angrily in our room, insisting that I speak to her on his behalf. I confess that I was a wimp. I didn't agree with his way of handling her back talk, which I felt was authoritarian and rigid, but I knew this was not the time to criticize. On the other hand, I wasn't willing to "march in there and tell her that she needs to show her father respect!" as Steve kept insisting I do. I'm sure he sensed I was not on his side, which pissed him off even more. When I finally did go into Maddie's room to smooth things out, I found myself somewhat guiltily whispering to Maddie that "Dad had a bad day," as though to excuse his anger. Let me say right now this was neither mature nor helpful.

A few nights later I happened upon Steve playing a new video game with Nick that featured the kind of blood-and-guts violence I absolutely deplored. "What game is that?" I asked hotly.

"Oh, it's really cool, Mom," Nick answered as a hail of bullets from his machine gun ripped through Steve's combatant.

"A guy at work gave it to me," Steve added, eyes fixed on the screen.

"I don't want Nick to play games like that!" I shouted over the din. "Turn it off!"

"Oh, Mom!" Nick whined. "C'mon. Paul and Alex—everyone has this game."

"It's not that bad," Steve said weakly. But, sensing the hail of bullets shooting from my eyeballs, he turned it off.

Although Steve and I had occasionally slipped into the Good Cop/Bad Cop trap during the kids' toddler and preschool years, hot-button issues like whether to let one of the kids sleep in our bed or how much TV time to allow or how to handle tantrums rarely pitted us against each other. We both agreed that spanking didn't work; neither of us subscribed to the Clean Plate Club; and we were equally inept when it came to enforcing a rigid bedtime. But once the discipline challenges took on a more moralistic tone, once the kids' attitudes, values, basic *goodness* seemed to be at stake, I often felt as though we struggled with teamwork. We could agree that Nick had an infuriating tendency to have the last word in an argument or that Maddie's homework habits regularly sucked us into late-night screaming matches, but when it came time to lay down the law, we often had very different styles.

I wasn't always the softie, but I tended to have a much longer fuse, especially when it came to back talk or homework meltdowns. Steve was incredibly patient to a point, but during an argument he would occasionally lose it—suddenly and loudly. He hated to yell and I hated to hear it, but we rarely sat down to discuss better approaches.

To make matters worse, Maddie and Nick, like most school-age kids, had learned to play us off each other. "But Mom lets us" or "Dad said I could" are guaranteed triangulators, but they're also an inevitable part of this phase. We learned quickly to check out their claims (it was amazing how quickly rules were "remembered" differently as soon as I picked up the phone to call Steve), but it took a little longer to accept that our having different styles wasn't necessarily a bad thing. As Harriet Lerner wisely notes in her book *The Mother Dance,* "I would expect some disagreement about child rearing between any two parents, unless they're fused at the hip and share a common brain and bloodline."[13]

Still, it's infuriating when the man you love most in the world says or does something that undermines your authority or, as one mom said, "when his lack of judgment makes you wonder if he's channeling Adam Sandler." The mother of two boys, Kerry shook her head in disbelief as she described an evening when one of her sons had come home with a note from his teacher: "We were talking to Austin about his behavior; he is a bit of a class clown. And I'm saying how it's fine to be friendly and jovial but that he needs to pick the time and place, and Chuck jumps in with this story about when he was in fourth grade and how he called his teacher a doofus. I just looked at him to say, 'I cannot believe you are telling Austin this!' I was furious."

What followed was a long conversation about what kinds of experiences it was okay to share with their children and the messages that Kerry and Chuck felt were central to the values of their family. (They included a sense of humor, something Kerry is proud to say she has in abundance.) "That particular argument was a real drop-dead moment;

it stopped us in our tracks. We had never had to talk about what to tell the kids about our pasts before, and it forced us to do just that."

Mary, who has three boys and an older daughter, admitted that discussing discipline issues with her husband was extremely difficult and had had a profound effect on their relationship: "Bill has a problem communicating discipline. He never had to be disciplined because he was such a good kid, so he just doesn't know how. Not that I was so sure, either. But when the kids got to be about nine, I felt like I was constantly saying to Bill, 'You need to talk to them about such and such.' And he would inevitably say, 'Okay, just give me a day. I haven't seen them.' So a day would go by and he still wouldn't have addressed their behavior. I think it stressed our marriage."

It also probably stressed the kids. There's ample research that shows how parental fighting, even bickering over discipline differences, is likely to lead to more acting out or to withdrawal. Even children who play one parent against another don't really want to get away with it. They don't want to control the emotional reins in the family or to suffer the pain of thinking they're the cause of their parents' conflicts. If you're constantly blaming your child for *causing* the strife between you, think again. Chances are there's something much deeper and more entrenched than your child's picky eating habits that's leading to constant battles at the dinner table. And while it may be enough to focus on practical solutions, the more you begin to wonder if you have a troubled kid, the more you blame your child for the constant battles with your spouse, the greater the chances you need help with your marriage, not with discipline.[14]

When my friend Jane found herself locking horns with her husband over their son's homework, believing that Ivan was way too tough on Jesse when it came to his writing, she tried to take a step back and understand where Ivan's intensity was coming from. "There was this pivotal moment when Jesse got his scores back on his third-grade aptitude tests. Jesse got 100s on everything, except the writing. And he got an 86 or something close to 90 on that. So I thought, 'That's great.' But Ivan launched into this speech about how Jesse should work more on his journal, that he has to really practice his writing, until Jesse shouted, 'You're constantly telling me I have to do my best every moment!' I realized that this was a real difference between Ivan and me. But when we talked about it, he revealed that when he was

Jesse's age, if he brought home a report card with even one A–, his mother's only comment would be, 'So, why didn't you get an A?'"

Our own family cultures are reflected every day in the way we interact with our kids. If you came from a household where getting A's or cleaning your plate or playing aggressive sports earned you attention and love, then it's going to be very hard to parent alongside a partner whose family embraced different values. The goal should be not to agree on everything or to win arguments over discipline but to accept—as your children will—that you're very different people, with different expectations. Knowing what are the top three most important rules for your spouse (and making sure he knows what tops your list) can defuse all kinds of potential land mines.

Susie, a working mom with two kids, credits her French husband, who does all the cooking, with teaching her to handle picky eating by simply ignoring it. "I would be bribing the kids with M&M's," she admitted, "but Daniel, because he was raised to appreciate the importance of good food, just serves up the sole meunière and if they don't eat it, tough. There have been times when I think he goes too far, when I definitely would have backed off, but I know how important this is to him, so I defer to his approach."

Steve's many strengths as a father include his amazing calm during crises, his unwavering generosity, his tenacity, devotion, and passion. He's much better than I am when it comes to helping one of the kids on a school project, he's more patient during late-night meltdowns, and he has a much better singing voice. I have my strengths, too. What we share is a willingness to draw attention to these gifts—to raise a glass and thank each other openly and often. "Here's to Mom for taking such great care of us!" Steve will say from his end of the table. "Thank Dad for working so hard to make this trip possible," I'll coach the kids—and mean it.

One of the nice things about this phase of motherhood is that it often affords us a little more time to nurture our marriage. You may feel a bit out of practice, distracted by the many pulls on your attention, but your child's burgeoning independence and increased time out of the nest make it possible to find ways to be alone. One spring, when Nick and Maddie were about six and nine, respectively, Steve and I managed to escape to Scotland for a much needed break. At one point we traveled along a road called the Rest and Be Thankful Pass.

None of our guidebooks explained the name, although the serene view provided a clue, but we took the pass at its word and stopped. We talked about Maddie and Nick, about each other and our almost seventeen years together, about the relatives and friends we loved, about our jobs, and about the many small, good things that punctuated our lives.

We also talked about aspects of our life we wanted to improve, about our hopes for our family in the coming years. As I recall, this prompted me to launch into a familiar speech about feeling guilty that I didn't have more time with the kids and about our need to cut back on commitments and the importance of family meals—and, and, and . . . Steve cut me off me with a hard look and a gentle admonition: "You know, Annie, you're an amazing mother. You really are." It was not the first time he had said this to me, but it was one of the few times I actually listened. Instead of responding with some self-effacing litany of "Yes, but . . ." retorts, I closed my eyes briefly and thanked him.

Most of the mothers I know are amazing—not perfect, not even close to perfect, but energetic, creative, passionate, wise, and far more competent than any of them ever admit. When our children turn seven, eight, or nine years old, we reach a motherhood midpoint of sorts. Yes, we will always love, anguish over, boast about our children, but in the years ahead, our pull on their lives will diminish dramatically. At this bend in the road, it pays to slow down long enough to gauge the distance we've traveled, to appreciate how much our driving has improved—as has our ability to hand over the wheel to Dad more. There are so many aspects of mothering we take for granted at this stage in our development that we tend to fly down the road without ever glancing in the rearview mirror. But that view is critical to the trip ahead. The more we can learn from the mistakes we've made along the way, the easier the preteen and adolescent years will be.

Accepting our children for who they are, letting go of fantasies or expectations of perfection—in them and in ourselves—is a critical challenge during this stage of motherhood. Just as they have had to adjust to the much bigger, often overwhelming world of "real school," we have been forced to let them find their way, to make decisions, forge friendships, take on responsibilities, formulate ideas, and articulate their values independent of us. At a time when our children often want more privacy, we may crave a deeper connection—not only with them but with an image of ourselves as central to their lives. Relinquishing that role is never easy, but when it goes hand in hand with the strength to set limits and the patience to really listen, our children benefit in ways that last a lifetime.

Stage 6

⋙

Living in the Gray Zone

The Preteen Years, Ten to Thirteen

Depending on how you look at (and live) them, the preteen years can be either the shortest or the longest chapter in your mothering story. "There is no such thing as a preadolescent," an editor friend of mine declared when I asked her about life with her ten-year-old son. "Ten is the new teen! He started fifth grade and it's as if he's plunged into high school. It's such a radical change from fourth grade. Oh my God!" Several other mothers concurred that their children, especially girls, seemed to catapult directly from playing with Barbies to wanting to dress like Barbie. In their case, the "tweens" felt like a long and scary prequel to the teen years.

During this stage of motherhood, the progression-regression dance our children perform daily can throw into question not only practical concerns like rules and routines but more profound issues like trust and boundaries. The challenge to know when to be your child's pal and when to assert yourself, when to push and when to protect, forces many mothers to question with renewed intensity their roles at work, their involvement in their child's school, and their connections with other parents, with their husband, and, of course, with their child.

It takes an ego of steel to navigate the preteen years, because one day your kid is going to wake up uncomfortable in her own body. And when she stands with one foot in childhood, the other in early adulthood, and struggles to maintain her balance, the person she will grab onto with a desperate, clawing intensity is you. Which may explain why one research study found that only 38 percent of women with children between the ages of thirteen and eighteen said they felt motherhood was very often rewarding, compared with 50 percent who had children in elementary school and 60 percent with preschoolers.[1]

I'm sorry to say, I would have to agree. For one thing, there's no consensus about how to handle tweens; you're as likely to be advised to empathize with your preteen and to reward positive behavior as you are to be told to stand firm and set rigid limits. Coverage of this age group in the leading parenting magazines is minimal, and compared with the growing list of books about teens, there's very little out there about eleven- and twelve-year-olds. At a time when you feel as though you're driving through a dense fog, the lines on the road can be frustratingly haphazard and difficult to follow.

A few years ago I met with a group of moms in St. Louis. Most of them had young children, but Sally, the mother of three, had a ten-year-old daughter who was beginning to test her limits, to strive for more independence. When the moms with babies and toddlers at home complained about their struggles with tantrums or toilet training, Sally let out an audible sigh. "I guess I used to stress out about potty training," she said. "And I certainly wouldn't have believed it if someone had said, 'Well, wait until she's ten,' because my thought would have been, 'Ten-year-olds bathe themselves, put on their own clothes, even tie their shoes.' But it's so much harder now."

The preteen years can feel a lot like the preview for a disturbing movie you're forced to watch—even though you've paid for a comedy or a heartwarming tale of love and reconciliation. You sit in the dark, bombarded by loud and ugly flashes of conflict, and when the trailer ends, you whisper to your husband, "Let's skip that one!" Of course, you have no choice but to live through your very own full-length teen feature, a movie that guarantees plenty of drama. But it's wrong to assume that the script will be devoid of laughs and love. In my experience—and from the stories I've heard from dozens of other moms— the preteen years are, like many movie previews, an exaggeration of what's to come.

Of course, it's very hard not to believe a trailer. Your child asks to walk to school alone or to get her ears pierced, and suddenly you're projecting an image of multiple piercings, blue hair, and *Night of the*

Living Dead eye makeup on her sixth-grade face. "I definitely blow up little things on a screen of the future," Dorothy confessed. "When he was little and wouldn't stay in his bed, he would be pounding on our door and I would think, 'This is the kid who wants the car so badly. In my mind, he was suddenly seventeen years old and saying, 'Give me those car keys!'"

Dorothy's tendency to "futurize" (and/or to "catastrophize") was echoed by Sara, a funny, ambitious mother of a twelve-year-old boy. Like Dorothy, she was very close to her one and only, and as a working mom, she took pride in the fact that her son had developed an ability early on to be independent and self-sufficient. Even so, when the weekend rolled around, she was loath to leave him alone. "It's really kind of nuts, because Avery hasn't had a full-time baby-sitter in a couple of years. And he's often home with our cleaning woman during the week—and, believe me, she isn't watching him like a hawk." Even so, on a recent Sunday Sara hesitated about leaving him at home while she went for a walk. "Avery was watching a video, so Charlie and I decided we'd go out, leave him alone for all of about an hour. When I asked him if he would be okay for a little while alone, he rolled his eyes and said, 'What are you worried about, Mom? That I might watch the porn channel or eat some food containing white flour?'"

Sara laughed as she told this story, but there were many more moms of preteens I spoke to who seemed frustrated, perplexed, or truly terrified. Jan, a mother of five, had boasted that her kids learned to be independent early "because they had to." She compared her household with that of her close friend, the mother of an only daughter: "She worries about every little thing—the girl's friends, her diet. I mean, at my house it's so different. You're hungry? There's the peanut butter and jelly." Yet when I asked Jan about her son's preadolescent years (he was then thirteen), her mien changed dramatically. "He's pretty mature for his age; he takes acting and he's in a band. We've always had a great relationship. I have fun with him, with his friends, we clown around. But now he's suffering from this testosterone poisoning. It's like, what *is* this? It's really kind of scary. His behavior has really thrown us into a tailspin."

Volatile and Not Always Nice

Sandra, a single mom with two daughters, compared her eldest's fifth- and sixth-grade years as "living *The Exorcist*." Shaking her head, she seemed to marvel at the fact that she and her daughter survived it at all. "I mean, I just felt as though Christa—who had been my sweet, obedient little girl—suddenly woke up with her head spinning around. I just wasn't prepared. Not at all."

What bothered Sandra the most was the unpredictability of her daughter's moods, coupled with the sense that she was constantly taking one step forward, only to fall back a moment later. "I would think, 'Okay, she's growing up,'" Sandra recalled. "And I'd give Christa more responsibilities at home or expect her to remember something—and then she'd be crying and carrying on like a baby the next minute. I thought I would lose my mind."

Having gone through the same developmental cha-cha with Maddie, I thought perhaps girls were more unpredictable than boys, but several moms convinced me otherwise. Dorothy, who lives and works in New York City, described how her son acts five years old one minute and fifteen the next: "The velocity of change is pretty astounding. It can happen within the same half hour. He'll take down all of his Beanie Babies and put them in a basket and carry them around or fold them in a sheet and walk around the house with them, and the next minute he's out there dancing in some cropped-off little T-shirt to the *School of Rock* soundtrack."

In addition to the "velocity of change," there's often a volatility and intensity mothers say they associate with the toddler years. "I just never know what's going to set him off," a friend said of her eleven-year-old son. "He can be sweet and easygoing one minute and a nightmare the next."

It's exhausting to navigate a minefield, never certain when you might trip the wire and set off an explosion. I spent much of Maddie's preadolescence with my shoulders tensed up around my ears and my antennae quivering in anticipation of a major mood swing. When your daughter freaks out because the shirt she's "gotta, gotta have right now" is still in the washing machine, or your son rants and raves when he realizes at 11 p.m. that his French quiz is *demain,* not next week, you're likely to blame those "raging hormones." And certainly the approach of puberty brings about dramatic changes in a child's endocrine system, changes that profoundly affect his ability to regulate his emotions. But it may actually be your preteen's brain that's short-circuiting, simply because the area that helps control emotions and make judgments (the prefrontal cortex) isn't as developed as the limbic system, where emotions originate.[2] The wet shirt or possibility of a bad grade on a test throws her into a tailspin because she can't stop and say, "Okay, this isn't the end of the world. I have a drawer full of other shirts," or "This is only one quiz out of eight we'll take this year. I'll set my alarm an hour early tomorrow and do the best I can." And while you may be tempted to use your own superior prefrontal cortex to offer solutions, don't. Any attempt to proffer advice during the heat of a meltdown will be about as effective as banging your cerebral cortex against a wall.

It's also crucial at this stage to let your preteen fall on her face once in a while, to muscle through a problem without a guaranteed bailout from Mom or Dad. Natural consequences are rarely easy to enforce, but they can work wonders during this critical time in your child's life and foster a sense of mastery and responsibility. Even as I write this, I'm well aware of how abysmally I failed in this regard, how often I leapt to the rescue when Maddie or Nick was teetering on the edge of a cliff. Sometimes the cry for help was fairly minimal ("Mom! I left my math homework on my desk. Could you please, please drop it off at school?"), but on other occasions my rescue effort led to late-night "helping" with an English paper and the midnight thanks followed swiftly by "I suck at writing. I could never have done this without you."

In her book *Spoiling Childhood: How Well-Meaning Parents Are Giving Children Too Much—But Not What They Need,* Diane Ehrensaft describes the tendency many of today's moms have to check out a book from the library (guilty!) or go online to help their child with a research paper (guilty!) or to automatically purchase a replacement baseball glove when the fairly new one gets lost (guilty!) or to dash out to buy a last-minute birthday card for a relative because their kids have ignored frequent reminders (guilty!).[3] As the title of her book implies, a tendency to be overinvolved in our children's lives often stems from the most loving of intentions: We want our kids to be happy. And when we see them swinging wildly (and *un*happily) between babyish dependence and more mature independence, it's natural and understandable to want to play Tarzan to their helpless Jane.

The problem, of course, is that when we help too much, we deprive them of a sense of mastery, of truly owning what they produce or create. The good grade Maddie earned on an in-class essay was so much sweeter than the better grade she got for a paper I had proofread or critiqued. Every constructive bit of criticism—no matter how minor—chipped away at her ability to say, "I did this all myself." As tough as it would have been to say, "You know, honey, I don't want to read your paper now. I'll read it after you get it back," I probably would have bolstered Maddie's self-confidence far more effectively had I done so.

Helping Versus Holding On

On the flip side of the overinvolvement coin is a reluctance to let go, a deep ambivalence about everything from physical separation ("Can I walk to school by myself?") to emotional independence ("That's private, Mom!"). The first time Maddie asked to walk to school alone, she was in the sixth grade, and as I recall, the dialogue went something like this:

"Can I walk to school by myself?"

"Not yet."

"Why not?"

"I don't think you're ready."

"I am ready, Mom!"

"Yes, but I'm not ready for you to be ready."

This last line didn't really escape my lips, of course. First I blamed several wide avenues too hazardous to cross during rush hour. Then, when the question came up again, about a week later, I said that maybe, when daylight saving time was over, she could tackle the bus ride and short walk *to* school in the morning, but not the trip home. When the question came up the next time, I passed the buck ("If it's okay with Dad, you can"), knowing full well that Steve was even more protective than I. By this time I was leaning toward a yes, but when Steve asked,

"Why does she *need* to go by herself?" I didn't have a ready answer. "She doesn't *need* to, but she wants to. She feels she's ready."

Poor Maddie. We must have gone back and forth about this at least a dozen times before a psychologist friend hit on an ingenious solution. "Why don't you have Maddie show Steve how to take the bus." I suppose I should explain that my husband loathes the bus. It had been so long since he had actually boarded one that he had no idea how much the fare was, nor did he realize that 90 percent of New Yorkers were using MetroCards in lieu of exact change, or that the stop near Maddie's school was a mere two blocks away. The teach-Dad approach worked brilliantly: Steve, duly impressed by Maddie's confidence and competence, agreed she could go to school alone, and after challenging her to a dozen "what if" scenarios, we launched her, armed with a brand-new bus pass, into the bad Big Apple. Only when an hour had passed and I knew that the school would have called to report her missing had she not shown up did I take a shower.

Was I ready for her to be ready? The answer is yes, but only because I still had Nick's little hand to hold. When he pushed to walk alone to school—even earlier than Maddie had, of course—I caved more quickly. For one thing, I had seen it coming. More important, I had survived my first summer with both children off at sleepaway camp— a watershed six weeks that had been excruciating much of the time. Not long after they had left, I made the mistake of spending a week-end in the country with a friend and her ten-year-old son, Matt, whom I kept calling Nick. Eventually, I stopped apologizing and announced, "Look, Matt. For this weekend, you *are* Nick." It had hurt so much to watch him romping in the pool with his mom that I was thrilled when Matt asked me to sing him a song before bed. I couldn't bring myself to sing one of Nick's favorite songs, but I ran through a few of the B-list favorites, fighting against my constricting throat.

I also wrote letters every day, even if I had nothing to report. The process of finding a cute card, sitting quietly somewhere and thinking about the kids, then filling every corner with choice inanities was extremely comforting. Not since I was sixteen and madly in love with a guy who lived far away had I felt this kind of loss and yearning. I lit-erally counted the days until the camp bus pulled back into town.

For Constance, who lives in the United Kingdom, an Easter holiday

break to a tiny fishing village in Cornwall afforded her two boys a delicious taste of independence. But Constance recalled only the bite of
panic and a profound loneliness. "It was a huge moment for me, actually," she said, emotion flooding her eyes. "We got to the house and I
opened the front door and the kids just flew out and disappeared. Of
course, that's what all the children do there. But when I got to the sta-
tion later to pick up my husband from the train, I was really upset. I
blurted out, 'I don't know where my boys are!' and he looked at me as
though I was mad and said, 'Fantastic!' He just didn't understand at
all. I know it sounds pathetic. There were no physical dangers, but it
was the first time I realized that they were their own people, doing
something that didn't involve me. I don't want to sound selfish, but I
just felt lonely and not needed, and it was a real shock to me."

One could argue that every stage of motherhood is characterized by
the conflicting desire to push and to coddle, to give our kids wings
but clip them ever so slightly. But during their preteen years, our
awareness of childhood's end is always present. It's like the fortieth-
birthday card I received that read, "Turning 40 isn't the end of the
world, but you can see it from there."

Yearning to Be Home More

The result of this consciousness, for several mothers of preteens, is a
fierce yearning to be home more, to splurge on that European trip
now—not when the kids are grown and out of the house—to dramatically change the way they live their lives. Dorothy, whose son attended
sleepaway camp for three summers and loved it, decided that he would
only go for one month, rather than two, the summer he turned eleven.
"I decided when I visited him last summer and I thought, you know,
'Okay, that's enough of that experience. I want him around more. I'll
take my vacation during August with him.' Because I know from even
little trips we've taken together that he's at an age when he's just soaking up every experience. And I just thought, 'Oh, man. It's fleeting.
It's slipping away.'"

I experienced similar feelings of sadness, nostalgia, anxiety, even
mild dread as Maddie's sixth-grade year came to an end. Having
worked full-time throughout my children's lives, I was definitely at

the top of my game. I had been the editor in chief of *Parents* magazine for ten years and had put together a dream team of editors and art directors. I loved my colleagues, believed in the mission of the magazine, learned something daily from the articles we published, was well compensated, even somewhat well known. But when I got home from work, Maddie had already disappeared into her room. Nick, then seven, was likely to greet me at the door with a big hug and an uncontrollable need to share the details of his day. If I was dumb enough to ask Maddie, "How was school?" or, worse, "What did you do in school today?" the pat responses ("Fine" or "Nothing") felt sadder and emptier than they had before.

Although there had never been a year—make that a week—during which I had not played the familiar work-versus-family-you-can't-do-it-all theme song, this was the first time in my life that I began to feel I was running out of time. The fact that Steve had just started a new and highly demanding job made the clock tick even louder, especially on nights when I had to work late and would call to explain miserably that the kids should eat dinner without us.

"Okay. Bye," would be about all I'd get from Maddie as she hung up the phone and closed the window on my attempt to connect. I didn't blame her. I'm not a big phoner myself. But I knew that she needed me in ways she would never articulate directly. I could have asked a hundred open-ended questions and never have elicited more than a series of monosyllabic responses, which made me ache to be around her more, not less. Knowing that seventh grade was typically the nadir in terms of social angst, I began to consider other alternatives. I wanted to write this book, badly, but I certainly didn't want to compromise my already limited free time. As I launched this project, it launched me through a door I had only cracked open in years past.

I wish I had saved the two-column list I made one memorable Sunday morning at Steve's prompting. "Write down all of the pluses of your work now and all of the pluses associated with staying home and writing a book," he suggested. Under "Current job," I managed to list about a dozen concrete "pros." Under "Stay home," I could summon only three: "More time for kids. More couple time. More time for myself." Granted, those were the Big Three, but my failure of imagination underscored my ambivalence and anxiety. When a friend, a fellow magazine editor and writer, came for dinner that night and I confided my plan, she was unabashedly envious and enthusiastic. "Oh, my God!" she gushed. "You are so lucky! I wish I could do that." We went upstairs so I could show her the guest room I hoped to make my office. "This is perfect!" she continued as we stood in the small, dark space. As she regaled me with all the benefits of working from home in this quiet, upstairs aerie, all I could think of was Sara Crewe in *The Little Princess* or the mad, attic-bound wife of Rochester in *Jane Eyre*.

The week I told my boss and staff my plan to take a few years off to write this book was marked by meetings that started on a professionally even keel and inevitably dissolved into weepy hugs. More than once I phoned Steve to whisper, "Are you sure this is a good idea? Do you think anyone would ever hire me again?" More than once I felt a sense of panic—never more than when my wonderful art director put her arm around my shoulders and said, "You know, you'll never have this again. This is really special." She was right. It's very hard to find a team of coworkers as amazing as the women I worked with at that time—not to mention a job that was so compatible with my role as a mom. But I was still convinced that if I didn't take this opportunity to be home more, to strengthen my relationship with my kids, I would never have *that* again, either.

All of these feelings came back recently when I interviewed an old friend, a woman who had lost her high-profile job about three years earlier. On the way to lunch I recalled seeing Sarah not long after she had been fired, when her anger and determination to fight her way back into the game generated palpable heat. I knew she had been busy with a variety of impressive freelance and consulting projects, but I also knew she had turned down several prestigious job offers. Having always thrived in the spotlight, Sarah at this point had been quietly working from home and spending time with her daughter, Eliza, for a lot longer than I had ever imagined she would.

"Well, it's funny," she explained. "Mine's an unusual case, because I've always worked. And I had no desire when Eliza was younger to be home. I really wasn't torn the way so many of my friends were. But when I lost my job, Eliza was about ten. And a month or so after I had been home, we were driving someplace and she cracked a stupid joke and then I cracked an even stupider joke and we were laughing loudly and she said, 'You know, Mom, you've actually become quite entertaining since you were fired.' And then, about a month after that, we were having some argument and Eliza said, 'Look. You think you know me, but you don't know me as well as you think you do. But that's okay, because I don't know you as well as I should. So now is a time when we should really get to know each other better, because if we really understand each other, we're definitely not likely to have as many arguments.'" Sarah's characteristically animated face and hands suddenly stilled. She looked up and said, "That's when I stopped looking for a job."

The window Sarah realized might have been permanently shut had been thrown wide open by Eliza. Not that there wouldn't have been opportunities to connect, but—as Sarah sensed—her daughter was telling her straight out that she wanted her around more. When a few months later a nasty rumor was circulated about Eliza in school and she called Sarah to meet her and walk her home, the emergency hot chocolate and "good long talk" they had that afternoon felt like an unexpected gift. "Would she have talked to me the same way had I been working at my old job and staggered in around seven?" Sarah mused. "I really doubt she would have said what she did four hours later. I suspect that months would have gone by before she said anything. That's the tricky thing with kids this age, which is not to say people shouldn't work, but things pop up when they pop up."

For Dorothy, the sense that she would miss something, not know what was going on, or fail to connect at some critical time made her feel increasingly insecure about herself as a mom. "I feel way less sure about the right thing to do. I think every mom, if she's really honest, goes through these hard, dark nights of the soul. I feel that more these days. In the past there was always something I could do—buy him the funny little thing, tell him a story—and I could enter into his world, transform a moment into a common experience. Now I'm not so sure I know the thing that's going to delight him."

Of course, it's often a fantasy that your chances of connecting with your preteen increase in direct proportion to the hours you spend warming up the hearth at home. Don't forget, it's your child's job to push you away at this age, to guard secrets, forge new friendships, figure out who the hell he is, often in direct opposition to you.

As many times as I managed to "be there" for Maddie during her preteen years, she was just as likely to be elsewhere. The phone was permanently attached to her head, often in tandem with an online chat or a must-see television show. If there was a sound to signal a child's entry into the preteen years, it would be the slam of a door. Deb, who often picks up her son at Nick's school to drive him to various sports activities, shook her head when I asked how Jack was doing. "I have no idea! We could spend hours together and I wouldn't have a clue. He doesn't tell me anything." Deb didn't feel hostility from her son; what upset her was the sheer suddenness of the shift to silence. It was as though a Plexiglas shield had descended between her and her highly gregarious, easygoing boy. "I'm shut out. I'm really shut out."

Marie, who lives in a suburb of Chicago, sounded the same bell when I asked about her relationship with her two boys. "My sons? They just clam up. They won't speak. It used to be a very easy conversation: How is everything? What did you do today? Now all I get is 'Fine,' and then they go to their room."

For Constance, who works part-time, the most frustrating afternoons were those she orchestrated specifically to be home with her kids, only to find her efforts rebuffed. "My husband and I work funny hours so we can have two afternoons off to be home with the children after school. And inevitably I have these visions of baking a cake together or playing some sort of game, and the last thing they want me to do is ask about things they're up to. They want to be in their bedrooms doing whatever they want to do. So I'm sitting downstairs thinking, 'I left the office, even though I'm not finished with my work, so I could be here, and nobody wants me here.' But, of course, that's the point: It's not true that they don't care. I think they very much do want you to be there—just in case."

The Don't-Touch-Me Phase

Sitting alone, hoping to be called on—or simply acknowledged— reads a lot like a scene from *Sex in the City,* in which one of the girls is waiting haplessly by the phone. The analogy becomes even more apt when your child moves into the "Don't touch me in public!" phase. As one parent described it, "It's a little like we're carrying on this illicit affair. We now go as far from school as possible to have a soda together. And I can never, ever touch him in public."

There's no question that as your child hits ten or eleven, his need to appear more James Dean–cum–lone wolf increases in direct proportion to how many of his friends may be hanging around. Try to give him a hug or even tousle his hair at the bus stop or in the mall, and he's likely to flinch as though you've zapped him with a cattle prod. "I couldn't believe it when Jack stopped letting me give him a kiss in public," Deborah recalled. "It was really, really hard. Because he was so physical and affectionate just a year ago. I knew why he didn't want me to touch him in front of his friends, but it still hurt."

Hand in hand with the "don't touch me" message is the "you're so embarrassing" complaint, leveled several times a day. Suddenly, you're dumb and dumber. Maddie remembers all too vividly an unfortunate faux pas I committed the afternoon I managed to carry on a lengthy conversation with a dark-haired girl I repeatedly called Claire, even though, according to my mortified daughter, Rachel (her actual name) bore absolutely no resemblance to Claire. "She has *way lighter hair*," Maddie hissed as she dragged me away, insisting in her next breath that I henceforth pick her up around the corner.

My friend Kate's daughter presented her with a list of phrases never to be uttered in front of school friends. They included any reference to mother-daughter conversations; for example, "Hayley tells me" or "Hayley and I were talking about . . ." or "I understand from Hayley." Kate isn't quite sure if this caveat was designed to mitigate suspicions that Hayley shared her friends' secrets or if it was just an attempt to shut Kate up as much as possible when her friends were over. "I'm also not allowed to talk above a whisper on the street. She'll say, 'Mom! Do you have to talk so *loud?*' when the only other person within a five-block radius is a sleeping wino."

Jessica, ten, simply handed her mother a list labeled "Rules of Conduct" to be followed during any and all visits to school. It read:

1. Do not, under any circumstances, mention my name or say anything about me.
2. Wave to me, do not come over and say hello.
3. Do not call me honey, sweetie, or any other name apart from Jessica. If you edit my work, concentrate on the editing.
4. Act pretty much as if I were any other student. You can wave to me and all that, but nothing else.

"The biggest source of embarrassment for my kids is the car," Gail, an adoptive mom in Chicago, told me. "I love my car—it's an '85 Cadillac. It's totally cool. In fact, I drove it all the way from Arizona, feeling like an aging actress driving this vintage wreck. And I pull up into the driveway and the kids scream, 'This is *it?*' They make me park around the block, rather than chance someone seeing them get into it after school. And if they happen to luck out and get a ride home with someone else, I'm tailing behind alone!"

One mom admitted poignantly that she now cuts her sons' hair because "it's the only way I get to touch them." Another confessed she sneaks in at night just to kiss her ten-year-old's cheek. "He'll sometimes let me do it when we're alone at home, but not very often," she said wistfully.

As painful as it is to repress the urge to grab your growing boy (boys tend to be more cuddle-shy than girls during this phase) and beg an indulgent snuggle, respect his need for boundaries. His abhorrence of public hugs is in no way an indication that he wants less of your loving attention. Susie, whose daughter Caroleen began pulling away when she was nine, struck a bargain. "She would say, 'Don't kiss me when the camp bus comes, because the other kids will laugh, but you can kiss me before or at home as much as you want.' So I maul her before, and then I let her go. I don't know if I appreciate that she can say it to me or if I feel bad because she's still so young. But that's who she is and I appreciate that. She isn't telling me to go away, just to do it in private."

Wendy's son, also closing in on eleven, shrinks from any physical contact: "I can't hug him without feeling like I have leprosy. But my husband goes up to his room at night and lies next to him, and he's okay with that. I could never do that, because he would be so uncomfortable." I asked Wendy if she was envious of their bond. "On one level it really hurts," she admitted. "But then I know this is just a phase he's going through. He's very sweet in other ways—brings me a bouquet of flowers he's picked and occasionally lets me give him a kiss. But I definitely miss the physical cuddling." His twin sister, on the other hand, still sought physical closeness. "She'll climb into bed for a morning cuddle," Wendy said with a smile. "Every day like clockwork! But that's just what she's about—always has been."

Happily for me, Nick's headlong plunge into adolescence hasn't included a dramatic Mom the Leper stage. Still, there are limits. Singing along with U2 in the car is permissible, if it's just us; otherwise, the slightest rhythmic motion of my neck is enough to generate a complaint from the backseat. I have to watch what I do when we're in public, but as long as I don't try to hold his hand or push his hair out of his eyes, I'm usually allowed to give him a quick kiss, even a hug in front of his friends. Greeting said friends with chirpy questions about school or, God forbid, homework is verboten, but it's not too corny to offer them milk shakes and snacks when they come by after school. In fact, I recently managed a minor miracle when one of Nick's newer and clearly cool friends crossed the threshold and immediately asked if we had any of "that awesome chocolate cake" I had served during his last visit. I told him no but suggested that he and Nick make a cake. "Who, me?" he asked.

"Yes, you guys could bake a cake," I said as matter-of-factly as possible. There was a moment of stunned silence before Nick's friend turned to him and said, "Hey, man, whaddya think?" Nick shrugged nonchalantly, then led the way to the kitchen, where they spent a noisy forty-five minutes with the ultra-*un*cool Betty Crocker.

My sweet sense of triumph that Nick and his pal were experimenting with pots, not pot, soured only slightly when the warm aroma of cake drew me into the kitchen. A chocolate-splattered assortment of discarded cake pans and utensils loitered around (not *in*) the sink, while the still-warm cake—two gaping chunks gouged from its side—sat like an old battered hat on the counter. The boys' whereabouts were apparent from the conspicuously large brown crumbs that trailed up the stairs.

I kept my cool until the friend had departed, then invited his host to clean up with me. There were audible groans and a few lame complaints about having a lot of homework, but Nick finally agreed to join me in the kitchen. As we attacked the mess, I was reminded of advice given to me by William Pollack, a renowned expert on the psychology of boys, about ways to get even the most recalcitrant preteen to talk. "The vast majority of boys are not taught to open up, to say, 'I feel this way, Mom,' or 'There's something bothering me I'd like to talk about.'" He explained, "They're much more likely to express their feelings while they're doing something with you. If a boy has something else to focus on as he talks—shooting hoops, playing a game—then he successfully protects himself from the possibility of experiencing shame, which is paramount during the preteen years."[4]

Creating what Pollack calls "shame-free" zones—situations when your conversation appears as off-the-cuff as possible—is critical with boys. My friend Nicole, who has four kids, found it close to impossible to get ten-year-old Henry to talk. "Then I made a point of meeting him after school once a week and taking him to his music class a few blocks away. We go to a coffee shop or a pizza place and we just sit there together. Sometimes he doesn't say a word, but more often he'll see a kid from school out the window and that will prompt him to share something that happened—even things like teasing or malicious mischief."

For suburban moms, long drives to soccer practice or even to the mall provide a chance to be part chauffeur, part shrink. "Maybe because we're sitting side by side—not face-to-face—Jonah feels much more comfortable chatting," Ronnie, who lives in Connecticut, observed. "But he's definitely more likely to open up during those twenty-minute drives to baseball practice than if I ask him flat out what's up at school or with his friends." There's no question that 90 percent of what I would consider important conversations—about peer pressure, school, drugs, sex—have taken place when one of the kids and I were playing backgammon or watching television or setting the table for dinner.

In many ways Nick has always been more of an open book than his sister. Or perhaps, as with every other mothering challenge I've faced, I had to practice with Maddie—and to learn from my mistakes. By the time Nick's preteen years rolled around, I had witnessed not only the power of "action talk," as Pollack dubs it, but the value of timing. When Maddie had a bad experience (a certain piano recital from hell comes to mind), I had a tendency to rush in, not only with encouraging platitudes ("You'll do better next time") but with a barrage of questions about her feelings. The more I tried to walk silently beside her, to let her know I was available—when she was ready to talk—the more likely she was to open up.

Reading Between the Emotional Lines

Of course, there were many times when my kids retreated to their rooms or created a high-tech barricade that was tough to scale. How does one engage a ten-year-old when he's playing Mortal Kombat (a game you loathe), pausing only to type an instant message on his laptop or to adjust the gigantic "I can't possibly hear you" headphones cupping his ears? According to Ron Taffel, another gentle giant in the adolescent-psychology field, you create "comfort time" by pushing through those barriers and joining your kids in whatever activities they seem to enjoy. "Comfort time is sitting next to your daughter while she reads the biographical information about Freddy Prinze Jr. on the Internet," Taffel says. "Comfort time is having your son teach you how to play whatever video game currently captures his imagination and interest. Comfort time even includes occasionally going to a rock concert with your twelve-year-old."[5]

Taffel probably should have added ". . . even if he doesn't want you around," because there's no preteen on the planet who's always going to welcome his mom into his world with open arms. One of the most depressing afternoons of my life was spent in a little repertory theater watching a singularly inept staging of the movie *Seven Brides for Seven Brothers*. Maddie, then eleven, and I knew the film—a classic kitschy Hollywood musical—by heart. We had watched it so many times that it had become a kind of cult flick for us, the one movie we could recite and ridicule with hilarious abandon. So I thought it would be a kick to see a campy production of our campy favorite. And it *would* have been a riot, had Maddie not decided to bring along a friend from school. Her friend was a lovely girl, but she just didn't get it; she was bored and not even faintly amused by the fact that the leading lady weighed more than her seven brothers put together or that their faux beards kept slipping out of place. During intermission Maddie asked sheepishly if they could skip the second act and go shopping in town.

I sat grimly through act 2, while the girls wandered through the tiny summer-resort shops, browsing and giggling and having a lovely time. As far as Maddie was concerned, it had been a great day; for me, it signaled how quickly the ejection seat could fling me out of Maddie's kids-only world—and how hard that was to stomach.

Claire, a social worker and divorced mom of two, who lives in Washington, D.C., recounted a similar story with a slightly sweeter finale. Her preteen, Sam, was going on a field trip to a local Mexican restaurant. Having learned the hard way to always ask before volunteering, Claire had gotten the nod a few weeks earlier to be the class parent that day. But the night before the trip Sam seemed agitated and kept asking questions like "So, Mom, are you definitely gonna go on the trip? Are you sure you want to go on the trip? Don't you have a meeting or anything?" Claire didn't need her advanced degree to sense that Sam was conflicted at best, unhappy at worst, about her going, so she provided an out by saying, "Sam, honey, it sounds like maybe you'd rather I *not* go on the field trip." At first Sam demurred, insisting that it was fine. But when Claire looked him in the eye and said, "Listen, honey. Please know it's totally fine with me, I will not take it personally at all, if you don't want me to go. What's most important to me is that you feel you can tell me what you want and what's best for you." Sam burst into tears. He apologized profusely but confessed that he would rather she not come along. They hugged and all was well, but when Claire went up to bed, there on her pillow was twenty dollars and a note that read, "Dear Mom: Please go and buy yourself a nice lunch tomorrow, while I'm on the field trip."

As Claire recalled, she didn't know whether to laugh or to cry. "It was so sweet, so thoughtful, but I was also worried by how racked with guilt Sam was. I thought, 'Wait a minute. Something is wrong here if he feels that I am going to be so devastated at having to skip this trip.'" Along with the twenty dollars, Sam had given his mom an invaluable opportunity to reflect on why he felt responsible for her happiness. As a divorced mom, she was well aware of the risks of children feeling responsible not only for their parents' breakup but for their future happiness.

As self-centered and egocentric as preteens can be, they're also highly tuned in to the moods and attitudes of those around them. The same antennae that pick up a rival's sarcastic tone of voice quiver with emotion when your reaction to something registers even slightly out of the normal range. Looking back, I definitely recall times when Maddie's guilt over upsetting me took me by surprise—not only because I wasn't *that* upset but because I was stunned that she felt responsible. More than once I realized that I needed to give her some emotional breathing room, to let her know that despite my anger, I appreciated her apology and could move on. The message needed to be: Even the people we love make us really angry, and it's far better to get those feelings out in the open where we can deal with them than to waste time trying to read complicated signals. This is a particularly important message for young girls, who tend to avoid confrontation or to see it as catastrophic. Girls are insanely sensitive to social clues because they dare not say aloud how upset or angry they're feeling. Boys keep their feelings buttoned up, and as Claire wisely concluded, "It's very tough at this stage to read their cues, to know when and how to respect their boundaries."

It's especially hard with a child like Sam, whose ambivalence and anxiety about growing up are so poignantly on display. When our children are teetering on the edge of adolescence, their half-child half-adult behavior makes it tricky to know where to draw the line emotionally and physically. One mom confessed that her eleven-year-old son still liked to "hug and snuggle" before bed. "He would die if he knew I was repeating this," she told me. "But his bedtime routine is pretty much the same as when he was a little boy."

Lines and Limits

At what point does it become inappropriate to let your preteen snuggle and hug you—even sleep with you—as Nick and Maddie often asked to do during this stage? With Maddie I rarely hesitated. But when Steve would travel out of town on business and Nick would hang around in our room, reading before bed, and then ask, "Hey, Mom, can I just sleep here tonight?" I was always torn. We had been having "sleepovers" since he was a little boy. Like Maddie, he loved our "gigantus bed"; like me, he relished telling stories and giggling in the dark with me, drifting off to sleep holding my hand. Steve was adamant that at ten Nick was too old to sleep with his mom; his insistence that I send Nick to his own room made me feel slightly guilty about a routine I knew in my gut was soothing, not sexual.

I begrudgingly agreed to end our sleepovers, but I missed them—

even though, I have to admit, I rarely slept well during them. More than once I considered going against my word, but that would have made me feel as though I were doing something illicit. I realized that Steve—like many fathers—was probably a little jealous of my relationship with Nick, who made no secret of how much he adored me. Also, we were both products of a society that pushes independent sleeping arrangements from infancy, not to mention the macho notion that big boys aren't supposed to want to sleep in Mommy's bed.

According to William Pollack, "There is absolutely nothing wrong with a ten-year-old sleeping with his mom, as long as there is nothing sexual or even vaguely uncomfortable about the arrangement." Unless a parent is coercing or pushing a child to share her bed or the child's need for physical closeness includes "inappropriately exciting snuggling or rubbing," then Pollack believes the emotional closeness is a highly positive experience.[6] Any dad who has bunked with his kid and awakened to a sleepy smile and a sweet hug would no doubt agree.

Of course, by the time Nick turned eleven, the closest he wanted to be to me at night was on the chaise in our bedroom. When I came home from dinner one evening, I found him there, this hulking boyman, his enormous feet dangling off the end. He looked so uncomfortable, I actually thought to myself, "I should carry him up to his room." Who was I kidding? He weighed almost as much as I did.

The bed-chaise debate soon became moot (he wanted to sleep in his own bed, preferably with the door closed), but the issue of boundaries persisted well into the teen years for both my children. Ironically, the challenge derived partly from their charm. Tantrums and moodiness notwithstanding, preteens can be a blast. They're curious, passionate, desperate to *know* about the adult world, and intellectually capable of sharing everything from politics to movies to music to museums. I adored palling around with Maddie, shopping or taking in a photography exhibit or talking about a movie. But if I happened to mention that I thought a particular actor was "really hot," and she agreed, I immediately questioned whether I should have kept that to myself. Maddie was such great company, so mature and poised, that I would often talk to her as though we were friends, share my feelings about something, and then worry that I had overstepped my bounds, burdened her unnecessarily. Or I would make a sexual joke in front of her and an hour later refuse to let her watch something slightly racy on TV.

Not long ago I was interviewing University of Chicago sociologist Barbara Schneider about her five-year study of close to seven thousand teenagers. At one point she said, "You know, a lot of kids will tell you, 'My mom's my best friend.' Well, that's not a good idea. It's not a mother's role to be her child's best friend. You have to stay the mom; you have to be authoritative *and* understanding."[7]

Schneider allowed that the mandate to be flexible yet firm is hard enough with toddlers but practically impossible to pull off consistently with preteens. As I type this sentence, Nick (almost thirteen) is reading *A Clockwork Orange* in a chair in my office. The book is brilliant but unremittingly violent. He loves it, even as he admits, "It's pretty rough, Mom. I can't believe you liked it." When he finishes the book, I know he'll want to rent the movie, which I remember as one of the most disturbing films I've ever seen. I can script the argument, see the frustration and fury on his face, and know in all likelihood that I'll cave. But that's largely because I gave up a long time ago, letting him see *The Terminator* and several other "cartoon-violence" flicks on video. He still harbors resentment for the year I stood my ground and refused to take him to *The Matrix,* despite his claims that I was the "only mother in the entire world" who wouldn't allow her ten-year-old to go. My compromise was to wait until it came out on video, then screen it myself and eventually let him watch it with Steve. By that time, I rationalized, he was a year older and, perhaps, better able to see the movie as a fantasy, not an endorsement of mindless violence.

Was I sure about that? Only for about six minutes. Then I immediately felt the ground shifting beneath my feet and the doubt squeezing the back of my neck. Claire knows exactly what that's like: "I feel like I'm living in this gray zone, and I hate it," she told me. "It's not a good place to be as a parent. Especially when you have a kid like Sam, who has always needed stability, predictability in his life. Just when he most needs me to be in control, to know what I'm doing, I feel like I'm constantly struggling to figure out what the right answer is to the myriad of questions and requests I am confronted with on a daily basis. This is brand-new territory, and I can't go on my instincts, so I get really stuck."

What Claire sensed—and what every parent of a preteen will confirm—is that showing indecision or weakness is like sticking your
head in a shark's mouth. A tenacious, self-righteous eleven-year-old
can smell equivocation from a mile away and, like a hungry predator,
will move in for the kill: "You don't know anything!" "Why are you
doing this to me?" "But everybody else is!" "What's your problem?"
and "I hate you!" are just a few of the choice bites you're likely to feel.

Even if you know in your heart that your preteen loves you, it's
never easy to be sprayed with venom and not feel paralyzed by indecision or, worse, convinced that it would be a lot less painful to just lie
down and admit defeat. As Claire wisely noted, "Now every day there
is something I don't know the answer to. It's not like you read a book
and it says, 'At twelve, kids can do such and such.' It all depends on
your child's temperament, their resourcefulness. Are they kids who
can think on their feet? Handle stress when they are by themselves? Is
my kid a follower or a leader? There are so many more variables beyond their chronological age."

Rather than react the minute her son starts to lobby ("And, believe
me, it's a constant barrage!"), Claire takes a time-out. "I've learned
that whenever he starts to push me to make a tough decision, I need to
say, 'I understand this is important to you, so I have to take it under
advisement.'" If Claire decides that the answer is no, she takes "a deep
cleansing breath" and steels herself for battle. Her son, like most preteens, negotiates, pushes, and schemes. "He'll come back again and
again with a different reason why I'm wrong. Or he'll scream, 'I hate
you!' And at that point the only thing I can do is say, 'I understand
you're disappointed and angry. I'm sure you're going to hate me a
lot over the next few years, but I'm not intimidated by that because
it's my job to set these limits.'" According to Claire, sometimes Sam
sulks and is resentful for a few hours, but most of the time he gets over
it. In fact, once he knows that the negotiations are over, he stops. "It's
like the textbooks say about toddlers," Claire said with a smile. "They
want the limit; they want to know what the deal is. And when you're
in the gray area, it's distressing."

Behind every preteen who claims to have a mother who is "a bitch,"
"so incredibly annoying," "clueless," or worse is a kid scrambling for a
toehold on a very slippery slope. Even if the hand they grab on to grips
a bit too tightly, it's nonetheless warm and sure. But the only way to

maintain your own footing is to give yourself time to take that cleansing breath before responding. If "I'll get back to you" works at the office, why not use it at home? The answer, of course, is that we're not managing a mature, competent coworker; we're trying to stay in charge in the presence of a highly irrational, red-faced preadolescent. Only rarely will it be possible to cling to the rock while your child's fury storms around you. Only rarely will it be possible to do exactly the right thing, to stand firm and not doubt yourself a minute later. The ten-year-old who wants to get her ears pierced might have a long list of perfectly reasonable arguments to support her request. Your response may be as simple as "I want you to wait" or "I don't like pierced ears." But if you trust your gut, avoid the "Am I being overprotective and neurotic about this?" bug in your ear, chances are your child will back down. Will she thank you later for taking a sure and loving stance? Not a chance.

What's Pushing Your Buttons—and Theirs?

But she may teach you something about the skeletons in your own closet and about the ways they tend to fly out and dance on your head when certain arguments veer out of control. That is, of course, if you're willing to open that closet during calm, solitary moments (or with the help of a loving spouse or friend or a competent therapist) and reflect on what drives you crazy and why.

In her book *The Mother Dance,* therapist Harriet Lerner describes a power struggle with her son, Ben, during which she "hit rock bottom." The battle, which raged for months, centered around Ben's tendency to ignore his mom's daily requests to pick up his clothes or put his dirty dishes in the sink or to simply help out a bit around the house. Lerner recounts how she tried everything from typing long lists of detailed instructions to demanding Ben look her in the eyes when she ordered him to do something to pleading with him "as if I'm a helpless victim of his inconsiderateness: 'If you *love* me, if you *respect* me, if you *care* about me, why don't you do what you're supposed to do!?'" The drama spilled over to her marriage, pitting her against her husband; it affected her work and deeply undercut her self-confidence as a mother. At the rock-bottom moment, she got on Ben's case "but in a singularly awful way," reducing him to tears. He rightly accused her of being so focused on whether or not he cleaned up that she didn't recognize his many strengths, didn't really know what he was doing in school. "When Ben starts to cry, it breaks my heart," Lerner writes. "As he exits from the conversation and the kitchen, I understand, maybe for the first time, that I am really hurting him, that if someone needs to grow up and be responsible, it's me."[8]

Lerner's take-away from that experience—and from years as a family therapist—includes the sage advice to "pay attention to the big picture," to recognize that when you're so entrenched, something else may be going on. "We become riveted on our child when we are not paying attention to issues in our marriage, our divorce, our stepfamily, our family of origin, and our own life plan."[9]

Ironically, when we focus obsessively on a child's slovenliness or poor eating habits or laziness, we stop listening. During Maddie's middle-school years, she would often take hours to get dressed, especially when we had a party or special event to attend. Aware that we were running late, I would stand in a sea of discarded clothes, listening to her rant about having "nothing to wear." My blood would boil in my deaf ears, as I picked out shirts and skirts and angrily tossed them her way. "We just bought this!" I would say tensely, knowing full well that she would find some reason to reject it. The fact that this happened on a weekly, sometimes daily basis should have been enough to force me to step back—preferably out of her room altogether—and figure out what might really be going on ("I don't like my body" or "I don't want to grow up yet") and how I might help.

What I did in the heat of the moment was in many ways far less important (and always less effective) than what I tried to do when Maddie was calm and able to listen. Getting her to focus on those aspects of her life in which she took legitimate pride—her piano, her artwork, her gift for languages—mitigated her age-appropriate insistence that she had nothing going for her. Sharing some story of my own preadolescent angst or, better yet, some can-you-top-this social blooper I had made in sixth grade usually made her laugh with a mixture of relief and empathy. And letting her find ways to connect with Steve, whose opinion of her carried far more weight than mine, guaranteed that she would be showered with compliments from the man who loved her more than anyone in the world.

Hitting double digits is a watershed moment, one that some children embrace aggressively, while their less-ready friends inch backward toward the nest. "The day Eliza turned ten, she burst into tears," Sarah recalled. "Some kids are eager to be heading toward their teens. She got depressed; she was just miserable. She did not want to stop being a little kid. She could see the pressures that were coming down the road, the sexy fashions—belly shirts and short skirts and low-slung pants—and she didn't want to be all sexy and stressed."

Sarah was lucky. At least Eliza's blatant ambivalence about the preteen years led to a clear cry for help. More often a child's mixed feelings parade around in a variety of guises: insecurity, vanity, apathy, self-centeredness, obsessiveness, and anxiety. When your body is out of control and there is not a single part of that body you particularly like, then what you put on that body takes on biblical importance. And this is true for girls *and* boys. Girls may script an entire chapter of their lives around the tragic consequences of having to wear Payless shoes (as Sandra's daughter did the last time they went shopping), but boys can be just as confused and freaked out; they simply hide their fragile egos in oversized layers.

For the mothers of preteen girls I spoke to, clothing battles were a daily occurrence. Lois's older daughter, Emily, had always been quiet and compliant, so their "nightmare mornings" represented a complete reversal in the family's dance. "Just today we had a major fight about what Emily was wearing to school," Lois told me, the exasperation in her voice pitching it high and shrill. "I'm yelling, 'The shirt's too short and the pants are too low!' and she's screaming that all the kids dress like that—and they do."

As I told Lois, the fact that she had been spared these clothing combats until Emily's sixth-grade year was amazing. Most of the moms I interviewed reported a shift much earlier. "Adolescence has gotten younger. As early as first or second grade, children are influenced by the *tyranny of cool,* a standard bearer of the pop culture that we formerly associated solely with teens," says Ron Taffel in *The Second Family: How Adolescent Power Is Challenging the American Family.* As his title implies, Taffel believes that teens don't choose a rebellious wardrobe or music or lifestyle out of revenge or animosity toward their parents. "They're merely drifting away, desperate to find a place where they're known and where they feel comfortable."[10]

Dorothy described how her son—"still developmentally a little boy at ten"—had a new and vaguely disturbing ability to just soak up teen culture like a sponge. "He's got the moves that are scary to me, the cultural messages that he reacts to. He'll sniff it out, interpret it, make it his own at a startling rate. He's much more affected by pop culture and by music now than I ever imagined he would be. He's always walking around with a Discman, spends hours making compilations. He would much rather do that than ride his bike in the neighborhood. And he's totally clothes-obsessed. I'm so glad he goes to a school where he wears a blazer, because otherwise he'd be in the ripped T-shirts and baggy jeans."

But school uniforms don't solve the problem. For my friend Nicole, whose daughter dons the regimental navy skirt and white blouse of her all-girl private school, the shop-till-you-drop-addiction has hit with a vengeance. "I'll say, 'Let's go to a museum,' and Isabel will roll her eyes and say, 'Oh, Mom. Can't we go to Bloomingdale's instead?' And if we do go, it's a nightmare. She's obsessed with finding just the right outfit, and even if I can buy the exact same thing at Target or Daffy's, she wouldn't be caught dead in those stores."

When I met with Jacqui, a very attractive, chic Londoner with two children, she was bemoaning her daughter's recent descent into the grunge look: "It's terrible. She's sort of into a mixture of Goth and God knows what, which involves cutting up tights and making garments out of them. It's awful actually." As Dr. Kenneth R. Ginsburg, a specialist in adolescent medicine, sagely puts it, "This is the dawning of the independence spurt. 'I don't need you anymore, Mom and Dad. I'm going to be my own person, an individual.' In reality, that translates to 'I'm going to be an individual—*just like all my friends.*'"[11]

But conforming is hard; you have to know the rules, anticipate subtle style shifts, avoid deviations from the norm, and most of all, live in an almost-constant state of anxiety that you'll mess up and experience the shame all middle-schoolers dread. When your daughter blames you for her bad-hair day ("You bought the wrong shampoo!") or when your son claims that his brand-new pants suddenly look dorky because you washed them all wrong, it's tempting to shout, "Well, then buy your own goddamned shampoo!" or "Want to do your own laundry? Be my guest!" But most of us manage to stand by, understanding all too well that these outbursts about appearance bubble up from a well of insecurity and confusion. We remember what it was like because we may have felt exactly the same way—not decades ago, but days ago.

"What's really awful about Chrissie's clothing meltdowns is that she sounds exactly like me," one mom confessed. "I'm constantly asking my husband, 'Do these pants make me look fat?' or worrying about my hair. I'm sure she picks up on that."

There's no question that monitoring the body-image messages we send our children—especially our daughters—is critical during the preteen years. But this can be particularly challenging if you happen to have given birth in your thirties or later. In that case, you may find that your child's preadolescent awkwardness corresponds uncomfortably with your own conflicted entry into middle age. I can recall standing in front of my bathroom mirror, running my fingers along new wrinkles, while Maddie worried about a tiny pimple marring her otherwise perfect complexion. We both felt the pressure to measure up to some culturally imposed ideal of beauty, to conform to glossy standards that made my sagging skin and her blemished brow targets of unhealthy focus. As important as it was for me to reassure Maddie that her beauty would not be marred by occasional pimples, it was far more critical for me to lose my tendency to moan about looking fat or flabby or forty.

Class Cruellas and Cliques

There was nothing I hated more than clumps of whispering girls who got quiet when I passed. I felt half the time I was impersonating a girl instead of really being one.

From *The Secret Life of Bees* by Sue Monk Kidd[12]

More than anything, tweens want to belong, to be part of the in crowd or, better yet, a member of the most popular clique. To raise your head above the social sands, to stand out, guarantees banishment to the Land of Nerds. To wear the right clothes, talk the talk, walk the walk, increases your chances of acceptance, but there's rarely a guarantee, because cliques are, by definition, in constant flux.

There is a rich body of literature on clique dynamics; sociologists have parsed everything from "out-group subjugation" to violent bullying.[13] But most of us don't need a sociology lesson to remember how painful the fickleness of friends can be. Ask any mom about the "Cruella" from her sixth-grade class, and a name springs readily from her lips. Ask just about anyone to close her eyes and say the first thing she associates with "seventh grade," and she's likely to mention friends or cliques or fall back on a simple "Ugh!"

And the agonies and ecstasies of a tween's social life are hardly unique to the United States. Jacqui, whose daughter spent hours on the phone each night with her friends, practically shouted her frustration when I asked about cliques: "Oh my God! The intensity! It drives you mad. Who is being horrible and bitchy to whom? Who's going to be invited to so-and-so's party, or 'Mum, I'm not going to the sleepover, no matter what!' They talk furiously on the phone, pass notes in class about one another. It's horrible. Girls are horrible."

Girls do tend to be meaner—or at least to operate in very different ways from boys. Girls' friendships tend to be intensely close and exclusive; the group may occasionally let in someone who's liked by someone else in the clique, and—despite what they say behind one another's backs—to be nice, as opposed to tough.[14] Their aggression is emotional. Boys' groups are often bigger, more fluid, and physically competitive or playful.[15] Although their friendships are less emotionally charged, their blowups more straightforward and short-lived, boys can certainly be cruel. Name calling hurts just as much when it's in your face on the playground as it does when you hear it thirdhand from a "friend." The only thing that possibly hurts more is being the mother of the victim and having to sit helplessly by while your child's ego is eviscerated.

I can recall choking back waves of anger and frustration when Maddie would recount some insanely complicated lunchroom dance that had left her outside the circle of "friends" on whom her fragile self-esteem depended. "They didn't even talk to me, Mom," she would whisper, the pain traceable from her hairline to her small, clenched fists. "No one likes me. I'm such a loser!" I knew better than to argue, to shower her with compliments or list her many wonderful qualities. With her emotional earplugs in place, Maddie was definitely *not* open to gratuitous advice; the best I could do was zip my mouth, shake my head sympathetically, and perhaps share some tragic story from my own sixth-grade memory bank.

I also had to remind myself that despite Maddie's maturity in many areas of her life, she was incredibly naïve about how and why girls use gossip and scorn to manipulate their friends. She acted as though I was a genius one night when I pointed out that by putting someone else down, a bully elevates herself and that the girl who seemed to know a lot about other kids was probably not the best choice of confidante ("But she said she wouldn't tell anyone!"). She even grudgingly admitted that she engaged in her share of gossip and badmouthing.

It was equally important for me to admit that Maddie could be critical, competitive, jealous (all I had to do was ask Nick), because assuming she was the innocent victim got me nowhere. I had heard her talking about other kids, complaining about teachers, joking about a celebrity's hideous outfit or latest romance. And of course, she had heard me talking about my friends, complaining about my boss, joking about a celebrity's hideous outfit or latest romance. When it came to gossip I was hardly a Liz Smith, but I'm sure both kids heard their share of stories around our dinner table or witnessed my siblings and me teasing one another—usually, but not always, "all in good fun."

By the time Nick entered middle school, I so hated the kids' gossip that I instituted a fine for every nasty comment I happened to catch. Although this tactic primarily served to redirect the nasty comments my way, I made my point. Of course, there were several occasions when a phone conversation with one of my friends was interrupted by a shrill voice from the couch shouting, "I heard that, Mom! Fifty cents!"

I made sure they also heard me and, more important, saw me working on my relationships with close friends. The kids know how much I adore these women, many of whom I've been lucky enough to know since childhood. When one of them needed my attention or child-care help or career advice, I tried to be there and to describe how helpful or attentive or caring she was in return. I made no secret of the times I was angry with a friend, especially if I had taken steps to remedy the situation. I also shared stories about times when I had hurt a friend's feelings and had to face up to my mistake and apologize. "I didn't like it when Jane told me I had been tactless, but she was right to say,

'Look, I have to clear the air about something' and set me straight," I remember telling Maddie one night after a long (and hard) phone conversation with one of my oldest and dearest friends.

One of the reasons Maddie at ten or eleven was so interested in these stories of hurt feelings and reconciliation was that her life was consumed with choosing and being chosen by the girls in her circle. This new dance of intimacy was agonizing, but it was also thrilling. As Linda Perlstein aptly notes in *Not Much Just Chillin': The Hidden Lives of Middle Schoolers,* "Social scientists explain that being eleven means that you put friends number one on your list of priorities, that for the first time you perceive intimacy as a desirable state, not just within your immediate family but in your very own world outside it, that what you're doing is less important than whom you're doing it with. You pick your friends not just because they live near you or happen to be in your ballet class but because, well, *you pick them.* You want to share. You learn that making them happy makes you happy."[16]

Figuring out what to do when they make you desperately unhappy is another story. Most of the time Maddie and Nick lived in dread of my interference. They would preface a tale of woe with "Don't do anything, Mom, but . . ." So I was unprepared for what happened one afternoon of Maddie's seventh-grade year. She came home that day looking particularly hangdog and recounted how hurt and upset she had been by a girl whose thirteenth birthday was a few weeks away. Apparently this child, understandably excited about the big party her parents were throwing, spent every free moment regaling her classmates with the details (the games they would play, her parents' celebrity friends, the party favors), all well and good for those who happened to be invited, which Maddie was not. "It really hurts my feelings, Mom," Maddie said, quickly adding, "I mean, I don't care if I don't go, but she's inviting half the grade and then she talks about it right in my face."

I hesitated before asking, "Do you want me to call her mom?" And was totally stunned when Maddie looked up and said, "Would you, Mom?"

Now what? How would I tell this woman that her daughter was acting like a tactless brat? Then a technique Steve taught me years ago came sprinting to my rescue. I picked up the phone, and when the mom answered I launched into a friendly spiel: "Hi. This is Annie, Maddie Murphy's mom. I'm calling because I'm a little confused . . ." I explained the situation, adding, "Rena has been talking to Maddie about her party so much we just assumed the invitation got lost in the mail." The mom apologized profusely and said she would double-check the list. "No, Maddie's not invited," she said, again apologizing. "I'll tell Rena to be more careful." There was a slight pause before she added, "But who *is* Maddie?" My smugness evaporated as I found myself tripping over adjectives that might counter her implication that my daughter was a nobody. I hung up, furious that I had not retorted: "Don't you see? That question says it all! Whom do you think your daughter takes after?"

Recently, I shared this story with a friend whose own daughter is experiencing the same pain whenever a big party rolls around. "It's incredible to me how thoughtless these parents can be," Sarah complained. "Just this past weekend Eliza called in tears because she had been invited to a friend's bar mitzvah ceremony and the big party that night but not to the luncheon in between. So she's standing alone in the foyer of the synagogue watching half her friends and their parents skip off to the lunch. It was totally humiliating."

Sarah came to the rescue, canceling her own afternoon plans and taking Eliza to a movie. When I asked how she felt about that, she was quick to point out that "total self-absorption" defined this phase: "It was all about Eliza—one hundred percent, the whole weekend. And that's a really important point. I've had to recognize that in order to get her through this time, I need to be there. At the end of the night, she came and gave me a big hug and said, 'Thanks. I had such a fun weekend.' But that doesn't always happen."

"Losers," Laziness, and Learning to Step Back

We agreed that that *rarely* happens. More likely your SACRIFICIAL MOTHER sweatshirt will get lots of wear during the preteen years, not necessarily for large and memorable acts of incredible altruism but for small, exhausting, and quickly forgotten sacrifices. "I know it sounds petty," Martha told me. "But my big problem is how often he calls me from school to bring him the book he left or the uniform he forgot."

Dorothy echoed the "raising a loser" theme: "The very idea of collecting himself and his papers—making it to school intact—then getting it out of his backpack and to the teacher and then getting it home again—this has proven to be the most difficult thing. He just can't wrap his mind around it. We're doing everything we can. But I'm a little bit preoccupied with it right now."

According to several psychologists I asked about this, the middle-school years are notorious for rendering kids hopeless when it comes to organizing, tracking, or even accomplishing certain daily tasks. All you have to do is check out the lost-and-found at your kid's school to see years of brain-development research reflected in the uncollected jackets, gloves, sweatshirts, and notebooks. The parts of their brains that affect organization, logic, judgment, and short-term memory are not firing at a rate that enables them to keep track of all the balls they're juggling—especially when their emotional pistons are working overtime.

What can be a lot more troublesome than a lost backpack is the lack of motivation that often strikes at this age. "I worry about how he's going to do because he's so, so lazy," Jacqui complained about her son when we commiserated about school and the frequent home-work hassles we had encountered with our kids. "He's quite clever and he could be very good at academics if he could bring himself up!" Her frustration was echoed by a group of moms with preteen and teen kids in Chicago, whose conversation turned into a group chant when I mentioned school. "Homework is a nightmare!" said Anne, who called to ask my advice about motivating her son. "Every night we're bugging him to turn off the tube and hit the books. Or he'll lie and say, 'I already did it,' and then we'll get a note from his teacher saying he never handed in such-and-such an assignment. It's driving us crazy. I really don't know what to do."

According to Linda Perlstein, who followed a group of preteens for a year, "The collective eighth grade of the United States could be labeled 'doesn't work to potential.' Decline in motivation from elementary school to middle school is universal and documented. Thirteen-year-olds can't get interested in anything that bores them, no matter how many times they're told, *this is important, you'll see why in ten years.*"[17]

If your child happens to hate a certain teacher or thinks he "stinks at math," odds are his report card will bear the bad-news ending to his negativity. "My son is very intelligent," an energetic single mom from Chicago told me, "but all he talks about is how much he hates school. He's always complaining about his teachers. He doesn't want to be there. But my attitude right now is, that's *his* problem. He may hate to go to school, but he has to go. So deal with it!" I wish I could have been more like that—able to toss the hot potato right back into the kids' hands. "Deal with it!" just wasn't my style, and may not be yours.

What I did manage to communicate, first to Maddie and later to Nick, was that deciding a teacher was "a total jerk" or that one's classmates were "really dumb" didn't get you off the hook. In fact, if one of the kids pronounced a certain teacher "mean" or "boring" or "clueless," I learned that that was the class to track. We had to remind the kids at the start of each semester (and many times during the year) that it was easy to get an A in a class you loved, taught by a teacher you respected, surrounded by classmates you liked. The challenge was to hunker down and work at the subjects that were boring, poorly taught, or both.

But once we had shared our words of wisdom or met with a tough teacher or probed about assignments, we had to step back. And I don't do "step back" with grace or alacrity. So, yes, there were some very ugly nights during which Maddie ranted and raved about flunking a particular class and I prodded and pushed her to sit her butt in her desk chair and write the paper already. Or I put up with the tears, sarcasm, or self-indulgent whining until Steve appeared at the door and dragged me out of the dance that was clearly getting Maddie nowhere.

With Nick, either because of temperament or learning curve (his and mine), homework has not been an issue. Unlike his big sister, Nick will casually mention that he got an A on an essay I never even knew was assigned. It occurred to me only recently that he probably swore a secret oath early on to avoid what he witnessed too many nights in the room across the hall. He recognized—obviously better than I did—that what Maddie was going through was probably exacerbated by my interference. Watch someone throw gasoline on burning coals once too often, and you learn to keep the gasoline thrower at bay.

What did I learn? First and foremost, the preteen years taught me that my children are not me. They won't do their homework, practice piano, sketch a still life, make a friend, or write a letter the same way I would. And they certainly won't do any of those things just because I say to. When you've asked your eleven-year-old to do something fifty times and he's still not doing it, maybe *he's* not the slow learner!

I also heard the rattle of childhood ghosts, witnessed the spillover from my own life onto the kids, and learned that when the going gets tough, the tough stop going. They pause, breathe, exit. Choosing to step out of an unproductive or, worse, destructive dance with your preteen is an extremely powerful strategy during this phase of motherhood. So is flexibility. I found that a willingness to bend a bit, even to surprise my kids by demonstrating that I actually *had* been listening and could be convinced to change my mind, defused many potential conflicts.

Living in the gray zone meant recognizing that what worked on Monday might prove totally useless on Wednesday or that the child who seemed unfit for more responsibility one day could act with stunning maturity the next. Similarly, even if a minor missile launched at the end of a day from hell caused my heart to bleed, I could still be counted on to pull the troops through on days when I was calm, rested, and undistracted. Or when I had had the time to talk to Steve, the benefit of a friend's advice, a chance to meet with one of the kids' teachers, or perhaps a consultation with a therapist. Any of these lifelines might alert me to hot spots, help me stop and reflect on how to better negotiate the daily challenges and relish the fun of living with a preteen.

Stage 7

❦

It Gets Easier . . .
and Then They Leave

The Teen Years, Thirteen to Eighteen

A normal adolescent isn't a normal adolescent if he acts normal.
From *Necessary Losses,* by Judith Viorst[1]

Mention that you have a teenager at home, and you can expect one of several responses:

1. audible groans, often accompanied by dramatic sighs
2. chortling and/or sneering (think Marquis de Sade)
3. head wagging, sympathetic shoulder touching, or sudden weeping
4. commiserative comments ("Oh, yes. We have one, too.")
5. empathic probing ("How's it going?")

One or all of these reactions may make you feel as though you've contracted some widespread but often fatal disease. Or that you're on a forced march toward an emotional abyss guaranteed to make the next five years a living hell.

What I've come to realize as Maddie approaches her eighteenth birthday and Nick his fourteenth is that during this phase of motherhood we relive all of the other stages, experience everything from the panic of our children's infancy to the frustrations of toddlerhood to the loneliness of the preteen years. The difference is that now the risks are ramped up. Even if you worried constantly about your baby's safety, from a purely statistical vantage point she was at very little risk; during adolescence, the fact is, she *can* die. During your child's toddler years he tested limits, pushing you away, then running back. Teenagers today *do* run away, and while they usually come back, there is the scary possibility that they won't. When our children enter preschool, we're faced with being on display in a whole new way; adolescents display their dissimilarity by shoving it in our faces. The child who at age seven shocked you by shouting "Shut up!" is likely at fifteen to tell you to "Fuck off!" And the preteen, though a challenge, didn't have keys to the car.

Then there's everything you hear from relatives, total strangers, and the news media about the teen years. During the weeks leading up to Maddie's thirteenth birthday, I fully expected to wake up and discover my heart lying on the ground next to my bed. I imagined the worst: My sweet, loving daughter would metamorphose into an extra from *Traffic* or *Thirteen*. Our relationship would be characterized by suspicion, screaming matches, shocking revelations, sleepless nights, separations, and accusations, not to mention heartbreak.

I was pretty sure I could handle rebellion, even the occasional catastrophic fight. What I dreaded most was "having your heart wrenched from your body and ground into bits." That's how my friend Maxine, then the mother of seventeen-year-old Ben, described his descent into adolescence. Maxine exudes the kind of savvy, slightly sassy self-confidence of many urban moms. I had seen her with Ben often enough to know that, although they respected each other's relative independence, theirs was a close, loving relationship, so I found the pain etched on her face as she described his teen years surprising and a little scary. "No one prepared me," she explained softly. "No one said, 'Look, you're going to fall madly in love. And this person will think you're the sun and the moon; he'll worship the ground you walk on for about twelve years. And then one day he'll wake up and think you're disgusting. He'll break your heart, and you're supposed to think it's okay, accept that this is what teenagers do." The tears spilled down her cheeks as she assured me that life was better now that he was approaching eighteen. "He's grown out of the really ugly period—when he was thirteen, fourteen, fifteen, and uncomfortable in his own skin. That was the worst."

Having lived to tell about Maddie's teen years (and, thus far, having survived the first year of Nick's), I would concur with Maxine that early adolescence and the later teen years differ as dramatically as the first and last six months of your child's first year. Just as you walked the high wire in a high wind during the "fourth trimester," only to look back in amazed appreciation at how far you had come, you will sit in that high school auditorium on graduation day and tolerate, even welcome, the conflicting realities of this stage of motherhood: You've succeeded in building a harmonious relationship with your teen only to have to say good-bye. In the process you will have reshaped not only your relationship with your child but your identity as a mother.

In an effort to describe how tumultuous, unpredictable, and painful the teen years can be, people often compare adolescents to toddlers. The authors of *The 8 Seasons of Parenthood* dub parents of teens "volcano dwellers" and emphasize the necessity for "damage control."[2] But that's a fairly superficial and tactical approach. The critical challenge at this stage of motherhood is to let go of one's self-image as a mom—totally—and remake that image just as your daughter is remaking herself.

I discussed this transformation—or, rather, laid bare my own grief over Maddie's imminent departure from the nest—recently with an old friend, a wonderful writer whom I had not seen in over five years. Anna Quindlen had always been something of an idol to me, certainly an inspiration, and I was eager to hear how she had handled her children's teen years. She had provided some clues in a column she writes for *Newsweek,* which she said had garnered such an outpouring from mothers that her e-mail system had crashed. In her essay "Flown Away, Left Behind," Anna writes, "It's not simply the loss of these particular people, living here day in, day out, the bickering, the inside jokes, the cereal bowls in the sink and the towels in the hamper—all right, on the floor. It was who I was with them: the general to their battalion, the president to their cabinet. The Harpo to their Groucho, Zeppo and Chico."[3]

Scripting Your Part

Trying to figure out who you are with your adolescent children will trigger feelings of resentment, loss, panic, and anger—but also joy, pride, and astonishment that these towering almost-adults have rich and complex lives over which you exert very little control. What you can control is the role you choose to play in a tragicomedy with a constantly changing script. Maxine said that when her son "turned from absolute hostility to bemused tolerance," she often felt as though their roles had reversed: "He's tall enough to literally pat me on the head and say, 'That's nice, Mommy.' And when he does that, I feel like the child in the relationship with him. I'm totally aware that he is doing that on purpose. But I don't mind it, because I see that he's so confident, so knowing, and so self-assured. When he says, 'Mom, why don't you wear your little hat,' I feel as though I've been cast as this little woman—but that's okay."

Other moms were far less sanguine about their role as the "little woman." Anna talked about one of her sons, whose break from her during the teen years was particularly tough to handle. "I had been the wellspring of love for him, the emotional center of his life, but when he started to break away—as most teenage boys do—he adopted this kind of patronizing, 'Isn't Mom cute' bit, which I knew was the socially acceptable way to act toward your mom, except I wasn't going to accept it. I had to find another way to help him make the transition from relating to me as his mom to something that would be comfortable for both of us." Anna's solution was to consciously work on moving from a mother-son dynamic to a writer-writer relationship. "We went on this trip to London together, because I was working on a book, and I made Quin my assistant. He's a fantastic writer himself, so we were suddenly interacting as colleagues. Of course, I was still his mom, but it was great for both of us—and for our relationship during his high school years."

What impressed me in Anna's story was the deliberate choice she had made, the conscious shift from a role of passive, patronized mother to a more mature and mutual dynamic. As she would be the first to admit, there was no guarantee that the sarcasm, impatience, even contempt wouldn't surface another day, but her experience serves as a reminder that we have options. We can reject or, at the very least, make clear what we will and will not tolerate in our teens' behavior toward us. We can choose to play certain roles and reject others.

Describing a recent incident with her fourteen-year-old son, Chloe realized that behind her feelings of anger and alienation were far deeper hurts. "Tom has some friends who are really into the locker-room humor stage. One of them gets pretty worked up when he's around Tom—cracks lots of obscene jokes, makes homophobic comments. Chris and I were playing a word game with the boys, and when they started with that kind of talk, it made me really, really uncomfortable. What made it worse was that Chris laughed along with them, which juiced them up even more. I didn't think it was funny or fun."

Having grown up in a strict Catholic home, Chloe had never wanted to impose the kinds of restrictions she felt had stifled family life during her childhood. "But at the same time, I don't like it when they disparage women or act that way. It made me feel totally alienated from them and very flat-footed when it came to knowing how to respond." What came out in our conversation was the association Chloe made between "feeling powerless while these guys made me incredibly uncomfortable" and her tragic and painful experience of having been sexually abused as a child. "What I was able to do—which, of course, I never did when I was a girl—was tell them the next day why I had been so upset. I'm pretty sure the boys heard me—as did Chris."

Chloe's back-to-the-future vision of her son knocked her sideways, because suddenly she was faced with the very real possibility that the boy whose personality she not only knew but felt she had played a role in shaping might turn out to be decidedly different from her fantasies. "When I went to bed that night," she said sadly, "I wished with all my heart that I could turn back the clock."

Her comment brought back a vivid memory I have of sitting on my mother's lap when I was about eight years old. This spontaneous snuggle was her idea ("Come give me a little loving"), and it came close on the heels of a screaming fight she had had with my then sixteen-year-old sister. Holding me a bit too tightly, she whispered, "Oh, how I dread your teen years. Do me a big favor, darling: Please, please, don't grow up." I have breathed similar prayers, forced my five-feet-ten-inch son to sit on my lap and begged him not "to get big and mean," but I know that my Peter Pan fantasies are for naught. At some point he will disappear—not entirely, not irreparably, not forever—but long enough and with enough drama for me to ask, "Who *are* you?"

When Life Gets Ugly

In this sense, living with a teenager is very much like the toddler years. I remember staring at Nick as he wailed his way through a major meltdown and asking myself (or a passing stranger), "Who *are* you?" But my frustration or anger was followed quickly by the question "What did I do wrong?" Some of the time I could acknowledge that his struggle to bloom independently required him to dig in his heels, so I strove to give him air and plenty of sun. Even on bad days, when I wondered how I could possibly hold myself up as an exemplar of good mothering to millions of trusting *Parents* readers, his Caliban outbursts rarely overshadowed his delicious displays of love. I would sit with my face in my hands, hating the way I had yelled at him, choking on fatigue or frustration, and I would feel two pudgy hands peeling my fingers away, smell his salty, tear-stained face before it was pressed nose-to-nose with mine. "Are you smiling yet?" Nick once asked after a particularly ugly evening. "Are you ever gonna smile again?" And inevitably, I did.

The point is, whenever I felt myself sliding into emotional quicksand, there was almost always a little handshake of peace extended my way. During the teen years, when our children struggle once again to construct a sense of self—usually in direct opposition to qualities we pride in ourselves—we're treated to countless outbursts, often over such life-threatening issues as frizzy hair or fickle friends, but it's far less common to find a hand offered as a truce. In the book *Ophelia's Mom*, a collection of letters, e-mail messages, essays, and interviews with mothers of adolescent girls, one woman vented about her daughter's behavior by completing the sentence "I hate it when":

- you tell me you hate coming home and being home.
- you accuse me of yelling when I haven't raised my voice.
- I feel like a failure as a mom because of something you've said.
- you take my time for granted.
- I put my own things aside to be there for you and you turn around to accuse me of not "having a life."

- you repeatedly tell me to "fuck off" or to leave you "the fuck alone."
- I feel like becoming a parent was the worst choice I ever made.[4]

Just as the rapture of loving our children makes us feel passionate, proud, inspired, radiant, and hopeful, the experience of hating them pulls little stinging wires around our hearts. We feel worthless, inadequate, unlovable, raw. Beth, whom I met in Chicago, prided herself on being the kind of no-nonsense mother who had little trouble letting go. "With five kids, you really have no choice but to let them fend for themselves a lot more than if you have only one," she said. Unlike his four older sisters, Beth's son, then fourteen, "rarely bickered," but the explosive quality of his rage, combined with his physical size ("he is bigger than me, he is taller than me, and I can't physically make him do anything he doesn't want to"), made his occasionally violent outbursts "really frightening." As Beth described an incident when Peter, enraged by a friend's behavior, had smashed his phone into pieces, this confident mother of five burst into tears.

When we can't contain our anger or control our kids, we slide back, lose our footing on a path that, although rocky at times, had seemed until now fundamentally progressive. As the mom of a preschooler, you felt far more confident and empowered than you did as the mother of a newborn. By the time your child's school years rolled around, the wind in your sails kept you more or less on course. Even the challenges encountered during the preteen years rarely made you feel as though you were moving backward. But when our teens act like toddlers or when their behavior is hostile and ugly, the loss is twofold: We're forced to give up a way of loving them and we're expected to renounce an image of ourselves as competent that we've spent the better part of a lifetime developing.

"Christa and I are very much alike—both strong and stubborn," Sandra, the single mother of two daughters, explained. "So when she was going through that phase when I was the Enemy and she just pushed back about every single thing I said, I dealt with it by pushing that much harder. Eventually I learned to let up on her a little, to let go. It was really hard for me, because I am one controlling person. And I was scared to give her too much independence. So I held on real tight, too tight. I see that now." Sandra was able to shift from an authoritarian ("Do it because I say so!") to a more authoritative style ("Do it because you know it's right, and I trust you to do the right thing") only when she was willing to accept that she could not control what Christa did or did not do.

For mothers of teens, letting go is the seminal challenge of this phase of our lives. And only the superhuman—or the comatose—can pull it off without experiencing feelings of loss, resentment, anger, and exhaustion. On the other hand, if this process of change and separation produces a well-deserved feeling of pride and accomplishment, not to mention the pleasure of sharing life with an almost-full-fledged adult, then the teen years can be golden ones.

In fact, you may find that the same behavior that one day drives you screaming from the house can actually prove exciting, even charming, the next. For example, as your teenager's brainpower develops, so does her ability to formulate more mature opinions. She may still assume you're "totally wrong" before you've even opened your mouth, but the argument that follows has the potential to be far more engaging, interesting, and adult than discussions were a year or two ago. Your child's growing brain contributes to her improved debating skills, her ability to employ sarcasm, appreciate a pun, and maybe, just maybe, concede that you have a point. In fact, if your teen is going through a particularly belligerent phase, picking fights, mouthing off, and finding something as innocuous as "Hi. How did you sleep?" the equivalent of throwing the gauntlet, then it may help to see her argumentativeness simply as showing off newfound skills. Just as her ability to recite the alphabet at five meant you had to endure seventeen hundred renditions of "Now I Say My ABC's," her maturing cognitive skills need a workout now as well.[5] Personally, I would much prefer to engage in a heated conversation with Nick than experience an icy "Whatever," followed by a view of his back.

Unfortunately, certain aspects of your teen's growing brain may lead him to do some incredibly lamebrained things. Adolescents are notorious risk takers, a tendency that neurologists are beginning to explain by actually looking at the physiology of those areas of the brain that are associated with decision making. Researchers at Temple University found that even teens who demonstrate relatively good judgment in normal, low-arousal states are lousy "executive thinkers" when they're overly excited, stressed, or highly emotional. Put a teen with a bunch of boisterous friends in an unsupervised situation, and you're looking at a pretty typical "high-arousal" state. The fact that American teens have access to cars, alcohol, drugs, and guns at a time when they're supremely ill equipped to make sound judgments has deadly consequences. Once a child enters adolescence, his mortality rate soars by 300 percent.[6] The vast majority of teens (78 percent) try alcohol in high school, with some five million admitting to binge drinking at least once a month. One out of every five kids has sexual intercourse before turning fifteen—and far more are engaging in oral sex or other sex play they think "doesn't count."[7]

A Mother Bear Once More

Reading these statistics or, worse, recognizing that your kid is in pain or in trouble, as many are during adolescence, can make this phase of motherhood feel less like the toddler years and more like infancy. Just as you were probably advised to "trust your gut" or to "read your baby's signals" at a time when your gut twisted into a pretzel every time your newborn cried, your attempts to read your teen's behavior now inevitably run headlong into a wall of self-doubt and insecurity. When Maddie was a fragile, helpless newborn, exquisitely ill equipped to tell me what she needed, how could I know for sure that I had done the right thing? When she was a young teenager, increasingly independent, vulnerable, and unwilling to tell me what she needed, how could I know for sure that I had done the right thing? Panic attacks, which I associated with my first months as a mother, were part and parcel of my experience of the kids' adolescence. If Nick is late getting home or highly distressed, my mother-bear instinct to protect him produces the same rush of adrenaline that sent me running to his cribside or to the pediatrician's office during his infancy.

Every mother I know who has raised a teen can recall a moment in her teen's life—particularly when he went MIA—when she was "up all night," "frantic with worry," "a maniac," or "out of my mind." According to Pulitzer Prize–winning science writer Natalie Angier, the fight-or-flight feeling we get when our adolescents are out of the nest is intimately connected to the depth of our love for them. "Love is the child of outrage, arriving most readily in the wake of crisis," she writes in *Woman: An Intimate Geography*.[8] Just as, during birth, the fear and pain we feel trigger responses in our neurochemistry that, postpartum, are often experienced as blissful, joyous love, it's also true that the challenges of living with a teenager (including the moments of panic, rage, and fear) stir up feelings that make us want to "flee." But as much as we may give lip service to the notion of "giving up" or running away from our infuriating adolescents, we are much more likely to grab them by the shoulders and scream, "Where the hell were you last night? Don't you know you had me worried sick?" and then hug them hard to us. The hugging is born of the hurt; the intense love and desire to protect often come on the heels of imagining the worst.

I'll never forget how helpless and miserable I felt one night when Maddie, then thirteen, was unusually late returning from her piano lesson. When forty-five minutes slipped by, I phoned the music school, but the switchboard was closed for the day; then I tried one of her classmates, who said she had seen Maddie leaving the building right after their lesson. The school was located in a nice part of the city, about eight blocks away, but it was already dark outside, and in my panicky brain her walk home was getting darker and longer by the minute. Nick was helping me with dinner, and reluctant to alarm him, I tried to keep my cool, but the banging of pots and pans barely camouflaged the pounding in my head. I phoned Steve, but of course there wasn't anything he could do, except to suggest calmly that I go upstairs and try to reach the piano teacher at home.

We live in a fairly large house, and because the kitchen is one flight down from the front door, I sometimes don't hear when Steve or the kids enter or leave. So I suppose it should not have come as a total shock to discover Maddie sitting quietly at her desk in her room, oblivious to my near hysteria. Of course, she wasn't oblivious for long; I stood with my mouth agape, staring at her as though seeing a ghost, then I let loose with a tirade about how incredibly irresponsible she had been to not say hello, how thoughtless and selfish and God knows what to go straight to her room. Within seconds we were both crying and apologizing and embracing, because no sooner had my rage subsided than my feelings of love and need came flooding in.

Sandra, who grew up in a tough neighborhood, one of two girls in a family of six children, recalled the visceral reaction she had when her teenage daughter admitted that she was planning to fight a gang of girls in her school: "One day she calls me at work and she's yelling about how I have to braid up her hair. 'When you comin' home? You have to come home early so you can braid up my hair, Mommy, okay?' So I drag in around nine that night and she's all over me to do her hair in braids. So I ask her straight out, 'Are you planning to fight someone?' because I know that's what you do so they can't pull it. You wear a shirt they can't rip up; you even put Vaseline all over your face so you don't get scratched. You know what I'm saying? So she tells me that these girls are coming after her, because they think she ratted out their friends for a boy who she considers her best friend. It's not true, and she's telling me she tried to explain it until she's blue in the face and they don't believe her and they're meeting her the next day at school."

At first Sandra tried to reason with Christa. "Kids have guns and knives these days. It's not like when I was her age, but she kept telling me to stay out of it. That I'd only make it worse. That she could handle it." Sandra tried yelling, but Christa only yelled back. "Look, they're just trying to mess with me, Ma," she said—as though that would be good news.

"I was terrified," Sandra recalled. "I started to panic. I begged her and cried and hollered. I even called my ex—her dad—so you *know* I was upset!" When her ex-husband and several streetwise friends and relatives asked, "Does Christa seem upset and scared?" Sandra had to admit the answer was a definite no, and the next day she decided to let her go to school. "I did call a teacher there, who's like a guidance counselor to Christa, but she wasn't in." Sandra confessed that she spent the entire day imagining the worst. "But something in my gut told me she would be okay. And she was. Those girls backed off."

Denial Is Not a River in Egypt

Sandra's inner voice told her to back off, but more often we hear the buzz of misgivings or sense that something's just not right—and we don't listen. Gavin de Becker, best-selling author of *The Gift of Fear* and *Protecting the Gift,* has devoted much of his career to exhorting women to trust their intuition, to pay attention to the voices in their heads in order to protect themselves and their children. Frequently during our kids' teen years we ignore a nagging feeling or bury our mounting anxiety; we push aside some vague suspicion or choose not to follow a hunch. But all these signals, including doubt, hesitation, apprehension, and fear, which de Becker calls "messengers," are telling us to stop and pay attention.[9] In Sandra's case, her inner voice told her to let go and trust her daughter's judgment. But most of the moms I interviewed said their biggest mistakes came from not listening to what their hearts were saying—often loud and clear.

I thought about this recently when an old college friend called to say that her daughter was in rehab. Although I bit my tongue, my first thought was "At last!" Instead of blurting out the obvious, I listened sympathetically as she admitted to years of making excuses, rationalizing, and simply ignoring the signs. "I guess I knew something was going on, but I honestly never considered drugs," this highly educated, sophisticated *therapist* confessed. Recalling how she had actually accepted her daughter's explanation that the rolling papers in her purse belonged "to a friend," or that her violently upset stomach was caused by food poisoning, I marveled at the tenacity of denial.

As de Becker notes, "Just as intuition protects us from danger, denial protects us from something too: unwanted information. Denial serves to eliminate the discomfort of accepting realities we'd rather not acknowledge."[10] He goes on to parse the five key signals of denial—rationalization, justification, minimization, excuse-making, and refusal—all uncomfortably familiar to me. I have definitely dismissed as "no big deal" missed curfews or mood swings; rationalized as "okay this one time" an inadequately supervised party; excused behavior that my little inner voice told me to watch out for. Happily or luckily, when that voice was shrill enough or when Steve's excellent radar kicked in, we were able to step in and communicate our concerns.

More important, we were occasionally able to help the kids counter their own tendency to rationalize, minimize, make excuses, or justify a situation that was not a good idea. I'm thinking of a summer when Maddie was heading to Florence to study Italian and art for a month. She would be living in an apartment with older girls, navigating a city that was beautiful but totally unfamiliar, making friends with kids who spoke very little English, and keeping up with a rigorous schedule of classes.

Months before she left, I had warned her about Italian men, a stereotype that every woman I know who's been to Italy confirmed by sharing an anecdote about some guy's unrelenting pursuit of her or aggressive flirting or worse. But I didn't need their stories, because I had spent the July of my sixteenth summer in Venice, living with a family and tutoring their twelve-year-old son in English. Suffice it to say, I spent the entire month fighting off the sexual advances of the older brother, the father, the riding instructor, the painting teacher, the family doctor. This "How I Spent My Summer Vacation" sounds funny in retrospect, but I was not laughing back then. More important, my parents—who were exceedingly liberal when it came to sex—found my tales of hot-blooded Italians hilarious. So, of course, I played them for laughs. It was not until years later that I realized how confused and miserable I had been at times during that summer, and how unwilling I was to admit I needed help.

What I wanted Maddie to be able to do was very simple: trust her gut and avoid any and all situations that put someone else in the driver's seat, literally and figuratively. I also wanted her to know that whatever happened, she should never hesitate to ask for help. Steve and I rehearsed various scenarios with Maddie; talked about the importance of traveling around in groups; armed her with a cell phone; and, once she had left, said daily novenas.

Maddie had a fantastic experience, but what amazed me was how maturely she handled several encounters, asserting herself in ways I would never have managed at her age. "There was one day, Mom, when I was out with my friends," she recalled recently. "And a bunch of guys stopped us and were flirting and trying to get us to go out with them. I couldn't believe it, but one of the older girls in my group actually gave one of them her phone number. And then she was complaining when he called every night and drove her nuts."

Remembrance of Not-Nice Things Past

Recalling your own adolescence is always a mixed bag of emotions. You may peer through that looking glass and understand why Rapunzel was banished to a tower. (It wasn't Maddie's hair I worried she'd let down.) When the kids hit their teens, I often told myself that I was so much more mature at thirteen or fourteen or sixteen, but I know damned well that that was pure rationalization. I just pretended I knew how to handle myself. Once amusing, Steve's stories of leaving a party to drive six hours with friends to visit girls at a boarding school rattled around like large stones in my head.

I was sharing the dilemma of discussing one's past with Rachel, a friend whose children (a boy and a girl) are on the verge of adolescence, and when I broached the subject of afraid-they'll-ask questions ("How old were you the first time?" or "Did you ever smoke grass?"), she moaned. "The thing is, I was such a fucked-up adolescent! It was the seventies, so we all drank too much, we all took drugs, we all smoked. And it was a very promiscuous time—I mean it was like Studio 54. Everybody slept around, and we did, too. I was very sexually active, so I have a lot of fears that I project onto Molly, which isn't really fair. I mean her reality will be her reality, and there will be sex and drugs and all kinds of stuff in it, but it's not going to be my reality."

Rachel is right. Your child is going to star not in the movie of *your* life but in the music video of his. Your daughter may be just like you—a wild thing who wore too much makeup, ignored her curfew, and locked horns with her Republican parents—or she may be a total square, captain of the volleyball team, politically right of Ann Coulter. Your son may remind you of your cousin Mike, who dropped out of high school and did some time, in which case his occasional misdemeanors will set off alarms in your head. Or his behavior will seem just fine (especially compared with the kid next door) and it will be his dad or your sister who seems ready to label him no good.

The bottom line is that our teens probably *will* try drugs, get drunk, and have sex before they're in college (we hope not all on the same night). The most we can do is try to arm them with enough self-esteem and good sense to make only a few stupid decisions—none of them life-threatening—and to have the courage to learn from their mistakes. In fact, we really shouldn't aspire to raise Prince Perfect or Miss Goody Two-shoes. Why? Because there's compelling evidence that teens who *never* break the rules, who refuse *every* beer and cigarette and come-on, don't fare so well when they're out on their own. Think about the kids who die each year from binge drinking. Inevitably, there's an article citing the child's unsullied past. His parents or close friends appear totally flabbergasted. "He was always such a good boy . . . he never drank or did drugs—never." Apparently that's the problem. According to researchers at Boise State University who studied the drinking behavior of 266 incoming freshmen, the model students were less likely to know how to handle their liquor or how to pace themselves than veterans of the party scene. Also, they were less likely to have had a discussion about binge drinking with their parents.[11] Mom and Dad just assumed they knew better. After all, why would you have to tell an A+ student that drinking successive shots of vodka can kill you?

You have to talk to your kids for the simple reason that all teenagers say they have good judgment when they don't. All teenagers engage in risky behaviors, because they believe they're invulnerable. And all teenagers lie to their parents, even when it's patently obvious that they're guilty. "The thing that I find most frustrating with Rubin," one mom told me, "is that he will lie right to my face, even when I have incontrovertible proof that he's done something wrong." Your teenager will lie because he wants to avoid punishment, and he will cling to his version of the story with ever-mounting tenacity if he thinks there's even the slightest chance you might believe him. The key is to avoid the trap of focusing so intensely on the lying that you lose sight of the behavior behind it. As Anthony E. Wolf explains in *Get Out of My Life, But First Could You Drive Me and Cheryl to the Mall?*, "getting caught up in the issue of lying can become a snare, leading to long harangues that go nowhere. The lies can take precedence over the problem at hand, namely, whatever the teenager did that was forbidden."[12]

When you find yourself caught up in the heat of an argument or, as often happens, put on the spot or cornered, find a way to stop the music and step out of the dance. There's absolutely no way to communicate effectively with a teenager who is screaming "You don't trust me! You never believe me! I'm never, ever telling you anything again!" Nor is there a way to keep your cool and say exactly what you want when the top of your head has just flown off.

Faced with the challenge of staying calm and focused during "the worst experience of my whole life," Nina was able to discuss with her fifteen-year-old son the fact that she knew he had been drinking and drugging. Despite the fact that she felt "as though someone had cut the elevator cable," despite the murderous rage she felt toward her live-in niece, who had supplied her son with grass, despite her frustration with her husband, who "went into a blind panic," Nina didn't waste her energy on venting or blaming. And she chose not to punish her son for his lies or for his actions. "Initially he was very defensive, but once he broke down and told us what was going on, he was in such agony, so racked with guilt—he adores his cousin—that punishing him for getting high didn't seem appropriate. I felt that would push him away." Instead, she and her husband had a series of talks with their son about drugs and alcoholism, the family's history with the disease ("there's a long line of bad drinkers in our clan"), and the rules they expected their kids to follow. "We established some clear consequences, and frankly, we started doing a better job of calling the parents of friends he was hanging out with, of monitoring where he was going and with whom. But the reality is, we just had to trust him and pray that if he's having a hard time, he'll come to us again."

When It Comes to Sex

I told Nina I would join her in prayer, because more than anything these days, I worry that I won't know what's going on. Or I won't want to know. Or my kids won't want me to know what I know— particularly when it comes to sex. It's not so much the door to their room that I worry about them shutting but the door to our continued communication about a subject that's increasingly difficult to discuss. Embarrassment isn't a problem for me; I've had candid talks with the kids about everything from intercourse to STD's to oral sex. Maddie and I read The "What's Happening to My Body?" Book for Girls when she was in the fifth grade, and I've casually left other excellent books on sex lying around their rooms. Thanks to the content of 90 percent of the shows they watch on television, we've discussed date rape, masturbation, penis size, contraception, vibrators, and what I think "going to third base" really means.

But as the kids mature, I'm faced with the conundrum (a word that sounds vaguely X-rated) of trying to provide the right information without crossing the line into conversations that are gratuitously revealing or unnecessarily personal. In Everything You Never Wanted Your

Kids to Know About Sex (But Were Afraid They'd Ask), Justin Richardson and Mark A. Schuster note, "It's one thing to say, 'Sex can be wonderful,' to your six-year-old, who is making puke sounds about it in the backseat. It's another to say it to the sixteen-year-old seated up front next to you. You know and she knows that you didn't just read about this in a book. As your child grows older and more sophisticated in her thinking, you may begin to sense that when you talk to her about sex, she sees through to this little truth: what you say is informed by your own sex life."[13]

At our house, anything beyond a peck on the cheek is guaranteed to elicit groans of disgust. "I wish you had been there on New Year's Eve," I overheard Nick tell Maddie last January 1. "I had to sit and watch Mom and Dad make out." Believe me, our purported "make-out" session lasted about five seconds, but Nick's heightened sensitivity to our displays of physical intimacy was clearly related to the complicated and dramatic changes he was experiencing every day.

Richardson and Schuster attribute teens' aversion to accepting their parents' sexuality to the incest taboo: "A parent and a child will try to keep their sexual feelings private from each other, because to share them would raise the fear that something in the way of arousal could pass between them. As children grow older and more sexually developed, and as their sexual appetites strengthen, efforts to prevent this worrisome possibility get stepped up."[14] As they explain, even talking about sex makes parents and teens uncomfortable because it requires recognizing and imagining the other as a sexual person. And no one—particularly a teenager—wants to picture his parents getting it on.

For several single moms, the old saw "Do as I say, not as I do" echoed down a particularly empty chamber during their kids' teen years. "I haven't been dating for over a year," Sandra, who has two daughters, told me. "But I was thinking recently, 'How would I do this?' When they were little, and I was in a serious relationship, if the guy I was seeing slept over, I just had to get him out of the house before they woke up. They were basically clueless. Now that they're both dealing with their own sexuality, I feel like they're much more impressionable. I really don't think I would be able to be comfortable in bed with someone in my room next to theirs."

When she heard recently from her niece that her youngest, Moriah, "thirteen going on ten," had been sitting on a boy's lap, "reaching out for attention from boys," Sandra sat her down for a talk about "respect and what's appropriate touching and sex." But as Sandra was quick to admit, her daughter listened attentively, only to point out that she had seen her mom sit on men's laps, "so what's the difference?"

Three thousand miles away in London, Morven echoed Sandra's ambivalence when she talked about the challenge of raising her teenage son alone. "I don't have a life!" she said. "Basically I come to work, go home, and once in a blue moon I sort of arrange to go out and see friends. But I haven't had a real relationship since Thomas was born." Her conviction that she needed "to bring some other strands" into her life, to date more, was tempered by her awareness that Thomas's adolescence, his budding sexuality, might make this the worst time for her to focus on her own social life. "It's so difficult to know what they need at this stage," she said with a sigh. "You know, I wonder if there will be a time when he wants to talk about whether he should sleep with the girl he's dating. And if I'm not there at the right time—if I'm out with some guy—I'll miss this incredibly important opportunity. How ironic!"

The irony at our house is the fact that my children's sexual development coincides with my approaching menopause. This, as Mary Kaye Blakeley points out in her memoir, *American Mom,* is proof that God is not a woman.[15] The hormones roaring through our house at certain times of the month make Dorothy's ride atop the cyclone look mild. And there's no question that as much as I savor my children's physical beauty—find myself admiring the lovely curve of Maddie's waist or the toned firmness of Nick's arms and back—I also envy the promise of their bodies. I would love to wake up and look the way Maddie does even when she shuffles into the kitchen, hair unwashed, no makeup; I wish my neck, thighs, breasts looked like hers or that I could still attract the looks she doesn't even notice when we walk into a restaurant together. In *Fruitful,* Anne Roiphe eloquently describes the experience of walking down the street with her pubescent daughter: "I know she's releasing a barely decent scent. It precedes us, it follows us as we walk around. I feel old, dowdy, slightly envious of the way the sun shines on her skin, the way the muscles in her legs flex, the way she walks trying out a discreet hip swing from side to side, the way her hand flips through her hair."[16]

Even movie stars are not immune. In an interview about playing an older woman, the beautiful Brooke Adams talked about her feelings toward her then fifteen-year-old daughter: "It's just very hard to suddenly become invisible when you walk on the street, not to get those looks from men—all of that stuff that you kind of take for granted and pretend you don't care about or don't like, but you rely on a lot."[17]

For some mothers this awareness of their "sexual devolution," as one friend put it, brings out competitive or even inappropriate behavior. "I realize now how often I flirted with the girls' boyfriends," the mother of twins told me. "I wasn't aware of it until my own mother pointed it out. And though I was really defensive and angry at first, I had to admit I turned on the high beams around certain of their male friends. I'm really quite ashamed of it, looking back."

Feeling envious, competitive, or suddenly displaced when your teenager falls in love for the first time may be natural, but it's usually unexpected and often guilt-provoking. Even if you think the young man or woman in question is a doll, you're suddenly relegated to a sad and awkward corner. Even if you swear your child's happiness makes you happy, the longing for a time when nightingales sang from blossoming trees the minute your beloved entered the room may render your own garden sadly in need of weeding (or planting). Even if you think you're prepared to deal with the inevitable break your adolescent's first romance produces, think again.

"Every time Will would go to a school dance, I hoped he would meet a nice girl, but then when he did, I was stunned," Sharon, the mother of an adorable sixteen-year-old admitted. "He would have these whispered phone conversations for hours, and I would find myself getting more and more pissed off. I was jealous—I was definitely jealous."

Chloe's daughter, Becky, came out during her junior year in high school, and for Chloe the hardest part of accepting Becky's sexual orientation was realizing that another woman had taken her place in her daughter's heart: "I never had a problem with Becky's lesbianism. In fact, I bent over backward making her friends feel comfortable and letting them know that I was PC. But it was very hard to accept that I was no longer the primary woman in her life, that I had been replaced by another female. It helped that I really, really liked her girlfriend.

And I thought, 'Well, I would hang out with her if I were eighteen, too.'" When I pointed out that this relationship clearly went beyond "hanging out," Chloe laughed and admitted that she was somewhat lax in establishing boundaries, because "the girls had been going up to Becky's room for years, giggling behind closed doors." Then one afternoon the giggling from the other side of the door stopped her in her tracks: "I was going up the steps to her room, and giving them plenty of notice by walking loudly before actually knocking. I remember that I stopped on the steps and actually reversed, because I could tell from the whispering and laughing that they were having an intimate moment. But I needed Becky for something, so the second time I really stomped and banged my way up the stairs before knocking. When she came out, she was buckling up her pants and she had this, well, post-sex look about her. It was very stunning; it made her sexuality concrete, not abstract."

The writer Erich Fromm once described the difference between erotic and motherly love this way: "In erotic love, two people who were separate become one. In motherly love, two people who were one become separate."[18] When one's child becomes one with someone else, you can't, nor should you want to, be a part of that. Still, for some mothers, accepting their child's outsideness is particularly tough, as a letter I received from a *Family Circle* reader aptly illustrates: "My seventeen-year-old daughter is madly in love with a really nice boy she's been seeing for close to a year. The other night she got back from a date and I could tell from her behavior and not-so-subtle remarks that they had had sex. My daughter shares everything with me—we have a wonderful, loving relationship and have always talked openly and honestly about sex—but I didn't want to hear about her 'big night.' I went to bed feeling just miserable."

In addition to struggling with her feelings of having been suddenly displaced by her daughter's boyfriend, this mom sensed the need for boundaries at a critical turning point in her and her daughter's life. Should she let her daughter talk about her "big night"? And, more important, what about discussing her own sexual history? Several experts advocate sharing your experiences—including admitting your mistakes or recounting regrets—as a way of communicating the fact that you know what you're talking about, but only if you're able to draw the line when your teen's curiosity invades your privacy. Richardson and Schuster recommend that if your daughter or son asks an awkward question, you handle it by "asking him how he would react if the answer was yes and if the answer was no."[19] I think it's also okay to just say, "That's private. But why do you ask?"

What strikes me as most critical is that you communicate the message that communication *is* the message when it comes to good sex. Being able to talk to the person you love, to make certain that sex is always consensual and that both partners feel comfortable expressing what they like and what they don't, should be the headline every time our kids broach the topic of relationships. Long before they get involved with someone sexually, they'll be practicing and demonstrating their skills at asserting themselves, listening, empathizing, and negotiating with their friends and family.

When Sandra's daughter Christa stood up for a boy, a troubled kid whom she had tried to help, only to have him dismiss her efforts and fail to reciprocate, she cut him off completely. "What really impressed me was how strong and sure she was with him. She phoned him and said, 'Don't ever call my house! Don't contact me! We're through!' And this is someone she had cut classes for to help. I was proud that when she saw he wouldn't be there for her, she said, 'Forget you!' I would never be able to do that. I can't even do that now!"

I felt the same way when I overheard Nick telling a friend why he was angry with him. His clear, unapologetic, highly constructive feedback was simply mind-blowing. When he got off the phone, he actually asked me why I was staring at him. "Because I could not believe how maturely you handled that conversation, honey."

"Whatever."

I Love You When You're Like/Not Like Me

We love the better halves of our teens, the parts we lack or envy or through which we taste a vicarious thrill. We loathe and fear those things that remind us all too vividly of ourselves or of our mothers and the hatred we harbored for these qualities when we were teens. In an essay entitled "One Week Until College," Sandi Kahn Shelton describes the torture of having her eighteen-year-old daughter suddenly shut her out, become distant and angry, at a time when she longs for "smiles through tears, bittersweet moments of reminiscence, and the chance to offer the last little bits of wisdom I might be able to summon for her." At one point she turns to her younger daughter, age nine, for a little of the affection and love her teenager can't provide: "I hug her to me ferociously, as though I could hug all daughters trying to break away. I am not unaware that I am hugging my long-ago self, standing there so furiously, glaring at my mother, unable to forgive her."[20]

There's no question that our relationships with our own mothers— that hot or cold wind that blows throughout our lives—churns the waters with particular power during the teen years. For mothers of daughters this is especially true, because our identification with our adolescent girls is, by definition, more complete and more intensely felt. And as many of us learned when we were teens, our effort to form an identity that was as different as possible from that of our moms drove us to act in ways that were, let's just say, not always pretty.

"I hated my mother—really, really hated her—throughout my adolescence," a close friend recalled. "I couldn't wait to go to college and move out, to be as far away from her physically and emotionally as possible." Living halfway across the country from her mom was the easy part; having a rebellious teenage daughter brought the unresolved emotional connection screaming back into the house. "Sometimes I feel as though I'm channeling my mother—not just in the clichéd sense of sounding just like her when I talk to Angela—but in the ways I silence my anger, usually by denying it."

Having grown up with a mother who, despite her many extraordinary qualities, had a terribly hard time expressing her anger, I knew immediately what my friend was describing. And I also knew that I had modeled exactly the same kind of behavior with Maddie. "Are you mad?" she would ask me after doing something that any sane mother would have found infuriating, and true to Mama's model, I would inevitably reply, "No. I'm just tired." Anger, dressed in fatigue, would creep back down, leaving behind a tense and toxic silence.

Then one day I overheard Maddie talking to a friend, who I happened to know had done something really hurtful, about which— moments ago—Maddie had been bitterly complaining. "No, I'm not pissed," I heard her say. "I'm just really tired." It was a big "oh, no" moment for me, not only because I suddenly heard that my-mother-myself tune blaring loud and clear but because I had just spent forty-five minutes coaching Maddie on what to say to her friend, how to be more assertive and honest about her feelings. I should just have shut my trap and called a good therapist, who might have helped me exorcise my own ghosts.

My mother used to compliment me by saying, "You've inherited all of my worst characteristics." I say "compliment" because she would say this affectionately whenever I reported that I had volunteered for yet another nonprofit organization or had stayed up all night making crêpe-paper toques for Nick's birthday party or had performed any number of self-sacrificial acts typical of hers truly. Looking back, I realize the powerful sway her identification with me had on the choices I made—both good and bad. Only when I veered into territory of which she disapproved (certain boyfriends come to mind) or refused to confide my feelings (a cardinal sin in my family) did she suddenly profess to be "tired."

But because my mother and I rarely locked horns, I never went through the kind of turbulent rebellion considered the norm. Throughout my teen years I rarely experienced my mother as an embarrassment or an intrusion. I not only loved her, I liked her. And while she certainly didn't make it easy for me to break away, she only rarely clung with a bit too much force. Of course, the question remains—perhaps for the therapist's couch—whether I see myself as a lot like my mother because she made sure I grew up that way or if my development was free of the message "I love you the most when you're most like me."

I came face-to-face with the ugly possibility that I was sending just such a message to Maddie one summer early in her teen years. She was weeping into an uneaten bagel, begging, "I don't want to leave . . . I want to go home with you." We were in the American Airlines terminal, hiding from the teen tour group she would be hiking around the West Coast with for a month. She had been looking forward to this trip for six months, corresponding via e-mail with some of the kids, making meticulous multicolumn lists of to-dos, laughing off my jokes about stowing away in her backpack. But now she was trying to crawl into my pocket, regressing, her face crumpled and trembling, her tears abundant and real. "I wish I didn't feel this way. I wish I was more confident. More like you, Mom."

This last comment broke my heart. I wanted her to feel more confident, too. But did I want her to be more like me? Had I made her feel inadequate because she couldn't plunge into a group of peers, stick out her hand, and smilingly say, "Hi! I'm Maddie." She couldn't camouflage her insecurity by turning up the charm dial, the way I can.

As the tears continued to fall, I tried a little rah-rah speechifying ("You're going to have a fabulous time . . . everyone's nervous right now . . . this is the toughest part . . . you're going to see incredible sights . . . it's only four weeks), but when nothing seemed to bolster her confidence, I began to lose my patience. With her departure time nearing, I veered uncomfortably into the annoyance lane. "This isn't how we planned it," I thought miserably. "Why can't she just shake it off?" And then, of course, I felt like an ogre and contemplated whisking her back to the car and home for the summer.

When our children are not like us, when their personalities begin to take shape and the qualities we associate with a successful adulthood—integrity, intelligence, thoughtfulness, tenacity, determination, ambition, affection—are in low gear or in reverse, we often panic or become infuriated. How many times have I heard a parent vent, "I can't believe he thinks that dressing that way is attractive." Or, "He just doesn't seem to care about anything! He's so unmotivated, it drives me nuts." Or, "The only person she cares about is herself." Or any number of complaints about a teenager's lack of character, conviction, or compassion.

Teenagers can be self-centered, willful, moody, and rebellious; they're reinventing themselves every day, trying on different roles, struggling to stitch together an identity that is uniquely their own. The reason they act like two-year-olds at times is because they're going through a psychological adjustment very much akin to the I'm-my-own-person transformation of toddlerhood. And just as it was you whom your toddler pushed away, then ran back to find, it will be you who, by turns, drives your teenager crazy or inspires him to excel.

When your recalcitrant seventeen-year-old refuses help in math even though he's been getting C's, or when your fifteen-year-old daughter, the chess prodigy, decides slide guitar is more her thing, you may feel as though the ground has splintered under your feet and your chances of climbing back onto a happy, grassy knoll are nil. But the cavern you're peering down into isn't as bottomless as you imagine. Underneath the Mohawk is a kid with whom you may still have much in common; in fact, recognizing that your teenager is quite separate and different from you is a gift. It spares you the curse of unrealistic expectations, of trying to force your teenager into a mold defined by your fantasies, not by hers, of sending the destructive message "If you will bury the parts I don't like, then I will love you."[21]

Whose College Application Is It?

We all know parents who send this insidious message, who wear their children's accomplishments like a designer blouse. One mother I know actually called me recently to say, "We got into Yale!" Her narcissistic boast is the extreme of our natural tendency to overidentify with our teens. As a woman I met at our twenty-fifth college reunion confided, "I'd like to say that I want her to do whatever makes her happy, but that's not completely true. I want her to do whatever makes her happy—as long as it helps her get into a good school." Too often we give lip service to this "whatever makes you happy, honey," ideal while we're pushing our children along a path dug deep and long ago.

Try as I might to send the message to Maddie that there wasn't a cell in my body that cared where she went to college—"as long as it makes you happy, honey"—I know from the (thankfully) few times she screamed, "I can't get into that school! Stop pressuring me!" that I probably deserve a B-minus for my behavior during her senior year. The truth is, I really, really didn't care what bumper sticker we slapped on the back of our car, I really did want what she wanted, but it killed me to see her fall into despair and cry, "I'm not good enough for that school!" or to watch her awareness of her own strengths melt into a puddle of self-doubt and anxiety.

The college-application process forces teens not only to articulate a flattering portrait of themselves but to "sell" that image to others. It is cruel and unusual punishment, particularly for kids who haven't a clue who they are or want to be. (And that covers just about 90 percent of the teens I know.) Even for those with a highly inflated sense of self-worth (that covers the remaining 10 percent), the experience of watching the best and the brightest of their peers stumble and often fall can be painfully humbling.

It's painful for us, too. In that sense, the sacrifices we make—emotional and practical (it takes a lot of time and money to apply to college these days)—are not entirely altruistic. We strive to avoid suffering twice—for them and for ourselves. So if your child's idea of putting his best foot forward is to put his foot in his mouth, if he's loath to discuss his passion for the clarinet for fear of seeming un-cool, or if he tends to avoid eye contact with anyone over thirty, then the prospect of his interviewing for colleges may drive you onto a ledge. Don't go there. Don't offer "constructive criticism" as he heads into the admissions office. And definitely don't look over his shoulder through every step of the application process, unless you're invited to do so. Even then you'll be expected to walk that barely visible line between guiding and goading, coaxing and coauthoring, inspiring and interfering.

The good news is that by the time your child is applying to college, chances are the worst of the teenage years will be behind you. "They do come back," Dorothy said, sighing, as she recalled her stepdaugh-ter's journey through adolescence. "You think you've lost them com-pletely, or you wonder, 'Who is this?' But then they reappear, bigger and sometimes better."

Anticipating the Empty Nest

Of course, as the title of this chapter implies, by the time you've fig-ured it all out, they fly away. Phyllis Theroux wrote about the end of her kids' adolescence: "It is leaving me. The power I once held ab-solutely over my children's lives. I no longer hold a fat ball of twine in my hand but a fistful of string from the end of the skein."[22] As you trace the course of that ball of string, stretching back as it does through eighteen years of motherhood, you'll see tangles and tapes-tries and, one hopes, sense the strong, generous net you have woven for your children. That net will never go away; it will support them when you're not around and draw your children back to you in the years to come.

What's hard is learning to stop weaving that net yourself and letting your kids mend it themselves. And, at the same time, to imagine and plan for a life that will be as dramatically different as your years were before you became a mother. Just as we had to prepare ourselves for the tremendous impact our children's arrival would have on our identities and on our relationships, the end of this stage of motherhood requires an equally dramatic—and far more heart-wrenching—adjustment.

Few negotiate this transition without moments of sheer despair and longing for the past. I used to tease my friend Patty when, during the final months before her daughter went off to college, she filled her calendar with events made suddenly important by the fact that they would be "the last basketball game Meaghan will play against the Dalton School" or "the last time we'll attend a class play with Meaghan" or "the last time I'll be able to go shopping with her on the first Tuesday of the spring sales season." Now that Maddie's departure for college is just months away, I'm finding similarly desperate excuses to connect.

I'm also haunted by the memory of my own mother during the spring of my senior year in high school. She used to hang around my room, asking inane questions about school or my friends, coming in late at night to sit on the edge of my bed and pat my back or give me a kiss good night. I didn't think much of her slightly excessive attention until I happened to overhear her talking to my father late one night. Actually, she was shouting—shouting and sobbing—in a way I had never heard before. I couldn't discern every word, although I admit that I tried very hard, but her heartbreak was stunning to me. As she cried about wanting to get a job, wanting to fill the void my departure would bring, I sensed not only her panic and profound sadness but her anger at my father, who she believed neither understood nor really cared.

These days Steve is as likely to tear up about his adored daughter's imminent departure as I am. We're both stunned to have reached this place along the path and to sense the even scarier transition that lies ahead when Nick goes off to college. "I just can't believe it," I whisper across our pillows in the dark, and when Steve sighs like a lovesick teenager, I know he's heard me. I'm extremely grateful that we're on a similar emotional page, at least right now. For some mothers, saying good-bye to their grown children seems to shine a harsh light on their marriages. "I know Bruce is sad to see Rob go," the mother of an only son confessed, "but when he talks about the fun we'll have in our soon-to-be-empty nest, the trips we'll be able to take, and the kind of freedom we'll have next year, I feel as though we're shouting at each other across an ocean. I'm feeling miserable. And he just doesn't get it."

As is true during other phases of motherhood, the need to believe that your husband is feeling your pain, that you're in step during this last difficult adjustment, can lead to disappointment and anger. Which may explain in part why, despite an overall decline in divorce rates, there has been a 16 percent increase in the number of divorces among couples who have been married thirty or more years.[23] But it's unrealistic and unfair to expect your husband to "get it." His relationship with your children, his sense of himself as a father, and the degree to which that image is central to his identity are vastly different from yours. More important, he's not the man you married—just as you are dramatically different at this stage of your relationship than you were twenty or so years ago.

According to John Gottman, who has conducted several important long-term studies of marriage, "the Four Horsemen of the Apocalypse" in a relationship are criticism, contempt, defensiveness, and stonewalling.[24] If you never get beyond "He just doesn't get it," you effectively give up at a time when, more than ever, you need to find ways to express your feelings, listen with compassion, and hold on to each other for support.

Moms Need Friends at This Time

If your husband can't come through for you or if you happen to be single or divorced, don't try to go it alone during the teen years—especially when the going gets tough. Long before your teenager heads out the door, you will have experienced acute loneliness and a need for someone—anyone—to pull up a chair, make you a cup of tea, and listen to you vent. Just as it may have been the mothers you met in your Lamaze class who understood you best when you were together in the postpartum trenches, it may be the mom of another college-bound kid who looks you in the eye and lets you see yourself.

If you're fortunate enough to have a band of empty-nesting friends, seek them out. There's actual scientific evidence that suggests our instinct to "tend and befriend" when we're stressed is highly adaptive and beneficial. Our behavior may be driven by that friendly hormone, oxytocin, which women, unlike men, release in response to stress. Just as oxytocin made us feel warm and cozy while we breast-fed our infants, it makes our connections with other women particularly soothing.[25]

These days I don't need a neuroscientist to inspire me to pick up the phone and confess to my friend Val or Patty or Maxine that I'm already mourning Maddie's absence from my life, that I wish there was a way to reclaim my heart, mind, and soul from hers because it feels as though they're being wrenched out from somewhere very deep inside me. They never preach or try too hard to placate, but when I finally pause long enough to ask, "How's your life?" they inevitably shine a light into the dark. Having watched each of them and many others—my older sister, colleagues, cousins, and, of course, my own mother—find a way to redefine who they are during this last stage of motherhood, I am reminded of how resilient, powerful, creative, patient, and blessed mothers are. And how proud I am to be one.

Conclusion

When I started work on this book, I was naïve (or arrogant) enough to believe I could complete it in a couple of years. Then, as a couple of years became four and my patient publisher granted another extension, I would joke that "perhaps by the time the kids go off to college, I will have finished." (In darker moments it was "Perhaps by the time I'm a grandmother" or "Maybe before I die!") If all goes according to plan, Maddie will enter college the same month this book goes on sale and I will be able to make the honest claim that I've experienced all seven stages of motherhood. More important, I will confess unapologetically that, in the process of writing this book, I have learned as much as I have hoped to impart about what it takes to raise happy, healthy, confident children.

I have learned that motherhood is as much about autonomy, independence, and self-actualization as it is about connectedness, dependence, and self-sacrifice. It's about taking risks and lashing ourselves to traditions, tolerating lightning-speed changes and mind-numbing boredom, juggling the practical along with the ineffable, and learning how to push through when life is so full of pain or bliss it hurts to breathe.

It's also about living up to expectations that are cruelly unrealistic. Raising children may be the most gratifying experience available to women, but it's also the most challenging; believing that you can somehow avoid the anxiety, ambivalence, anger, and guilt that are endemic to motherhood only promises more of the same. That said, there is no reason to believe that you won't look back on the seven stages of your development as a mother and feel as though you could rule the world.

The mothers I interviewed for this book—and the millions of others like them—*could* rule the world. Their passion, determination, commitment, strength, energy, empathy, humor, kindness, wisdom, and courage were revealed in mundane and monumental ways. Just the other day I watched a young mom board a crowded bus, soothe her tired toddler, shoulder his screaming baby sister, and fold up their stroller in less time than it took the passenger behind her to mount the stairs. A few minutes later I glimpsed rapture on the face of a seven-year-old whose mother—dressed to the nines—was holding his hand and skipping idiotically down the street. And later that afternoon I witnessed the mother of a teenager finesse a tense moment in a boutique with diplomatic aplomb.

As always, I saw myself in each of these women, remembered what it felt like to drape exhausted children over my shoulders, to make their day by acting ridiculous, or to circumvent a meltdown by negotiating a compromise. But there are thousands of other memories that have been lost to time, boxes of snapshots I wish I could leaf through and appreciate not only for the sheer pleasure of reliving them but for the sense of accomplishment I would undoubtedly experience.

Like most mothers, I tend to sweat—not take credit for—the small stuff; I let should-have, could-have, would-have guilt overwhelm much-deserved feelings of pride. If there's one thing I hope you have learned from this book, it's that you need to pay attention to the little acts of caring you perform every day. Don't minimize what you do— even when you know things could have gone better—because when you take yourself for granted or when you focus only on your short-comings, the people you shortchange are your kids.

Every mother makes mistakes—big mistakes. But along with society's conflicting messages about what makes a good-enough mother, there's an implicit bias these days that the ultimate failure is to fail as a parent. We tolerate failed marriages and the concomitant high rates of divorce; we tolerate failed politicians, business leaders, priests. But we send the message to mothers that if their children mess up, it's their fault. Worse, long before a child stumbles, we fly the "mothering comes naturally" banner with aggressive cheer, failing to show moms what's printed on the other side: "If mothering doesn't come naturally, keep it to yourself." And in even smaller type: "Because asking for help is tantamount to admitting you've failed."

Burn that banner! There is nothing inherently "natural" about turning your life inside out, reshaping your identity, drastically re-aligning your priorities, rethinking your relationships, and assuming responsibility for people you love more than life itself. Every mother on the planet needs help and support, not only in the practical sense of sharing the load or lending a hand but in navigating the shadowy alleyways where guilt and self-doubt lurk. When we shine a light into those spaces and say, "Hey, you're doing a great job. We all go through this. Don't be so hard on yourself," or when we advise a mother to stop what she's doing and really think about what she wants, or when we tell her to put herself first on her list once in a while, we stand a better chance of practicing what we preach.

That's really why I wrote this book. I wanted other mothers to learn from my mistakes as well as from what I may have done right. I wanted readers to know that this crazy, messy, really tough business of raising our kids hardly ever progresses in a predictable way; we rarely move consistently forward through the stages of motherhood. There's as much circling, sliding, and falling back as there is surging ahead. Because our paths frequently double back, we revisit key issues and face seminal challenges at every stage of our development: how to bal-ance work and family; when to coddle, when to let go; how to trust your gut; nurture your marriage; get a grip on your anxiety; set limits; tolerate intense feelings of love and anger. For some mothers these challenges are greatest during their children's toddler years; for others their kids' adolescence remains the ultimate crucible. You may find that the phase you most dreaded was a walk in the sun compared with a period you fully expected to sail through. Although your child's behavior may be what you choose to credit or blame for your feelings, that suitcase of personal and cultural baggage you're dragging around has as much—or more—to do with your experience.

Unpacking those bags and taking a good, hard look at yourself is a lifelong process. You can't do it while the train is moving; often you can't do it alone. But if you do manage to stop and to pay close attention to how your own childhood experiences, current stresses, cultural expectations, hopes, and fears inform your interactions with your children, you'll stand a much better chance of putting those interactions into perspective. Until you know what you're about, you can't appreciate your child for who he truly is. And being accepted and loved—warts and all—is what every kid wants and deserves.

This past winter Steve and I celebrated our fiftieth birthdays and twenty-five years of marriage with a large party for family and friends. It was a magical evening, highlighted by the toasts Maddie and Nick gave. Along with plenty of jokes at our expense were generous and genuine expressions of their love and gratitude. But it didn't really matter what they said; just the vision of them, poised and beautiful and fully their own people, held me spellbound. Throughout the night I watched them—talking and dancing and laughing—and saw them not only as teenagers but as infants, toddlers, preschoolers, schoolchildren, preteens, and soon-to-be adults. They were all there, celebrating not only who Maddie and Nick were but the woman I had become.

No matter where we are in our development as mothers, we carry with us vestiges of our mother-selves from earlier phases. The skills we developed, the muscles we built, and the mistakes we made stay with us forever. Motherhood is the ultimate never-ending story; we may become less central in our children's lives, but we never separate completely and neither do they. In her book *Woman: An Intimate Geography,* Natalie Angier describes how years after we deliver our children, stray fetal cells continue to circulate through our bodies. Until recently, this "fetal-maternal cell dialogue" was believed to last only through pregnancy, but now we know that these cells last for decades: "A mother, then, is forever a cellular chimera, a blend of the body she was born with and of all the bodies she has borne. Which may mean nothing, or it may mean that there is always something there to remind her, a few biochemical bars of a song, capable of playing upon her neural systems of attachment."[1]

Our children's melodies enrich and haunt our lives from the moment we conceive until the end of our days. Sometimes they're in tune with our own songs, but more often they're set to a very different beat—one we may find frighteningly unfamiliar. No sooner do we pick out the rhythm and learn the notes than the music changes and we're expected to sing another tune entirely. No wonder we often feel out of breath. Sometimes the best we can do is close our eyes and listen; if we're lucky, by the time our children leave home, they may actually be singing our praises.

NOTES

Introduction

1. Erik H. Erikson, *Childhood and Society* (New York: W. W. Norton, 1950), p. 65.
2. Rozsika Parker, *Torn in Two: The Experience of Maternal Ambivalence* (London: Virago Books, 1995), p. 103.
3. Peter B. Neubauer, M.D., and Alexander Neubauer, *Nature's Thumbprint: The New Genetics of Personality* (Reading, Mass.: Addison-Wesley, 1990), p. 20.

Stage 1
Altered States: *Pregnancy, Birth, and the Fourth Trimester*

1. Daphne de Marneffe, *Maternal Desire: On Children, Love, and the Inner Life* (Boston: Little, Brown, 2004), p. 98.
2. Fay Weldon, from personal interview in Rozsika Parker, *Torn in Two: The Experience of Maternal Ambivalence* (London: Virago Books, 1995), p. 5.
3. Harriet Lerner, *The Mother Dance: How Children Change Your Life* (New York: HarperCollins, 1998), p. 57.
4. Daniel N. Stern, M.D., and Nadia Bruschweiler-Stern, M.D., with Alison Freeland, *The Birth of a Mother: How the Motherhood Experience Changes You Forever* (New York: Basic Books, 1998), p. 37.
5. I. Rodolfo A. Bulatao, "Values and Disvalues of Children in Successive Childbearing Decisions," *Demography*, vol. 18, no. 1 (February 1981).
6. Louise Erdrich, *The Blue Jay's Dance: A Birth Year* (New York: HarperCollins, 1995), p. 9.
7. John Updike, "When Everyone Was Pregnant," in *The Early Stories, 1953–1975* (New York: Knopf, 2003), p. 446.
8. De Marneffe, *Maternal Desire*, p. 83.

9. Robbie E. Davis-Floyd, *Birth as an American Rite of Passage* (Berkeley: University of California Press, 1992), p. 33.

10. Natalie Angier, *Woman: An Intimate Geography* (New York: Houghton Mifflin, 1999), p. 309.

11. Meredith F. Small, *Our Babies, Ourselves: How Biology and Culture Shape the Way We Parent* (New York: Anchor Books, 1998), p. 13.

12. Davis-Floyd, *American Rite of Passage,* p. 30.

13. Survey conducted by Harris Interactive for the Maternity Center Association (MCA) in partnership with Johnson & Johnson Pediatric Institute, *Parenting,* December 2002/January 2003, p. 96.

14. Lise Friedman Spiegel, "Planned Cesarean Delivery and Its Effect on Maternal Self-Esteem and Locus of Control," *Dissertation Abstracts International, Section B: The Sciences and Engineering,* vol. 56, no. 5-B (November 1995), p. 2888.

15. Centers for Disease Control data, 2000.

16. Anita Diamant, *The Red Tent* (New York: Picador, 1997), p. 226.

17. Joyce Block, *Motherhood as Metamorphosis: Change and Continuity in the Life of a New Mother* (New York: Penguin Books, 1990), p. 183.

18. Marshall H. Klaus and John H. Kennell, *Maternal-Infant Bonding: The Impact of Early Separation or Loss on Family Development* (St. Louis: C. V. Mosby, 1976), pp. 88–89.

19. Susan H. Greenberg and Karen Springen, "The Baby Blues and Beyond," *Newsweek,* July 2, 2001, p. 26.

20. Sarah Blaffer Hrdy, *Mother Nature: Maternal Instincts and How They Shape the Human Species* (New York: Ballantine, 1999), p. 167.

21. Elizabeth Berg, "'I Can't Believe You're Here!': A New Mother's Diary," *Parents,* April 1992, pp. 98–102.

22. Karen Binder-Brynes, personal interview, November 2001.

23. Kate Figes, *Life After Birth: What Even Your Friends Won't Tell You About Motherhood* (New York: Penguin Books, 1998), p. 41.

24. Stern and Bruschweiler-Stern, *Birth of a Mother,* p. 105.

25. Marnell Jameson, "A Natural Formula for Success," *Los Angeles Times,* September 4, 2000, p. S1.

26. Sally Tusa, "BabyTalk: Breast vs. Bottle Poll," *BabyTalk,* vol. 66, no. 7, September 2001, p. 38.

27. Mary Ellen Rodgers, "Like Mother, Like Child," *American Health,* July 1992, p. 30.

28. Erdrich, *Blue Jay's Dance,* p. 148.

29. Natalie Angier, *Woman,* p. 315.

30. Ibid., p. 316.

31. Parker, *Torn in Two,* p. 7.

32. Block, *Motherhood,* p. 17.

33. T. Berry Brazelton, *Touchpoints: Your Child's Emotional and Behavioral Development: Birth–3* (Reading, Mass.: Addison-Wesley, 1992), p. 38.

34. Parker, *Torn in Two*, p. 74.

35. Susan H. Greenberg and Karen Springen, "The Baby Blues and Beyond," *Newsweek*, July 2, 2001, p. 26.

36. Ibid.

37. Jay Belsky and John Kelly, *The Transition to Parenthood* (New York: Vermillion, 1994), p. 14.

38. T. Hakansson, "Sexuality and Lactation," *International Journal of Prenatal and Perinatal Studies*, vol. 4 (1992), cited in Figes, *Life After Birth*, p. 187.

39. Margaret A. De Judicibus and Marita P. McCabe, "Psychological Factors and the Sexuality of Pregnant and Postpartum Women," *Journal of Sex Research*, May 2002, p. 94.

40. Harvey Karp, *The Happiest Baby on the Block: The New Way to Calm Crying and Help Your Baby Sleep Longer* (New York: Bantam Books, 2002), pp. 94–98.

41. Brazelton, *Touchpoints*, p. 68.

42. De Marneffe, *Maternal Desire*, p. 128.

Stage 2
Finding Your Footing, Finding Yourself:
Months Four Through Twelve

1. Allison Pearson, *I Don't Know How She Does It* (New York: Anchor Books, 2002), p. 15.

2. Mary Elizabeth Williams, "The Working Mother's Survival Guide," *Parents*, June 2003, p. 55.

3. Kate Figes, *Life After Birth: What Even Your Friends Won't Tell You About Motherhood* (New York: Penguin Books, 1998), p. 79.

4. Jack P. Shonkoff and Deborah A. Phillips, eds., *From Neurons to Neighborhoods: The Science of Early Child Development* (Washington, D.C.: National Academy Press, 2000), p. 251.

5. Daphne de Marneffe, *Maternal Desire: On Children, Love, and the Inner Life* (Boston: Little, Brown, 2004), p. 108.

6. Lisa Belkin, "The Opt-Out Revolution," *New York Times Magazine*, October 26, 2003, p. 42.

7. Arlie Russell Hochschild with Anne Machung, *The Second Shift* (New York: Avon Books, 1989), pp. 286–94.

8. Harriet Lerner, *The Mother Dance: How Children Change Your Life* (New York: HarperCollins, 1998), p. 67.

9. Hochschild, *The Second Shift*, p. 118.

10. Jay Belsky and John Kelly, *The Transition to Parenthood* (New York: Vermillion, 1994), p. 35.

11. De Marneffe, *Maternal Desire,* p. 104.

Stage 3
Letting Go: *The Toddler Years, One and Two*

1. Judith Viorst, *Necessary Losses* (New York: Fawcett Columbine, 1986), p. 206.

2. T. Berry Brazelton, *Touchpoints: Your Child's Emotional and Behavioral Development: Birth–3* (Reading, Mass.: Addison-Wesley, 1992), p. 152.

3. Ibid., p. 155.

4. Selma Fraiberg, "Ghosts in the Nursery," in *Selected Writings of Selma Fraiberg,* ed. Louis Fraiberg (Columbus: Ohio State University Press, 1987), pp. 100–116.

5. Arietta Slade et al., "Mothers' Representations of Their Relationships with Their Toddlers: Links to Adult Attachment and Observed Mothering," *Developmental Psychology,* vol. 35, no. 3 (May 1999).

6. Joyce Block, *Motherhood as Metamorphosis* (New York: Penguin Books, 1990), p. 15.

7. Anne Lamott, "Mother Anger: Theory and Practice," in *Mothers Who Think: Tales of Real-Life Parenthood,* ed. Camille Peri and Kate Moses (New York: Villard Books, 1999), p. 92.

8. Harriet Lerner, *The Mother Dance* (New York: HarperCollins, 1998), p. 46.

9. Carin Rubinstein, *The Sacrificial Mother* (New York: Hyperion Books, 1998), p. 44.

10. Maureen O'Brien, *Watch Me Grow: I'm One-Two-Three* (New York: Quill Books, 2002), p. 6.

11. Ibid., p. 167.

12. Susan Lewis, *Reinventing Ourselves After Motherhood* (Chicago: Contemporary Books, 1999), p. 40.

Stage 4
Trying to Do It All: *The Preschool Years, Three to Six*

1. Allison Pearson, *I Don't Know How She Does It* (New York: Anchor Books, 2002), p. 1.

2. Roz Chast, *Childproof: Cartoons About Parents and Children* (New York: Hyperion Books, 1997), p. 2.

3. Diane Ehrensaft, *Spoiling Childhood: How Well-Meaning Parents Are Giving Children Too Much—But Not What They Need* (New York: Guilford Press, 1997), p. 74.

4. Ibid., p. 76.

5. Maureen O'Brien, *Watch Me Grow: I'm One-Two-Three* (New York: Quill Books, 2002), p. 602.

6. Kristin van Ogtrop, "Attila the Honey I'm Home," in *The Bitch in the House: 26 Women Tell the Truth About Sex, Solitude, Work, Motherhood, and Marriage,* ed. Cathi Hanauer (New York: HarperCollins, 2002), pp. 161–62.

7. Ron Taffel and Roberta Israeloff, *Why Parents Disagree and What You Can Do About It: How to Raise Great Kids While You Strengthen Your Marriage* (New York: Avon Books, 1994).

8. Elizabeth Thompson Gershoff, "Corporal Punishment by Parents and Associated Child Behaviors and Experiences: A Meta-analytic and Theoretical Review," *Columbia University Psychological Bulletin,* vol. 128, no. 4 (2002), pp. 539–79.

9. Patricia McCormick, "Oedipus Wreck," *Parents,* June 1995, pp. 79–80.

Stage 5
Reading the Compass to God-Knows-Where: *Years Six to Ten*

1. Erik H. Erikson, *Childhood and Society* (New York: W. W. Norton, 1950), p. 259.

2. Diane Ehrensaft, *Spoiling Childhood: How Well-Meaning Parents Are Giving Children Too Much—But Not What They Need* (New York: Guilford Press, 1997), pp. 114–15.

3. Martin Seligman, *The Optimistic Child: A Proven Program to Safeguard Children from Depression and Build Lifelong Resilience* (New York: HarperPerennial, 1995), p. 35.

4. Ibid., p. 194.

5. Dan Kindlon, *Too Much of a Good Thing: Raising Children of Character in an Indulgent Age* (New York: Hyperion Books, 2001), p. 9.

6. Anny C. Dietz, "The Problem with Andrew," *Newsday,* January 10, 1994, p. 39.

7. David Elkind, *The Hurried Child: Growing Up Too Fast Too Soon* (Reading, Mass.: Addison-Wesley, 1981), p. 3.

8. Ehrensaft, *Spoiling Childhood,* p. 207.

9. Lucinda Franks, "Little Big People," *New York Times Magazine,* October 10, 1993, p. 34.

10. Kindlon, *Too Much,* p. 21.

11. Ibid., p. 198.

12. Nancy Samalin, *Loving Each One Best: A Caring and Practical Approach to Raising Siblings* (New York: Bantam Books, 1996).

13. Harriet Lerner, *The Mother Dance: How Children Change Your Life* (New York: HarperCollins, 1998), p. 274.

14. Ibid., p. 279.

Stage 6
Living in the Gray Zone: *The Preteen Years, Ten to Thirteen*

1. Louis Genevie and Eva Margolies, *The Motherhood Report* (New York: Macmillan, 1987), pp. 91–92.
2. Kenneth R. Ginsburg with Martha M. Jablow, *But I'm Almost 13! Raising a Responsible Adolescent* (Chicago: Contemporary Books, 2001), p. 33.
3. Diane Ehrensaft, *Spoiling Childhood: How Well-Meaning Parents Are Giving Children Too Much—But Not What They Need* (New York: Guilford Press, 1997), p. 135.
4. William Pollack, personal interview, May 2002.
5. Ron Taffel with Melinda Blau, *The Second Family: How Adolescent Power Is Challenging the American Family* (New York: St. Martin's Press, 2001), p. 83.
6. Pollack interview, May 2002.
7. Barbara Schneider, personal interview, November 2003.
8. Harriet Lerner, *The Mother Dance: How Children Change Your Life* (New York: HarperCollins, 1998), p. 119.
9. Ibid., p. 124.
10. Taffel, *Second Family*, p. 83.
11. Ginsburg, *But I'm Almost 13!*, p. 92.
12. Sue Monk Kidd, *The Secret Lives of Bees* (New York: Penguin Books, 2003), p. 9.
13. Patricia Adler and Peter Adler, *Peer Power* (New Brunswick, N.J.: Rutgers University Press, 2001), p. 64.
14. Judith Rich Harris, *The Nurture Assumption: Why Children Turn Out the Way They Do* (New York: Touchstone Books, 1999), p. 232.
15. Adler and Adler, *Peer Power*, p. 195.
16. Linda Perlstein, *Not Much Just Chillin': The Hidden Lives of Middle Schoolers* (New York: Farrar, Straus and Giroux, 2003), p. 35.
17. Ibid., p. 16.

Stage 7
It Gets Easier . . . and Then They Leave:
The Teen Years, Thirteen to Eighteen

1. Judith Viorst, *Necessary Losses* (New York: Fawcett Columbine, 1986), p. 206.
2. Barbara C. Unell and Jerry L. Wyckoff, *The 8 Seasons of Parenthood: How the Stages of Parenting Constantly Shape Our Identities* (New York: Times Books, 2000), p. 155.

3. Anna Quindlen, "Flown Away, Left Behind," *Newsweek,* January 12, 2004, p. 64.

4. Nina Shandler, *Ophelia's Mom: Loving and Letting Go of Your Adolescent Daughter* (New York: Crown, 2001), p. 60.

5. David Elkind, *All Grown Up and No Place to Go: Teenagers in Crisis* (Cambridge, Mass.: Perseus, 1998), p. 37.

6. Sarah Mahoney, "What Was He Thinking?" *Prevention,* March 2004, p. 162.

7. Henry J. Kaiser Family Foundation, *Kaiser Daily Reproductive Health Report,* Public Health & Education section, July 8, 1999, www.kff.org.

8. Natalie Angier, *Woman: An Intimate Geography* (New York: Houghton Mifflin, 1999), p. 302.

9. Gavin de Becker, *Protecting the Gift: Keeping Children and Teenagers Safe* (New York: The Dial Press, 1999), p. 26.

10. Ibid., p. 28.

11. Rob Turrisi et al., "Binge-Drinking-Related Consequences in College Students: Role of Drinking Beliefs and Mother-Teen Communications," *Psychology of Addicted Behaviors,* vol. 14, no. 4 (December 2000).

12. Anthony E. Wolf, *Get Out of My Life, But First Could You Drive Me and Cheryl to the Mall? A Parent's Guide to the New Teenager,* rev. ed. (New York: Farrar, Straus and Giroux, 2002), p. 85.

13. Justin Richardson and Mark A. Schuster, *Everything You Never Wanted Your Kids to Know About Sex (But Were Afraid They'd Ask): The Secrets to Surviving Your Child's Sexual Development from Birth to the Teens* (New York: Crown, 2003), p. 56.

14. Ibid., p. 57.

15. Mary Kaye Blakeley, *American Mom: Motherhood, Politics, and Humble Pie* (New York: Pocket Books, 1994), p. 245.

16. Anne Roiphe, *Fruitful: Living the Contradictions: A Memoir of Modern Motherhood* (New York: Penguin Books, 1996), p. 65.

17. Neil Genzliner, "An Actress of a Certain Age Eyes the Beauty Cult," *New York Times,* January 20, 2004, p. E1.

18. Erich Fromm, cited in Viorst, *Necessary Losses,* p. 210.

19. Richardson and Schuster, *Everything You Never Wanted Your Kids to Know About Sex,* p. 248.

20. Sandi Kahn Shelton, "One Week Until College," in *Mothers Who Think: Tales of Real-Life Parenthood,* ed. Camille Peri and Kate Moses (New York: Villard Books, 1999), p. 81.

21. Viorst, *Necessary Losses,* p. 63.

22. Phyllis Theroux, *Night Lights: Bedtime Stories for Parents in the Dark* (New York: Viking Books, 1987), p. 171.

23. David H. Arp Jr. et al., *The Second Half of Marriage* (Grand Rapids, Mich.: Zondervan, 2000), p. 31.

24. John Gottman, "Welcome to the Love Lab," *Psychology Today,* September 2000.

25. S. E. Taylor et al., "Female Responses to Stress: Tend-and-Befriend, Not Fight-or-Flight," *Psychological Review*, vol. 107, no. 3 (2000), pp. 411–29.

Conclusion

1. Natalie Angier, *Woman: An Intimate Geography* (New York: Houghton Mifflin, 1999), p. 319.

BIBLIOGRAPHY

Adler, Patricia, and Peter Adler. *Peer Power.* New Brunswick, N.J.: Rutgers University Press, 2001.

American Academy of Child and Adolescent Psychiatry. *Your Adolescent: Emotional, Behavioral and Cognitive Development from Early Adolescence Through the Teen Years.* New York: HarperCollins, 1999.

Angier, Natalie. *Woman: An Intimate Geography.* New York: Houghton Mifflin, 1999.

Arp, David H., Jr., et al., *The Second Half of Marriage.* Grand Rapids, Mich.: Zondervan, 2000.

Belkin, Lisa. "The Opt-Out Revolution." *New York Times Magazine,* October 26, 2003.

Belsky, Jay, and John Kelly. *The Transition to Parenthood.* New York: Vermillion, 1994.

Berg, Elizabeth. "'I Can't Believe You're Here!': A New Mother's Diary." *Parents,* April 1992, pp. 98–102.

Blakeley, Mary Kaye. *American Mom: Motherhood, Politics, and Humble Pie.* New York: Pocket Books, 1994.

Block, Joyce. *Motherhood as Metamorphosis: Change and Continuity in the Life of a New Mother.* New York: Penguin Books, 1990.

Brazelton, T. Berry. *Touchpoints: Your Child's Emotional and Behavioral Development: Birth–3.* Reading, Mass.: Addison-Wesley, 1992.

Bulatao, I. Rodolfo A. "Values and Disvalues of Children in Successive Childbearing Decisions." *Demography,* vol. 18, no. 1 (February 1981).

Chast, Roz. *Childproof: Cartoons About Parents and Children.* New York: Hyperion Books, 1997.

Csikszentmihalyi, Mihaly. *Flow: The Psychology of Optimal Experience.* New York: HarperPerennial, 1990.

Davis-Floyd, Robbie E. *Birth as an American Rite of Passage.* Berkeley: University of California Press, 1992.

de Becker, Gavin. *The Gift of Fear: And Other Survival Signals That Protect Us from Violence.* New York: Bantam Books, 1997.

———. *Protecting the Gift: Keeping Children and Teenagers Safe.* New York: The Dial Press, 1999.

De Judicibus, Margaret A., and Marita P. McCabe. "Psychological Factors and the Sexuality of Pregnant and Postpartum Women." *Journal of Sex Research,* May 2002.

Dellasega, Cheryl. *Surviving Ophelia: Mothers Share Their Wisdom in Navigating the Tumultous Teenage Years.* Cambridge, Mass.: Perseus, 2001.

de Marneffe, Daphne. *Maternal Desire: On Children, Love, and the Inner Life.* Boston: Little, Brown, 2004.

Diamant, Anita. *The Red Tent,* New York: Picador, 1997.

Dietz, Anny C. "The Problem with Andrew." *Newsday,* January 10, 1994.

Douglas, Ann. *The Unofficial Guide to Childcare.* New York: Macmillan, 1998.

Ehrensaft, Diane. *Spoiling Childhood: How Well-Meaning Parents Are Giving Children Too Much—But Not What They Need.* New York: Guilford Press, 1997.

Elkind, David. *All Grown Up and No Place to Go: Teenagers in Crisis.* Cambridge, Mass.: Perseus, 1998.

———. *The Hurried Child: Growing Up Too Fast Too Soon.* Reading, Mass.: Addison-Wesley, 1981.

Erdrich, Louise. *The Blue Jay's Dance: A Birth Year.* New York: HarperCollins, 1995.

Erikson, Erik H. *Childhood and Society.* New York: W. W. Norton, 1950.

Evans, Patricia. *Teen Torment: Overcoming Verbal Abuse at Home and at School.* Avon, Mass.: Adams Media Corp., 2003.

Ferber, Richard. *Solve Your Child's Sleep Problems.* New York: Simon & Schuster, 1985.

Figes, Kate. *Life After Birth: What Even Your Friends Won't Tell You About Motherhood.* New York: Penguin Books, 1998.

Fraiberg, Selma. "Ghosts in the Nursery." In *Selected Writings of Selma Fraiberg,* ed. Louis Fraiberg, pp. 100–116. Columbus: Ohio State University Press, 1987.

Franks, Lucinda. "Little Big People." *New York Times Magazine,* October 10, 1993.

Fromm, Erich. *The Art of Loving.* New York: Harper & Brothers, 1956.

Galinsky, Ellen. *The Six Stages of Parenthood.* Reading, Mass.: Addison-Wesley, 1987.

Genevie, Louis, and Eva Margolies. *The Motherhood Report.* New York: Macmillan, 1987.

Genzliner, Neil. "An Actress of a Certain Age Eyes the Beauty Cult." *New York Times,* January 20, 2004.

Gershoff, Elizabeth Thompson. "Corporal Punishment by Parents and Associated Child Behaviors and Experiences: A Meta-analytic and Theoretical Review." *Columbia University Psychological Bulletin,* vol. 128, no. 4 (2002), pp. 539–79.

Gilligan, Carol. *In a Different Voice: Psychological Theory and Women's Development.* Cambridge, Mass.: Harvard University Press, 1982.

Ginsburg, Kenneth R., and Martha M. Jablow. *But I'm Almost 13!: Raising a Responsible Adolescent.* Chicago: Contemporary Books, 2001.

Gottman, John. "Welcome to the Love Lab." *Psychology Today,* September 2000.

Greenberg, Susan H., and Karen Springen. "The Baby Blues and Beyond." *Newsweek,* July 2, 2001.

Harris, Judith Rich. *The Nurture Assumption: Why Children Turn Out the Way They Do.* New York: Touchstone Books, 1999.

Henry J. Kaiser Family Foundation. *Kaiser Daily Reproductive Health Report.* Public Health & Education section, July 8, 1999, www.kff.org.

Hersch, Patricia. *A Tribe Apart: A Journey into the Heart of American Adolescence.* New York: Ballantine, 1998.

Hochschild, Arlie Russell, with Anne Machung. *The Second Shift.* New York: Avon Books, 1989.

Hrdy, Sarah Blaffer. *Mother Nature: Maternal Instincts and How They Shape the Human Species.* New York: Ballantine, 1999.

Jameson, Marnell. "A Natural Formula for Success," *Los Angeles Times,* September 4, 2000, p. 51.

Kaplan, Louise J. *Oneness and Separateness: From Infant to Individual.* New York: Touchstone Books, 1978.

Karp, Harvey. *The Happiest Baby on the Block: The New Way to Calm Crying and Help Your Baby Sleep Longer.* New York: Bantam Books, 2002.

Kidd, Sue Monk. *The Secret Lives of Bees.* New York: Penguin Books, 2003.

Kindlon, Dan. *Too Much of a Good Thing: Raising Children of Character in an Indulgent Age.* New York: Hyperion Books, 2001.

Kitzinger, Sheila. *The Complete Book of Pregnancy & Childbirth.* 4th ed. New York: Knopf, 2004.

Klaus, Marshall H., and John H. Kennell. *Maternal-Infant Bonding: The Impact of Early Separation or Loss on Family Development.* St. Louis: C. V. Mosby, 1976.

————. *Parent-Infant Bonding.* St. Louis: C. V. Mosby 1976.

Kunhardt, Jean, Lisa Spiegel, and Sandra K. Basile. *A Mother's Circle: Wisdom and Reassurance from Other Mothers on Your First Year with Baby.* New York: Avon Books, 1996.

Lamott, Anne. "Mother Anger: Theory and Practice." In *Mothers Who Think: Tales of Real-Life Parenthood,* ed. Camille Peri and Kate Moses. New York: Villard Books, 1999.

Lara, Adair. *Hold Me Close, Let Me Go: A Mother, a Daughter, and an Adolescence Survived.* New York: Broadway Books, 2001.

Lerner, Harriet. *The Dance of Deception: A Guide to Authenticity and Truth-Telling in Women's Relationships.* New York: HarperPerennial, 1994.

————. *The Mother Dance: How Children Change Your Life.* New York: HarperCollins, 1998.

Lewis, Susan. *Reinventing Ourselves After Motherhood.* Chicago: Contemporary Books, 1999.

Lombardi, Joan. *Time to Care: Redesigning Child Care to Promote Education, Support Families, and Build Communities.* Philadelphia: Temple University Press, 2003.

Mahoney, Sarah. "What Was He Thinking?" *Prevention,* March 2004.

McCormick, Patricia. "Oedipus Wreck." *Parents,* June 1995, pp. 79-80.

McMahon, Martha. *Engendering Motherhood: Identity and Self-Transformation in Women's Lives.* New York: Guilford Press, 1995.

Neubauer, Peter B., and Alexander Neubauer. *Nature's Thumbprint: The New Genetics of Personality.* Reading, Mass.: Addison-Wesley, 1990.

O'Brien, Maureen. *Watch Me Grow: I'm One-Two-Three.* New York: Quill Books, 2002.

Parenting magazine survey (December 2002–January 2003), conducted by Harris Interactive for the Maternity Center Association (MCA) in partnership with Johnson & Johnson Pediatric Institute.

Parker, Rozsika. *Torn in Two: The Experience of Maternal Ambivalence.* London: Virago Books, 1995.

Pearson, Allison. *I Don't Know How She Does It.* New York: Anchor Books, 2002.

Peri, Camille, and Kate Moses, eds. *Mothers Who Think: Tales of Real-Life Parenthood.* New York: Villard Books, 1999.

Perlstein, Linda. *Not Much Just Chillin': The Hidden Lives of Middle Schoolers.* New York: Farrar, Straus and Giroux, 2003.

Peters, Joan K. *When Mothers Work: Loving Our Children Without Sacrificing Our Selves.* Cambridge, Mass.: Perseus, 1997.

Pollack, William. *Real Boys: Rescuing Our Sons from the Myths of Boyhood.* New York: Henry Holt, 1998.

Pruett, Kyle. *Father Need: Why Father Care Is as Essential as Mother Care for Your Child.* New York: Broadway Books, 2000.

————. *The Nurturing Father.* New York: Warner Books, 1987.

Quindlen, Anna. "Flown Away, Left Behind." *Newsweek,* January 12, 2004.

Richardson, Justin, and Mark A. Schuster. *Everything You Never Wanted Your Kids to Know About Sex (But Were Afraid They'd Ask): The Secrets to Surviving Your Child's Sexual Development from Birth to the Teens.* New York: Crown, 2003.

Rodgers, Mary Ellen. "Like Mother, Like Child." *American Health,* July 1992.

Roiphe, Anne. *Fruitful: Living the Contradictions: A Memoir of Modern Motherhood.* New York: Penguin Books, 1996.

Rubinstein, Carin. *The Sacrificial Mother.* New York: Hyperion Books, 1998.

Samalin, Nancy. *Love and Anger: The Parental Dilemma.* New York: Viking Books, 1991.

————. *Loving Each One Best: A Caring and Practical Approach to Raising Siblings.* New York: Bantam Books, 1996.

————. *Loving Without Spoiling: And 100 Other Timeless Tips for Raising Terrific Kids.* Chicago: Contemporary Books, 2003.

Seligman, Martin. *Learned Optimism.* New York: Knopf, 1991.

————. *The Optimistic Child: A Proven Program to Safeguard Children from Depression and Build Lifelong Resilience.* New York: HarperPerennial, 1995.

Shandler, Nina. *Ophelia's Mom: Loving and Letting Go of Your Adolescent Daughter.* New York: Crown, 2001.

Shelton, Sandi Kahn. "One Week Until College." In *Mothers Who Think: Tales of Real-Life Parenthood,* ed. Camille Peri and Kate Moses. New York: Villard Books, 1999.

Shonkoff, Jack P., and Deborah A. Phillips, eds. *From Neurons to Neighborhoods: The Science of Early Child Development.* Washington, D.C.: National Academy Press, 2000.

Slade, Arietta, et al. "Mothers' Representations of Their Relationships with Their Toddlers: Links to Adult Attachment and Observed Mothering." *Developmental Psychology,* vol. 35, no. 3 (May 1999).

Small, Meredith F. *Our Babies, Ourselves: How Biology and Culture Shape the Way We Parent.* New York: Anchor Books, 1998.

Spiegel, Lise Friedman. "Planned Cesarean Delivery and Its Effect on Maternal Self-Esteem and Locus of Control." *Dissertation Abstracts International, Section B: The Sciences and Engineering,* vol. 56, no. 5-B (November 1995).

Stern, Daniel N., and Nadia Bruschweiler-Stern with Alison Freeland. *The Birth of a Mother: How the Motherhood Experience Changes You Forever.* New York: Basic Books, 1998.

Stevens, Patricia, ed. *Between Mothers and Sons: Women Writers Talk About Having Sons and Raising Men.* New York: Scribner, 1999.

Swigart, Jane. *The Myth of the Bad Mother: Parenting Without Guilt.* New York: Avon Books, 1991.

Taffel, Ron, and Melinda Blau. *Nurturing Good Children Now: 10 Basic Skills to Protect and Strengthen Your Child's Core Self.* New York: Golden Books, 1999.

————. *Parenting by Heart: How to Be in Charge, Stay Connected, and Instill Your Values, When It Feels Like You've Got Only 15 Minutes a Day.* Cambridge, Mass.: Perseus, 1991.

————. *The Second Family: How Adolescent Power Is Challenging the American Family.* New York: St. Martin's Press, 2001.

Taffel, Ron, and Roberta Israeloff. *Why Parents Disagree and What You Can Do About It: How to Raise Great Kids While You Strengthen Your Marriage.* New York: Avon Books, 1994.

Taylor, S. E., et al. "Female Responses to Stress: Tend-and-Befriend, Not Fight-or-Flight." *Psychological Review,* vol. 107, no. 3 (2000), pp. 411–29.

Theroux, Phyllis. *Night Lights: Bedtime Stories for Parents in the Dark.* New York: Viking Books, 1987.

Turrisi, Rob, et al. "Binge-Drinking-Related Consequences in College Students: Role of Drinking Beliefs and Mother-Teen Communications." *Psychology of Addicted Behaviors,* vol. 14, no. 4 (December 2000).

Tusa, Sally. "BabyTalk: Breast vs. Bottle Poll." *BabyTalk,* vol. 66, no. 7, September 2001.

Unell, Barbara C., and Jerry L. Wyckoff. *The 8 Seasons of Parenthood: How the Stages of Parenting Constantly Shape Our Identities.* New York: Times Books, 2000.

Updike, John. "When Everyone Was Pregnant." In *The Early Stories, 1953–1975.* New York: Knopf, 2003.

Van Ogtrop, Kristin. "Attila the Honey I'm Home." In *The Bitch in the House: 26 Women Tell the Truth About Sex, Solitude, Work, Motherhood, and Marriage,* ed. Cathi Hanauer. New York: HarperCollins, 2002.

Viorst, Judith. *Necessary Losses.* New York: Fawcett Columbine, 1986.

Weldon, Fay. Personal interview in *Torn in Two: The Experience of Maternal Ambivalence,* by Rozsika Parker. London: Virago Books, 1995.

Williams, Mary Elizabeth. "The Working Mother's Survival Guide." *Parents,* June 2003.

Wolf, Anthony E. *Get Out of My Life, But First Could You Drive Me and Cheryl to the Mall? A Parent's Guide to the New Teenager.* Rev. ed. New York: Farrar, Straus and Giroux, 2002.

ACKNOWLEDGMENTS

It's ironic to finish a book and then find oneself at a loss for words when it comes to thanking those who have helped along the way, but I cannot possibly do justice to my husband, Steven, and to our children, Madeleine and Nick. This book is about and in tribute to them; I hope I have managed to convey in some small measure how blessed I am as a wife and mother, how much joy they bring me every single day.

My agent, Kathy Robbins, not only coached, critiqued, and comforted me through this process, but she provided invaluable editorial input and shrewd advice. Every time I answered the phone to hear her signature opener ("So how *are* we?"), I knew I was one lucky writer. Given the fact that my superb editor, Jordan Pavlin, was supremely talented, warm, encouraging, *and* a young mother, I may just be the luckiest writer on the planet.

I also want to thank the surrogate kid sisters I was fortunate to call my associates when I set up shop at home: Kristen Schultz Dollard and, more recently, Cristen Calamari helped me cross the finish line. Blue Bista's countless acts of kindness and quiet generosity made even the most frustrating days bearable.

I doubt I will ever land a job quite like the editorship of *Parents* magazine. I owe my talented colleagues—Elizabeth Crow, Wendy Schuman, Sarah Mahoney, Maxine Davidowitz, Wendy Smolen, Janet Gold, and many others—thanks for their support and friendship during ten wonderful years and long past my exit. I also want to thank the extraordinary contributors and advisers to *Parents* with whom I had the honor to work: James Comer, M.D., Harold Koplewicz, M.D., Martin Seligman, Ph.D., Bernice Weissbourd, Nancy Samalin, Ron Taffel, Ph.D., Stanley Greenspan, M.D., and Elizabeth Berg, to name only a few.

My fellow board members at Zero to Three constitute a kind of Mount Olympus of child-development experts, yet they never make me feel like the mere mortal I am at our meetings. They and the staff of Zero to Three are my heroes.

For five years I have had the pleasure of working with a woman who is an exceptional producer, a wonderful mother, and a loving friend. Sandra Aiken makes me look good on *Good Morning America*. So do all my supportive and creative colleagues—Lisa Sharkey, Shelley Ross, Phyllis McGrady, Charles Gibson, Diane Sawyer, and the rest of the *GMA* family.

I am grateful every day for the presence in my life of my loving, smart, funny siblings, Mary and John, my in-laws, Ed and Gloria, Kevin, Jeanne, and Lois Murphy, and their wonderful spouses and children. Then there are the surrogate sisters I have been blessed to know and love for most of my life: Jane Rosenman, whom my father delivered; Nicole Bourgois Elliman, whom I met in kinder-garten; Ellen Iseman O'Neill, who rang my doorbell at age two and remained my neighbor and friend through high school and beyond; and the many other Dalton friends who generously gave of their time and contributed their mothering stories to this book. I could not have done this book without the encouragement and sup-port of several "newer" friends, all of whom I've loved for at least twenty years: Valerie Monroe, Patricia McCormick, Kate White. They are all talented writers, editors, generous listeners, wise advisers, and great mothers.

The mothers who shared their stories with me constitute another family to whom I owe an enormous debt of gratitude. Most of their names appear in this book, along with their candor, wit, optimism, pride, courage, and insight.

But the mother who towers above the rest was my own: Marjorie Pleshette. Her consistent, unconditional love informs every day of my life as a mother. I had hoped to finish this book before she died, because so much of her profound gift with children shaped these pages, but I'm sure she would have read it and called to exclaim, in her gentle Corpus Christi drawl, "Darling, your book is simply marvelous!"

INDEX

Adams, Brooke, 233
adoption, 43
advice, unsolicited, 17–18, 208
alcohol, 223, 228–9
ambivalence, 48
American Mom (Blakeley), 232
anger, xi, 44, 244–5, 246
  about baby with disabilities, 10
  breast-feeding and, 40, 42
  during preteen stage, 199, 209
  during teen stage, 220–3, 235–6,
    241, 242
  during toddler stage, 98–9
Angier, Natalie, 22, 223–4, 247
"Attila the Honey I'm Home" (van
  Ogtrop), 122–3

baby(ies), 67–87
  anticipating needs of, 62
  birth of, 3, 22–32, 60
  bonding with, 30–2, 83
  death of, 3–4
  "difficult," 44–5
  fantasizing about, 3–7, 9, 10, 12,
    36
  father and, 53–4, 55
  loss of structured time and, 63–6
  newborn, 29, 30–4, 35–8, 42, 54,
    61–3
  reading signals of, 61–3

  second, 128–32
  and toddlers, 98
  touch of, 57
  with disabilities, 10
  see also bonding; breast-feeding
BabyTalk magazine, 41
back talk, 125, 175, 176
bedtime, ix, 102, 175, 199
  importance of routine and, 89
  power struggles over, 92
Belkin, Lisa, 81
Berg, Elizabeth, 33
Binder-Brynes, Karen, 35
birth, 22–32
  anesthesia during, 24
  cesarean section, 27–8
  effect on libido, 60
  home delivery, 25–6
  pain during, 23–4
  shared experience of, 22
  "typical' reactions to, 29–30
  unforeseen events and, 3
Birth of a Mother, The (Stern), 9, 36
Bitch in the House, The (Hanauer, ed.),
  122
Blakeley, Mary Kaye, 232
Block, Joyce, 29, 45, 98
Blue Jay's Dance, The: A Birth Year
  (Erdrich), 13
body image, 14, 15, 58, 207

bonding, 30–2, 42–4
  birth and, 30, 32
  breast-feeding and, 42
  "difficult" babies and, 43, 44
  discipline and, 163
  father-daughter, 127
  independent children and, 127
  postpartum depression and, 51
  with spouse, 83
  with twins, 43
bottle-feeding, 40–1
boundaries
  anger and, 234
  respecting preteens' need for, 194,
    195
  setting limits, 199, 200–1
  unsolicited advice and touching, 18
bratty behavior, 162
Brazelton, T. Berry, ix, 62, 93, 135
breast-feeding, 38–43
  bonding and, 42
  challenges to, 38–40
  competition associated with, 41
  hormones and, 42–3
  self-confidence and, 48
  sex drive and, 57–8
bullies, bullying, 209

cesarean section, 27–8, 31, 41, 60
  control over decision, 28
Chast, Roz, 112
childbirth, 6, 13
  emotions during and after, 29–32
  euphoria after, 33–4
  fatigue after, 34–5
  lack of control during, 24–5
  pain management in, 22–6
  taking control during, 26–8
  trauma of, 35
child care, 67–8, 72, 76–9, 123
  asking for help with, 51–2
  choosing, 76

father's role in, 52, 82–3, 84
jealousy toward provider, 29, 78
relationship with provider, 77–9
Childhood and Society (Erikson), ix
choices given to toddlers, 97
chores, 82–4, 148–9, 174–5
cliques, 207–11
clothing
  during pregnancy, 15
  of preschoolers, 124–5
  of preteens, 204, 205, 206–7
  of school-age children, 163
college applications, 239–40
colic, 61–2
comparisons
  of adolescents with toddlers, 217
  by children ages six to ten, 164–5
  with mother's own parents, 119,
    159–60
  of toddler development, 104–6
competence
  of children ages six to ten, 148–50
  of mothers, 40, 62, 75, 179, 203,
    221
  of preteens, 186–7
  of toddlers, 102
competition, 41, 48, 83, 92, 104,
    121–2, 151, 164–5, 208–9, 283
control
  by babies, x
  during childbirth, 28
  shifting to children, 91–2
control, lack of
  during childbirth, 24–5, 35
  of children ages six to ten, 165–7
  postpartum, 32, 38, 51
  during pregnancy, 7, 8, 14, 21
  during toddler stage, 98–100
cortisol, 43
couch-potato kids, 171
Crawford, Cindy, 17
crying, responding to baby's, 62

dates with husband, 55–6
de Becker, Gavin, 225, 226
de Marneffe, Daphne, 4, 21, 64, 80, 87
denial, 10, 14, 226
dependence, 185, 186, 244
depression, 28, 50–1, 75, 81, 99–100
Diamant, Anita, 29
discipline, 173
    differing parental styles, 126,
        174–80
    for preschoolers, 135–7
    spanking, 136–7
drinking, see alcohol
drugs, 223, 228, 229–30

eating habits, xi, 102, 178, 204
Ehrensaft, Diane, 116–17, 151, 161,
    185
8 Seasons of Parenthood, The (Unell and
    Wyckoff), 217
Elkind, David, 161
emotions
    during breast-feeding, 39
    during childbirth, 13, 25–6, 30
    postpartum, 32, 38, 44, 51
    during pregnancy, 8, 14, 17, 21
    of preschoolers, 134–43
    of preteens, 184–6
    of teenagers, 220, 229, 236
    see also anger
empty nesters, 240–3
entitlement trap, 161–5
Erdrich, Louise, 13, 42
Erikson, Erik, x, 148
Everything You Never Wanted Your Kids
    to Know About Sex (Richardson
    and Schuster), 230–1
exhaustion
    during childbirth, 23, 35
    during infancy stage, 74, 81
    postpartum, 17, 19, 31, 32, 34–5,
        36, 37–8, 46, 50, 52, 58, 59–60

during preteen years, 184
during toddler stage, 100
during years six to ten, 161
see also fatigue

fairness, 173
Family Circle magazine, 151, 234
fatherhood, 10–13, 31–2, 52–6,
    59–60
    adjusting to kids' departure,
        241–2
    adjusting to new role, 10
    birth and, 23
    "expert/dumb apprentice trap," 53
    sharing child care, 13, 56, 82–6
fatigue, xi
    during childbirth, 30
    postpartum, 42, 51, 56, 67
    during pregnancy, 5, 6, 14, 16
    see also exhaustion
fertility treatments, 12–13
Figes, Kate, 36, 73
fighting, parental, 177
flexibility, xi, 64, 70, 201, 214
"Flown Away, Left Behind"
    (Quindlen), 217
friends
    after birth of child, 52
    help during teen years, 242
    preteen cliques, 208, 210, 242
Fromm, Erich, 234
Fruitful (Roiphe), 232
frustration
    of babies, 44
    of children ages six to ten, 148, 150,
        154
    of fathers, 51, 60
    of mothers, 38, 41–2, 44, 61, 76,
        81, 82, 99, 102, 127–8, 151–2,
        156–8, 183, 192, 208, 212, 220,
        229
    of preschoolers, 119–20

frustration (*continued*)
  of preteens, 201
  of toddlers, 93, 97, 101–2

*Get Out of My Life, But First Could You
  Drive Me and Cheryl to the Mall?*
  (Wolf), 229
Gift of Fear, The (de Becker), 225
Ginsburg, Kenneth R., 206
Giuliani, Andrew, 162
Giuliani, Rudolph, 162
Good Morning America, x, 82, 114,
  171
gossip, 208, 209
Gottman, John, 242
grandmothers, 47–50
gratitude, showing, 29, 84–5, 164,
  178–9
Grubman, Jack B., 120
guilt, 244–5, 246
  birth of second child and, 30
  bottle-feeding and, 41
  breast-feeding and, 38, 41, 42
  over death of child, 3
  formula for, 111
  of mother with multiple children,
    130, 131, 132, 133, 134
  of mother with teenagers, 233
  postpartum, 31
  during pregnancy, 10
  of preteens, 198–9
  self-doubt and, 167
  of teenagers, 230
  of working mother, 106–8, 111–14,
    123, 124, 127, 179

Happiest Baby on the Block, The (Karp),
  61
"happiness trap," 93
help
  from other mothers, 46–7, 49,
    246
  resistance to accept, 49, 51–2

Hochschild, Arlie Russell, 84
home
  office at, 189–91
  staying at, 21, 80–1
homework, 185, 195, 212, 213, 214
hormones
  friendly, 43, 243
  menopausal, 232
  postpartum, 30, 32, 35, 36, 40,
    43
  pregnancy, 14
  of preteens, 185
  see also oxytocin
Hrdy, Sarah Blaffer, 32

I Don't Know How She Does It (Pearson),
  71, 112
indecision, *see* self-doubt
independence
  of children ages six to ten, 144–5
  of newborns, 29
  of preschoolers, 128
  of preteens, 182, 183, 186–7, 188,
    205–6
  of teenagers, 220, 221–2, 223,
    244
  of toddlers, 88–9, 108, 109,
    119–20
  see also separation
infants, *see* baby(ies)
Internet, 138, 197
intuition, 225–6, 227
It's a Wonderful Life (film), 158

jealousy, 232–4
  of teens' romantic relationships,
    233
Journal of Sex Research, 56

Karp, Harvey, 61
Kennell, John, 30–1
Kidd, Sue Monk, 207
"kinderadults," 163

kindergarten, 120–1, 138
Kindlon, Dan, 161, 163, 168–9
Klaus, Marshall, 30–1

labeling children, 44–5
labor, 23–5, 26, 27–8
La Leche League, 39
Lamaze, 10, 23, 25, 27
Lamott, Anne, 99
laziness
  kids and, 211
  school and, 212–13
Lerner, Harriet, 8, 176, 203–4
Lewis, Susan, 107
Life After Birth (Figes), 36, 73
limits, 168–9
  discipline, 136
  for preteens, 182, 199–203
  for teens, 216
  for toddlers, 93
listening, importance of, 147–8, 180,
    204, 214, 242
  see also intuition
loneliness, 5, 12, 43, 53, 60, 65, 75,
    83, 172, 188, 215, 242
Loving Each One Best (Samalin), 133,
    173
lying, 229, 230

marriage
  challenges to, 54–5, 83
  nurturing, 178–9
Maternal Desire (de Marneffe), 87
Maternal-Infant Bonding (Klaus and
    Kennell), 30
menopause, 232
modeling behavior, 100
mother
  child's-eye view of, 157–9
  evolving role of, x–xi, 8, 45
  as friend to child, 200–1
  mother of, 45, 46–50, 52, 94–5,
    241

of multiple children, x, 130, 131,
    132, 133, 134
  pulled in different directions,
    144–5, 178
  reexperiencing childhood, 170–1,
    173–4
  remaking self-image of, 217–18
  "sleepovers" with, 199–200
  staying at home, 21, 80–1
  time-out for, 203
  working, x–xi, 15, 19–22, 49,
    67–75, 91, 106–9, 111–12,
    122–3, 156–7, 159–60, 178,
    183, 188–90
Mother Dance, The (Lerner), 176, 203
Motherhood as Metamorphosis (Block),
    29, 98
mother-in-law, 49
motivation, lack of, 212–14
Mrs. Doubtfire (film), 76

nagging, 162
Nature's Thumbprint (Neubauer and
    Neubauer), xi
Necessary Losses (Viorst), 215
newborns, *see* baby(ies), newborn
Newsweek, 217
New York Newsday, 162
New York Times Magazine, 81
Not Much Just Chillin' (Perlstein), 210
nursing, 38–43
  see also breast-feeding

Oedipal complex, 138–41
"One Week Until College" (Shelton),
    235
Ophelia's Mom (Shandler), 220
optimism, explanatory style and,
    156
Optimistic Child, The (Seligman), 155
orgasm, 43
overindulgence, 161–5
oxytocin, 43, 47, 243

parent coaches, 114–15
parenting style, 105, 126–8
Parents magazine, x, 21, 65, 70, 72, 99, 126, 136, 138, 150, 156, 168, 189, 220
Parker, Rozsika, x–xi, 44
Pearson, Allison, 71
peer pressure, 206
    among parents, 165–7
perfectionism, perfectionists, 114–17, 154–5, 179
    perfect-mom fantasy, 111, 112, 114–17
Perlstein, Linda, 210, 212
pessimism, pessimists, 156, 157
Pollack, William, 195–6, 200
postpartum period, 19, 30, 31, 32–8, 40, 42, 43, 44, 48, 49, 50–1, 67
    emotions during, 37–9
    fears during, 36
    helplessness and vulnerability during, 45–7
    and post-traumatic stress, 35
    psychological fragility during, 35–6
    sex life during, 17, 56–9, 60–1
    see also depression
power struggles
    with preteens, 203–4, 214
    with toddlers, 92–7
pregnancy, 3–22, 33, 45
    advice during, 17–18
    anxiety during, 5–6, 8–10
    fantasies about future during, 4–5
    language of, 6
    macho attitude toward, 5–8
    physical transformation during, 13–17
    sex life during, 16–17
    touching during, 18–19
    and work, 19–22

preschool, 145
    pressure of finding the "right," 120–3
    transition to, 123–6
preschoolers, 110–23, 124–5, 134–43, 182
    chores and, 115
    discipline of, 126, 135–6
    joyfulness of, 110
    need for down time, 117–18
    need for routines, 118
    neediness of, 111
    Oedipal complex in, 139–40
    reframing "bad" behavior, 125
    separation anxiety in, 123–4
    and sibling rivalry, 132–4
    spanking, 137
    tantrums, 135
preteens, 181–214
    attitude toward age, 205
    bedtime and, 199
    cliques, 207–9
    communication and, 195–7, 203–4
    confrontation and, 199
    discipline and, 202–4
    failure and, 185
    frustration with, 183–4
    guilt and, 198
    hormones and, 185
    independence and, 186–8
    limits and, 182–3, 201
    mothers' work and, 188–91
    overinvolvement with, 185
    responsibility and, 211–12
    showing affection and, 192–4
    social life of, 205–7, 210–11
    toddlers and, 184
    unpredictability of, 183–4, 192
Protecting the Gift (de Becker), 225
puberty, 185

"quality time," 116, 117–20, 122, 131
Quindlen, Anna, 217, 218

Red Tent, The (Diamant), 29
Reinventing Ourselves After Motherhood (Lewis), 107
responsibility, 163, 179, 198–9, 214, 246
    instilling an appreciation for, 161
    parents' influence on children, 95, 204
    preteens and, 184–5
    teens and, 149
    toddlers and, 149
Richardson, Justin, 231, 234–5
risk taking, 72–3, 222–5, 228–30, 244
Roiphe, Anne, 232
routines, 75, 80–1, 89–90, 91, 134, 160
    flexibility in, 118
    importance of, 63
    infants and, 63–4
    keeping sanity with, 100
Rubinstein, Carin, 99

Sacrificial Mother, The (Rubinstein), 99
Samalin, Nancy, 93, 133, 173
Schneider, Barbara, 201
Schuster, Mark A., 231, 235
Second Family, The (Taffel), 205
Second Shift, The (Hochschild), 84
Secret Life of Bees, The (Kidd), 207
self-doubt, 28, 37, 48, 165–6, 201–2, 203, 223, 239, 246
self-esteem
    of children ages six to ten, 155–6
    postpartum, 44, 48
    of preteens, 185, 186, 208–9
    of teenagers, 218, 228, 239–40
self-image, 59–60, 157–9, 217
Seligman, Martin, 155–6, 157
separation, 221–2
    at childbirth, 29
    from children ages six to ten, 145–7
    mother's anxiety about, 89

from preschoolers, 123–4, 138–9, 141–3
from preteens, 186–8
of siblings, 132
from teenagers, 217, 233, 234, 237–8, 240–3, 247–8
from toddlers, 88–92, 96, 108, 131
see also independence
Seventh Heaven (TV show), 155
sex
    postpartum, 56–8, 59, 60
    during pregnancy, 16–17
    among teenagers, 227, 228, 230–5
Sex in the City (TV program), 192
"shame-free" zones, 196
Shelton, Sandi Kahn, 235–6
sibling rivalry, 128, 132–4, 171–2
silence, of preteens, 192
Sixth Sense, The (film), 136
sleep deprivation, 32, 34–5, 37, 51
spanking, 93, 95, 135, 136–7, 175
Spock, Benjamin, ix
Spoiling Childhood (Ehrensaft), 116, 151, 185
Stern, Daniel, 9, 36–7
stress, 35–6, 89, 114, 154, 222
    bullying and, 172
    giving birth and, 29, 35
    hormones and, 43, 243
    infants and, 38, 72
    new fathers and, 86
    parental disputes and, 177
    toddlers and, 102, 108
structure, loss of, 63–6

Taffel, Ron, 126, 161, 197, 205
tantrums, 93–7, 98–100, 110
teenagers, 215–43
    alcohol and, 223, 228–9
    and anticipating empty nest, 240–1
    and college applications, 239–40
    envy of, 233
    letting go of, 222

teenagers (*continued*)
  lying and, 229
  overidentification with, 239
  parental denial and, 225–6
  parental role reversal with, 218
  personalities and, 238
  relationship to, 201, 235–7
  restrictions and, 219
  self-image and, 217
  sex and, 223, 227–8, 230–2,
    235
terrible twos, 97–100
Theroux, Phyllis, 240
time-outs, 100, 135, 136, 203
toddlers, 88–109
  adolescents and, 217, 220
  empowerment of, 102–3
  feeding of, 102–3
  independence of, 88–9, 108, 109
  separation from, 88–92, 96, 108,
    131
  speech of, 103
  spotting, 101
  teenagers and, 238
Too Much of a Good Thing (Kindlon),
    161, 168
Torn in Two (Parker), x, 44
touch, touching
  of babies, 57
  of preteens, 192–4
  unwanted, 17, 18
Touchpoints (Brazelton), 62
trust, 43, 181, 230

twins, xi, 33, 43–4, 54, 233
tyranny of cool, 205–6

unrealistic expectations, 111
Updike, John, 19

values, 164, 167–71, 176–7, 178, 179
van Ogtrop, Kristin, 122
Viorst, Judith, 88, 215
volatility, of preteens, 184–6
vulnerability, 22, 27–8, 45–7, 48,
    164, 223

Wasserstein, Wendy, 39
water, breaking of, 21–2, 23
Weill, Sanford I., 120
Weldon, Fay, 8
*"What's Happening to My Body?" Book
    for Girls, The* (Madaras), 230
*Why Parents Disagree and What You Can
    Do About It* (Taffel), 126
Wolf, Anthony E., 229
Woman: An Intimate Geography
    (Angier), 22, 223–4, 247
work
  balancing with motherhood, 70–5,
    91
  pregnancy and, 19–21
  pull toward home, 68, 74
  returning to, 65, 68–75
  stress and, 72
  see also mother, working
"wrong-movie syndrome," 159–60

extracts reading groups
competitions books new
discounts extracts extracts
competitions discounts
books new events
new
events books
extracts new titles reading groups
interviews
events extracts
discounts
new books events
events new
discounts extracts discounts
www.panmacmillan.com
extracts events reading groups
competitions books extracts new

reading groups
reading groups
events
books